Bullets, Babies, and Boardrooms

Bullets, Babies, and Boardrooms

SUCCESS SECRETS FROM A TEENAGE MOTHER

Dr. Angela D. Thomas

Thomas, Nelson, & Thomason Consulting
STAFFORD, VIRGINIA

Copyright © 2022 by Dr. Angela D. Thomas

All rights reserved. This book or any portion thereof may not be reproduced or used in any manner whatsoever without the express written permission of the publisher except for the use of brief quotations in a book review or scholarly journal.

First Printing: 2022

ISBN 979-8-9857341-0-2

Thomas, Nelson, and Thomason Consulting

2729 Richmond Highway

Suite 111-1043

Stafford, VA 22554

www.DrAngelaDThomas.com

Dedication

To my Lord and Savior Jesus Christ. Thank you for the gift of Salvation that restored me to my rightful position in God's Kingdom! To my husband David – for it ALL! To my son Nate whose life FUELS my passion. To my parents Victor and Denise for a solid foundation. To my brothers Aaron and Adam who have ALWAYS lived this "1% life" WITH me. To the rest of my village – my pastor, my bonus children, my family, my church family, and my friends (you know who you are) – there is no journey without you! THANK YOU for always pushing me to keep CRUSHING my dreams – don't ever stop pushing to CRUSH yours!

Table of Contents

Dedication vi
Table of Contents vi
Chapter 1 - Prologue 1
Chapter 2 - Introduction 5
Phase I: "Bullets" – The Mindset Phase 13
G.O.O.D.S. – Who You Are and What You Believe 15

    Chapter 3 - Introduction 15

Chapter 4 - Goal-oriented Dreams 22
Chapter 5 - Optimism & an Open Mind 33
Chapter 6 - Determination 44
Chapter 7 - Spirituality 54

    Conclusion – Phase I: Bullets 67

Phase II: "Babies" – The Resilience Phase 69
B.O.U.N.C.E. – How You Deal with Challenges and Adversity 71

    Chapter 8 - Introduction 71

Chapter 9 - Brave Realist 74
Chapter 10 - Obstacle Awareness 90
Chapter 11 - Uncovering Strategies 110
Chapter 12 - Never Quitting 123
Chapter 13 - Creating Champions 135
Chapter 14 - Expecting the Exception 144

    Conclusion – Phase II: Babies 154

Phase III: "Boardrooms" – The *Action* Phase 157
R.E.S.U.L.T.S. – How You Work and Remain Focused 159

    Chapter 15 - Introduction 159

Chapter 16 - Relentless Grind 161

Chapter 17 - Excellence and Evaluation 171
Chapter 18 - Swift Action 181
Chapter 19 - Understanding Failures 192
Chapter 20 - Listening and Learning 201
Chapter 21 - Tenacious Momentum 213
Chapter 22 - Smart Work 231
    Conclusion – Phase III: Boardrooms 242
Chapter 23 - Conclusion 243
Chapter 24 - Epilogue 245

DR. ANGELA D. THOMAS

CHAPTER 1

Prologue

I was clearly busted and I *knew* it! I walked through the back door of our home on Wildemere street at the usual time I was scheduled to come home from work. My mom was sitting right there in the kitchen waiting on me. That's when I *knew* I was busted.

I was 16 years old and coming home from my part-time job at TradeWinds Video on Livernois Road in Detroit, Michigan. I walked through the door around nine o'clock p.m., which was the time my mom usually expected me to be home from work. This time, she was sitting *right there* and this time I wasn't actually coming home from work. I was coming home from my boyfriend's house under the guise that I *was* at work. But what I didn't know when I came through the door was that my mother had gone up to my job to show me her beautiful new hairstyle, but when she got there, I wasn't there. My manager told my mother why I wasn't there. Earlier that evening, my manager let me go home early – I just chose not to go home.

The natural question in my mother's head when she received this news from my manager was, "Where is my daughter?" Her mother's intuition convinced her that I was up to no good, but she didn't quite know what. The reality was that my "brilliance" as a seemingly responsible 16-year-old earned me the privilege and trust of having my own car. I used that privilege and trust to drive that car over to my 19-year-old boyfriend's house and well – let's just say we did what two hormonal teens would do in a situation with no adult supervision in just enough time for me to make it home on schedule.

BULLETS, BABIES, AND BOARDROOMS

As I came through the door, my body language and appearance gave it all away. One of my earrings was missing and the lopsided placement of my shirt told the story of just what I was doing while not at work. I was shocked to see her sitting there and I'm sure she was shocked at the way I looked when I walked through the door. I *knew* I was busted! Yet, I *still* tried to convince my mother I was elsewhere.

She asked the natural first question a mother would ask in that situation, "So, where have you been?" I quickly replied, "At work". She said, "You're lying! I went up to your job to show you my new hairstyle and you weren't there. So, I'll ask the question again. Where were you?" I said, "Over Keisha's house". She said, "You're lying". Keisha's mom and my mom were good friends, so she already determined I wasn't there, but that lie was the best I could come up with on my toes. So, she asked the question again, "Where were you?" It was at that point that I conceded and said, "Over my boyfriend's house". She was extremely upset! She grounded me immediately! I stood there in the kitchen in two seemingly disparate mental spaces. One part of me was in disbelief that I got busted, yet the other part was in an odd space of relief that I now had a window to break "the news".

There was a hallway that separated the kitchen and the family room in our home. As my mom began walking out of the kitchen and down the hall, I decided to *finally* conjure up the courage to tell her what I wanted to tell her for the last four and a half months. I needed to tell her before it was obvious *what* I needed to tell her. I needed to tell her because this whole time I *knew* I needed my mother. But I also knew that what I needed to tell her would break her heart – would crush her. But I knew I *needed* to tell her. And in that moment, in my own sixteen-year-old, undeveloped brain, undeveloped sense of emotional intelligence, undeveloped sense of compassion, and undeveloped sense of wisdom, I stood in the kitchen and yelled to her while she was walking down the hall, "Since you are mad at me already, I might as well tell you that I'm pregnant!"

I could feel my mother's entire countenance freeze. I could feel the energy of her heart literally crush in that moment. I could feel her disappointment. I could hear the thoughts running through her head of how the hopes and the dreams that she had for her 16-year-old high school senior becoming a doctor was now GONE. I felt the weight of telling my *minister* mom that her child was not just pregnant, but was also *clearly* engaging in activities not becoming of a preacher's kid. I felt the weight of her now needing to figure out how to help her baby, who's now having her own baby, when she could barely make ends meet for her own children. I felt it ALL – all her hopes and dreams for me crush in one, single moment.

She took a breath and said, "Come here". At this point I was scared. I did not know what was going to happen next. Was she going to hit me? Should I run? Should I just stand there? Tepidly, I walked toward my mother and she walked toward me. When we met somewhere in that hallway, she said, "Lift up your shirt". I lifted my shirt. She touched my belly and said, "Yep! You're pregnant". She told me to go upstairs to my room. That's when I knew that the call to my dad was next and I had NO clue how that would go. I was nervous about it ALL! The secret I kept from my parents for months was now out! What was going to happen next for me? What was going happen next for this baby? What was going to happen next for my education? What was going to happen next for all my hopes and dreams? And what will my dad say? What will he think? Will his thoughts of his daddy's girl flutter away? Will my cool, calm, and collected dad get angry? The dad that I can truly say that I can count one hand in my entire life the number of times I've seen him angry – will THAT dad get upset? I was convinced that this was going to be one of those times. It had to be! He was the one who stood side-by-side with me just two years prior when I was 14 years old and convinced the video store manager to give me a job because I was *so* responsible! It was *his* word that vouched for my character that landed me that job, and now, on this day all his hopes and dreams for his baby girl would be crushed and disappointment would set in.

Minutes later, my mom called up the stairs saying, "Your dad's on the phone and he wants to talk to you". I picked up the phone. I didn't know what to expect, but what I heard next, I certainly didn't anticipate. He said, "It's going to be okay. Everything's going to be okay. We'll get through this!" And in that moment, he gave me something money can't buy. He gave me something to hold on to. I translated his simple, yet powerful words to mean that my hopes and dreams didn't have to be crushed. This didn't have to be the end. *Yes*, I was busted, but I was no longer hopeless. With his words, I had hope that everything was going to be okay. Despite the *horrible* way that I told my mother the news that I was pregnant and despite the journey we'd ultimately have to go through to heal from that horrible moment, my dad gave me hope and I've held on to that hope ever since. A few months later I officially became a teen mother, but I held on to that hope and used it along with some other key mindset lessons, some resilience, and a whole lot of action to earn four degrees while raising my son and ultimately accomplishing my dream of becoming a doctor!

DR. ANGELA D. THOMAS

CHAPTER 2

Introduction

The debate still stands! Can we really have it all? Is the term "work-life balance" a myth? Or is it achievable? There are several reasons why the debate continues to stand. One, the meaning of "all" is subjective. What I consider "all" is not necessarily what someone else considers "all". Two, the same holds true with the word "balance". What "balance" means in my life, may not be what "balance" means in someone else's life. Yet, what I have grown to *own* in my life is that the mystery of "me" is real. The mystery of "me" is that I do seem to achieve it "all" and have it "all", while keeping it "all" in "balance". I get it. I understand why the mystery of "me" exists. I was a teenaged mother who went on to earn four college degrees, including a doctorate, all while raising my son and often working a full-time job. I earned six figures before the age of 30. I completed a four-year doctorate program in 2.5 years as a full-time wife and mother, working as a full-time healthcare executive, teaching five college classes, directing the women's ministry at my church, singing on the praise team, consistently working out six days a week, reading on average 2-3 books a month, building a business, and *always* looking for ways to challenge and develop myself. So *yes*, I get it. I get why I'm often asked, "How *did* you do it?" and "How *do* you do it?"

For many years, I struggled with the answer to this question. When I attempted to even give an answer, I honestly didn't have a good one. I'd offer answers like, *"Oh, I just knew I had to do what I had to do."* Or I'd brush it off in humility with *"I had a lot of help"*. Or I'd even give the slightly arrogant answer of, *"It never dawned on me that I couldn't"*. Or give the slightly "Oprah-esc" answer of *"I didn't want one mistake to dictate my life forever"*. Or sometimes even the super spiritual answer of *"I really don't know, just...God"*. There are many more responses that I'm sure I've used in the past, and while all of these are true, they aren't mutually exclusive, and honestly not very *helpful* to those asking the questions. I believe that many of those who have the courage to ask are not only amazed at my accomplishments, but they too have goals that they are trying to achieve, have once tried to achieve, or are thinking about setting out to achieve. They are seeking to learn how they can apply lessons I've learned in *my* life to *their* lives. I believe that the heart of the inquisition is anchored in their desire to identify something that they can grab hold of, maybe a "magic bullet", or a key formula that would allow them to achieve their goals and dreams. And THIS is *why* I've finally chosen to sit down, write, and complete this book.

Starting with Why

In his book "Start with Why", author Simon Sinek emphasizes the importance of knowing the "why" behind an idea or activity before setting out to do the "what" and the "how". Many have asked me to write a book. The first requests came after I completed my bachelor's degree in four years after having my son at 16 years old. The requests continued over the years, growing exponentially as my list of accomplishments grew. Yet, no book. Now understanding Simon Sinek's concept of *starting with why*, I can now reflect and understand *why* it took me so long to finally write and complete this book. For years I understood the "what" (the book) and the "how" (write it and publish it), but still couldn't wrap my mind around the "why". *Why* is my story important? *Why* do so many care? *Why* does my life matter?

After years of reflection, I finally understand *why*! While I do believe that the mystery of "me" is more accurately the "myth" of "me" – I don't have it "all". I experience failures like the next person. I don't keep everything in "balance". I have moments where I feel overwhelmed just like anyone else. But what I know for sure is that I consistently lean on a set of life-changing principles that I've learned along the way. I took *years* to realize that this is what I was doing. Along the way, I've added to and refined those principles. Now that I know them and can articulate them, how dare I hold on to them and not share them! While I don't believe they are a "magic bullet", I certainly believe that these life-changing principles are principles that ANYONE can grab hold of, adopt, and apply to achieve their goals and dreams. THAT is my *why* for writing this book.

The Principles

For several years now, I've captured these life-changing principles into a three-word phrase that effectively captures significant periods of my life: "Bullets, Babies, and Boardrooms". Each of these phases are at the core of how I approach success. The "Bullets" phase represents when my mother was shot five times in her stomach by a hitman in front of my grandparents' house and survived. It was this phase that set the foundation for my developing the proper "Mindset". This "Bullets" phase gave me the "G.O.O.D.S." I needed to form a key foundation for success: Goal-oriented dreams; Optimism; an Open mind; Determination; and Spirituality. The "Babies" phase represents when I gave birth to my son at the age of 16 yet went on to accomplish seemingly impossible goals. It was this phase that allowed me to develop the proper "Resilience" to handle and rise above challenges and adversity. The "Babies" phase gave me the "B.O.U.N.C.E" I needed to be able to keep moving forward despite life's challenges: Barrier busting; Overcoming; Understanding reality; Never quitting; Creating champions; and Expecting the exception. Finally, the "Boardrooms" phase represents my career journey and the lessons I've learned along the way to take the proper "Action". This "Boardrooms" phase cultivated how I work and remain focused on my journey for success to get the "R.E.S.U.L.T.S" I need to ultimately achieve success: Relentless grind; going the Extra mile; Swift action; Understanding failures; Listening and learning; Tenacious momentum, and Smart work. Together, the Mindset and GOODS from the "Bullets" phase, coupled with the Resilience and BOUNCE of the "Babies" phase, and complimented with the Action and RESULTS from the "Boardrooms" phase, combine to create "Success". I call this the "Bullets, Babies, and Boardrooms Success Framework". Yes, this framework consists of several acronyms, but my purpose is to use these acronyms as easy-to-remember guides that help to explain what I've learned along the way, how I've used them, and how you can also apply these principles successfully. Your goal may not be to receive a college degree as a teen mother, but it may be to start a business, or to become debt free, or to go back to school, or to lose weight. Whatever you set out to achieve, this framework will help you. I do believe that God has purposed me to use my story to help others to accomplish their goals, realize their dreams, and achieve success. Thank you for trusting the God in me to help you on your journey. Because God has given me this framework to share openly with others, from this point on, I will no longer refer to the framework as "MY framework", but "OUR framework". You are now one step closer to greater success, but before we dive into the details, it's important that you understand how our framework goes beyond just achievement and success but allows you to achieve *sustainable* and *scalable* success.

The Success Stool

I want you to imagine a stool with three legs. For a stool to remain sturdy, all three legs must be present, in working order, and in balance. This is how I want you to think about our framework. It has three legs – Mindset, Resilience, and Action. For *sustainable, scalable* success, you need all three legs to be present, in working order, and in balance. What does it mean for something to be *sustainable*? One definition of *sustainable* is "pertaining to a system that maintains its own viability by using techniques that allow for continual reuse" (Dictionary.com). In our framework, this means that you must operate by a set of core principles that are timeless, viable, and can be used repeatedly. A lack of sustainability is the reason why some people achieve success and then lose it. Sound familiar? Have you ever met someone who lost weight and then gained it all back? Ever heard of one hit wonders in music or in business? Ever heard of 15 minutes of fame? All these situations reflect a lack of sustainability. The principles in our framework are sustainable, timeless, viable, and can be used repeatedly.

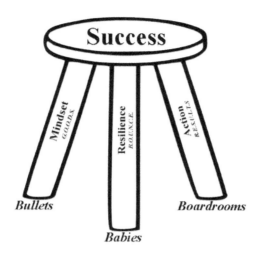

What does it mean for something to be *scalable*? One definition of *scalable* is "used to describe a business or system that is able to grow or to be made larger" (Dictionary.cambridge.org). Success principles that are scalable only matter to those who desire to be successful in more than one area of their life. That's certainly me, and I'm guessing that's you too! In our framework this means that you must operate by a set of core principles that are reliable enough that no matter what you're aiming to accomplish, you can apply those same principles to another set of goals, to another dream, to another vision, and be able to achieve success. These core principles must work together as a "system" to enhance and grow your level of success. A lack of scalability is the reason why some people are successful in some areas of their lives, yet not successful in others. Sound familiar? Have you ever met someone who is successful in their career, but failing in their family life? Ever met someone who is healthy and fit, yet their finances are a mess? This is because some goals require more *action* than *resilience*. Some require more *mindset* than *action*. Some require more *resilience* than *mindset*. Those who have all three can accomplish any goal. Without all three legs, just like a stool, you may run into trouble. This framework teaches you the elements of all three legs of the framework and how to apply all three to any situation. Therefore, the framework is applicable even if you're not a 16-year-old teenage mother trying to finish college!

We're almost ready to dive in, but before we do, I want to issue a warning. A huge temptation in reading this book is to skip right to "Action". Think of a home. What you "see" is the siding, doors, windows, and everything else inside the house that make it a home. But what you don't see is just as important as what you see. What you don't see is the foundation, the concrete, the plumbing system, the electrical system, and more. Without these components working properly, while you can build a house that looks pretty, it won't sustain changes in weather, won't function properly, and eventually will deteriorate over time. While "Action" is certainly the piece we "see", our "Mindset" and "Resilience" are absolutely critical to the sustainability and scalability of our success. As you read, be sure that you give equal weight and credibility to each of the three legs in the framework. You may find that you're stronger in one area than the other, about even in all three, or really need to work on one leg in particular. This book will help you uncover your aptitude in each of these areas and provide you with some tools that will help you increase your aptitude in each one.

About the Three Phases

This book is separated into three main phases. Phase I is "Bullets" and is all about the "Mindset" phase, Phase II is "Babies" and is all about the "Resilience" phase, and Phase III is "Boardrooms" and is all about the "Action" phase.

"Mindset" is the "foundational" phase. It focuses on *who you are and what you believe*. This phase will challenge you to be self-reflective. You must uncover some things about yourself in this phase. You must be honest with yourself. You really need to determine how you see the world and those key experiences that have helped to frame your perspective. You may find that your current perspective is ripe for achieving success. However, you may also find some areas of opportunity to shift your thinking that will subsequently increase your likelihood for success. Although this isn't the "Action" phase, you still must do some *work* in this phase. You must get "real". You must take an inventory. I'll challenge you to write some things down. You'll learn some new concepts and ultimately set the foundation and roadmap that you will need for success.

The "Resilience" phase focuses on *how you deal with challenges and adversity* and is the "core" phase. If you think of your body, your feet and legs are a foundation for how you stand, but it's your core – your abs, your back, and your chest – that allows you to stay balanced as you stand. A strong core allows you to have great posture, great balance, great kicks, and great form. It helps you to avoid an appearance of sloppiness and being out of shape. My husband is a trainer and one of the top questions he receives from his clients is, "How can I get a six-pack? How can I get great abs?" Have you ever seen someone who was thin but had a big stomach? It looks odd doesn't it? Like something is off, right? Nicer abs would probably do the trick to give them a better look. Well, that's how I want you to think about the resilience phase. It's like the "secret sauce" to giving your journey of success its balance, its posture, its sturdiness, and its form. During this phase you will learn the essential tools to overcome challenges and adversity. Again, you will need to get "real" in this phase. You will need to be brutally honest with yourself. You may even need to face some things that you've purposefully avoided for so long. This phase will show you the secrets to resilience and why it is the *core* of your success journey.

Finally, the "Action" phase is the "pinnacle" phase and focuses on *how you work and remain focused*. It's the phase that requires hard work, dedication, grind, and endurance. It also requires humility and wisdom. I would argue that for some goals, it is probably the phase that's the hardest – because it is the phase that ultimately will require the most work. I believe that it's the action phase where people get stuck or fall off the path of their goals. We see this every year, don't we? Think about New Year's resolutions. Even for those who have both mindset *and* resilience –they fall off by February or March because they did not have the action, the follow-through, the momentum, and the wisdom. It's the action phase that is the pinnacle of our success framework and in tandem with the other two phases, is so crucial to your ability to accomplish your goals and achieve success. Once you complete and understand all three phases, you will see that it is more than possible to achieve success in any area. It will take *mindset*, *resilience*, and *action*, but you can do it! If I can do it, so can you!

A Note on Faith

One last note. I'm *clearly* a woman of faith – a follower of Christ! Without apology, I am convinced that my faith has played and continues to play a critical role in my achievements. Therefore, there is absolutely *no way* that I can tell my story without referring to my faith. Therefore, I will reference my faith throughout the book. At the end of each chapter, I also reference a scripture that aligns with the concepts taught in that chapter. The goal of this book is not to "sell" my faith to you, but to tell my story. However, if the role of my faith in my story inspires you to want to know *more* about my faith, don't hesitate to reach out to me at www.DrAngelaDThomas.com . *Now* let's get started!

Phase I: "Bullets" – The Mindset Phase

Phase I: "Bullets" – The Mindset Phase

CHAPTER 3

G.O.O.D.S. – Who You Are and What You Believe

Exposure from a young age to the realities of the world is a super-big thing.
~Bill Gates

Introduction

Can you identify a pivotal moment in your life where you are *absolutely certain* that it was *that* moment that set the foundation for the rest of your life? *That* moment that formed how you would approach life from that moment forward. *That* moment that formed what you believe, your mindset, and how you would approach every decision in your life, good or bad. *That* moment that altered your life FOREVER. For me, I know *that* moment. In fact, there were two.

My life before the first moment looked drastically different. I am the daughter of Victor and Denise who were happily married when they had children. I'm the second child of three. After they married, they had my older brother Aaron, then me, and then my younger brother Adam. We are very close in age. I'm 22 months younger than my older brother, and 18 months older than my younger brother. We didn't have a whole lot, but we sure had fun times growing up as a nuclear family in Detroit, Michigan.

My parents set a good foundation for us. We were in private school in our younger years. For me, that was from preschool through second grade. It wasn't until third grade that I went to public school, but that stent in private school set the foundation for me academically. My parents also set a sound foundation for us spiritually. They kept us in church *all* the time. More on that later, but we had a good life. Again, we didn't have a whole lot, but we had each other. We had family, we had birthday parties, we had a bike rides, we had running around the track at the neighborhood high school, we had homemade pizza, and we had Friday trips to Dunkin Donuts before school and White Castle after school – just many fun times as a family.

It was this reality of having a cohesive family that originally allowed us to feel a sense of connection with a sitcom family named "The Huxtables" when a popular television show launched in 1984. This began one of the pivotal moments of my life. I related to the character Rudy. She was the youngest sister, five years old, and in 1984 that meant she was *my* age. I related to her having siblings, specifically related to having an older brother. But it was interesting that my relation to the show really didn't hang its hat on Rudy. I really began to focus on the main character Dr. Heathcliff Huxtable who delivered babies professionally as an Obstetrician. Now the show itself was both relatable and eye-opening simultaneously. While my family related to the fun times and the family dynamic, we did not relate to having a physician and a lawyer in the home. We didn't even relate to five kids in a home. We didn't relate to a reality of no financial worries. But I didn't focus on any of those things. I focused on the fact that Heathcliff Huxtable was in a profession where he could deliver babies and help women. He was a DOCTOR! I had never seen what a doctor really did, and it was great to see as a child a doctor who was my color on television. And that was it! I decided that I wanted to do what Heathcliff Huxtable did for a living. I wanted to be an Obstetrician. From that moment forward, that became my goal. My goal was to be a doctor. This was pivotal moment number *one*! It's when my dream formed, and it was because of a television family known as The Huxtables.

But I mentioned that there were *two* pivotal moments in my life. The second pivotal moment came in the year 1992 when it was clear that my family's ability to relate to The Huxtables' family cohesion was no longer a reality. It was absolutely broken! And THAT was absolutely devastating to me! My dad left the home and my parents got divorced. It was a new normal that I just did not want to get used to. It was awful! But if I thought that the divorce alone shattered this image that we had of this perfect Huxtable-type household, we were all in for a rude awakening for what was to come next!

I remember December 8, 1992 beginning as a *fantastic* day! I remember the sunshine. I remember having a great day at school and having fun on the city bus ride to and from school laughing with my friends. It was just such a great day until I got a call from my aunt. My aunt called to tell me that my uncle was coming to pick me and my younger brother up from the house because my mother had an accident. For context, this particular year had been full of "accidents" for my mom, especially with her knees. She fell and crushed her knees a couple of times that year. I just thought that it was related to her knees. So that news alone wasn't enough to ruin the day. I told my younger brother what was happening, and we got ready to leave.

My uncle came as my aunt promised and my brother and I got in the car. I sat in the backseat. When I sat in the backseat, there was a shotgun on the seat. That was my first clue that something was wrong. There had to have been something more than just crushed knees. And *that's* when it happened! I heard my uncle on the phone talking to someone when he said my mother had been shot. It was in that moment that I knew that it was serious. I began to cry.

He drove to my grandparents' house and when we got there, it was dark. It was dark physically and it was dark emotionally. There were sirens everywhere, police, ambulances, the media – it was pandemonium. I knew that the shooting must have happened right on my grandparents' street. It was later that I learned what really happened that day.

It was my aunt's birthday. My mom left work at her usual time. She was working as a probation officer in Detroit for the State of Michigan.

On the way home from work she was scheduled to pick up a cake for my aunt's birthday. When she went to the cake lady's home, she wasn't home yet. Since the cake lady lived right around the corner from my grandparents, my mother decided that she would head over to my grandparents' house because she needed to buy a ticket to my grandfather's retirement party.

When my mother arrived at my grandparents' house, she got out of the car, left her gun, her badge, and her purse behind. She took $20, balled it up in her fist, and began to walk toward the house. This meant my mom really had nothing of value on her besides the $20 bill in her hand and the gold stud earrings in her ears. She continued walking toward my grandparents' house when she heard something like a rustling leaf behind her. She turned around and she was met by an assailant who had a gun. The assailant pointed the gun to her chest and said something like, "Give me 'em." She said it was muffled. She couldn't quite understand. She perceived it as a robbery attempt. She was scared. In her fear, in front of her parents' house as any daughter would, she cried out for her mom and nothing happened. She cried out for her dad and nothing happened. Then she cried out "Jesus" as she was taught to do as a minister in church. She was taught that Jesus was the name to call when in trouble. When she did that, she said things started to change. According to her, the assailant's countenance grew incredibly scary. It was so scary that she began back away in fear. When she stepped back, she tripped and fell backward, hitting the ground, and landing on her back.

This fall shifted the gun from her chest to her stomach. It was at that point that the assailant was so upset that he decided to go ahead and shoot. He shot once, but the gun jammed. In this moment, she thought that calling on the name of Jesus actually helped the situation. But much to her surprise, he pulled the trigger again, and again, and again, and again, and again! Each of those next five shots were successful. She was shot five times in her stomach at close range by a nine-millimeter gun, on that cold night of December 8, 1992, in front of my grandparents' house. The assailant then ran away. In that moment, she laid on the ground cold and hoping somebody would help her. And what happened next, became the second pivotal moment in my life!

My mother says that in that moment where she was laying there on the cold ground in her blood, in front of her parents' house waiting for help, God gave her a choice. He gave her a choice to live or to die. She said that in that moment, she chose to live for her children. When she made the choice to live for her children, *immediately* help started to come. My grandparents came out of the house because they heard the shots. Neighbors started to come out of their homes – neighbors who she grew up with who became emergency professionals such as nurses and police officers. The paramedics also showed up on the scene. Collectively, they were all working together to save her life. She was rushed to the hospital and 12 days later, she was released. She recovered for a few weeks at my grandparents' house then came home to finish her recovery, and ultimately returned to work. It was at work that she received an anonymous phone call that the shooting was not an attempted robbery gone bad. It was a hitman who was hired by one of her probation clients to have her killed because she was going to recommend that the client to go back to prison for a probation violation. The client decided that having her killed would keep him out of prison. When she realized she was shot because of a hit on her life, she decided that it was safer for her to come home from work and end her career as an active probation officer.

You may be wondering which element of the story makes this a pivotal moment in *my* life. Maybe you're assuming it's the fact that she lived – my life would have been different growing up without my mother. Or you may assume that because she left work and was shot, our lives weren't the same – there were money issues and depression issues and much more. While all of that is true, the true reason I tell this story is because the pivotal moment came in her *choice*. This was a powerful lesson for me in the power of choices. She had a choice to live or to die and she chose to live not just for herself, but specifically for her children. Looking today at how her children turned out – pastors, ministers, world travelers, well-educated, great parents, great spouses, touching the lives of youth, and the lives of men and women and organizations nationally and internationally – I can only imagine how we would have turned out if my mother chose to die. We would have lost our mother right there on that cold ground in front of my grandparents' house on December 8, 1992.

Two pivotal moments in my life – the moment I started to dream and the moment that I realized the power of choices. When you pull those two things together, a dream and the reality that you have the power to choose your destiny, they become a strong foundation for success. This mindset carries you throughout your success journey. This mindset keeps you dreaming because you know you have the power to choose along the way. So that's why this particular phase is important.

Phase I: "Bullets" discusses the importance of your mindset and the foundation of the "GOODS" that you bring to the table – who you are and what you believe. We explore mindset in five different ways in the order presented in the acronym G.O.O.D.S – Goal-oriented dreams; Optimism, an Open mind; Determination; and Spirituality. Each of these is critical to your mindset and not even *one* can be overlooked. We'll start with diving into goals and end with spirituality. I personally like to start anything with a spiritual component, but the acronym simply didn't work out that way. My hope is that the section on goals will open new ways of thinking for you around familiar concepts. We'll then hit two "Os" along the way and explore them – optimism and having an open mind – as they go hand in hand. The section on determination introduces a new concept of *sustainable determination* and how to achieve it. Finally, we discuss spirituality. This is NOT a section about religion – I repeat, NOT a section about religion or my attempt to convert you, but an opportunity to explore how believing in something *greater than you* is critical for your success journey. When you have a sound grasp on these five critical elements and actively demonstrate each of them in your life, then you have the mindset necessary to achieve success. You have the GOODS!

DR. ANGELA D. THOMAS

And be not conformed to this world: but be ye transformed by the renewing of your mind, that ye may prove what is that good, and acceptable, and perfect, will of God ~Romans 12:2 (King James Version)

CHAPTER 4

Goal-oriented Dreams

If you can dream it, you can achieve it. ~Zig Ziglar

Have you ever taken inventory of your life and found yourself wishing you were so much further along? Are there dreams that you have yet to achieve? Maybe some dreams you even thought you would have achieved by this stage in your life. Have you set goals and have yet to accomplish them? Maybe you started but then stopped. Maybe you're still trying, but you're not seeing the results that you would have hoped to have seen by now. Maybe you see a bigger, grander plan for your life, but your current state seems so far from that vision. Maybe the thought of getting there seems so far away, that it seems like a daunting and nearly hopeless task. Does any of this sound like you? Are you in this head space for anything you are trying to achieve? This section should help you. Let's start with discussing dreams!

People have dreams for many reasons. For some, watching someone else helped to cultivate that dream – maybe watching a parent, a neighbor, a celebrity, a President, or a family member. For others, a God-given gift cultivates the dream and sparks a desire to do more with that gift. Other dreams are handed down by parents who have a very specific desire for their child to achieve a very specific dream. That child may or may not buy into that dream. Sometimes dreams are cultivated by the norms of society – to have a family, with a house, living financially sound, in good health, and as an upstanding citizen. Regardless of how dreams are cultivated, without a dream, goals don't have a lot of substance. They just become "things to do".

It's like driving a car down street after street with no destination in sight. You may land somewhere, but it's random. It may be a good neighborhood, but maybe not. Dreams are important. They become your destination point.

My Huxtable story highlights how dreams can be cultivated. Mine was cultivated by watching Heathcliff Huxtable in his profession as an Obstetrician. This became my destination – to become an Obstetrician. I didn't have much of a clue of how I was going to get there, but I knew that's where I wanted to eventually land. Whatever the stage in my life, this dream became the point of reference for me – for choices and decisions to come. Although this became a point of reference, I still had the unanswered question of, "How do I get there?" This is where goals become important. Without goals, a dream remains just that – a dream.

In business, one of the most popular and common acronyms for goal setting is S.M.A.R.T. There are some slight variations to the definition of S.M.A.R.T., but for our purposes we will use the following definition: S – Specific, M – Measurable, A – Attainable, R – Realistic, and T – Timebound. So, let's go back to the Huxtables before we jump into SMART goals. The show first aired in 1984, so that would mean I was five years old when it debuted. I mention this to give perspective. At five years old I didn't have the slightest clue about SMART goals. I was academically smart for a five-year-old, but I was not walking around at five years old with the SMART acronym in my head. I actually did not discover SMART goals until I was in my twenties and working in management positions. However, retrospectively, I do realize that there were some elements of SMART and "not so SMART" goals on my journey. It is important that you understand why you need SMART goals and how to use them on your journey to success.

Specific Goals

S – Specific! At five years old, I was actually specific. I wanted to become an Obstetrician. I wanted to be a doctor who delivered babies. A specific goal is just that – specific. I find it's easiest to understand specific goals by giving examples of *non*-specific goals. Let's take my specific goal of becoming an Obstetrician as an example. A non-specific version of this goal would be "I want to be successful". Or "I want to do something important". Or "I want a career". Or "I want to be a professional". Each of these are so broad, it becomes very difficult to create focus. It's like driving, looking for the next street to turn on, but you can't read the name of the sign. It's fuzzy. You're not sure if it actually represents where you want to turn or where you're trying to go. You may find that you're in the right neighborhood, but your actual destination is fuzzy and non-specific, leading you to turn on several random streets, hoping you eventually stumble across your destination. Sometimes, it takes you getting right up on the sign to realize that it's time for you to turn. You end up turning at the last minute – or even missing the turn altogether.

In general, I have 2020 vision. But there was a point in my twenties where seeing distances became increasingly difficult. Things were slightly fuzzy. I was prescribed some glasses for distances. These glasses became extra crucial when I was driving at night to a destination that was unfamiliar to me. When I was driving at night to a familiar place, I had no problems – no big deal. I knew each turn by heart, so I had no need to pay attention to, or to be able to see any street signs. But it was the unfamiliar destinations at night that were a problem. Being able to see and read each street sign at a distance became crucial! I needed to be able to properly prepare for a turn, properly notify other drivers with a turn signal, slow down in time, and not miss the turn! My glasses were so critical to my being able to read these signs. When I didn't have my glasses and found myself driving to an unfamiliar destination at night, it was a mess! I would miss streets or turn abruptly or just get completely turned around. This was quite dangerous. I could have caused accidents. I could have found myself in unsafe neighborhoods and situations. Yes, this was even before the popular use of the GPS. I had old-school maps and directions to follow, so being able to see clearly was crucial.

For your goals, if you have a non-specific destination, your journey will be filled with wrong turns, missed opportunities, and abrupt and sometimes hasty decisions. This too is dangerous to your being able to accomplish your goals. Think about what you want to do. Put your glasses of "focus" on and get specific. Try the *"What does that look like?"* test. To do this, you simply set the goal. For illustration, let's use a vague goal. Goal: "I want to lose weight". Ask the question: "What does losing weight look like?" Answer: "Being thinner." Ask the question: "What does being thinner look like?" Answer: "Fitting into the clothes I can't wear anymore". Question: "What does fitting into your clothes that you can't wear anymore look like?" Answer: "Fitting into a size 6 or 8." Question: "What does fitting into a size 6 or 8 look like?" Answer: "Losing about 20 pounds". *Now* we're specific!

The goal "I want to lose weight" actually functions more like a dream than a goal. One can see how if the goal was left at "I want to lose weight", it would be difficult to determine when that goal was achieved – thereby potentially becoming a perpetual dream. It's hard to know if the goal is achieved at 1 pound or at 100 pounds. For this person, it would be 20 pounds. That's a specific goal. It has successfully been converted from a dream "I want to lose weight"; to a goal "I want to lose 20 pounds". What goals do you have in your life? Are they specific enough? Are they really dreams that need to be converted to goals? Put them to the *"What does that look like?"* test. You may be surprised to find that they could be more specific. The more specific the goal, the safer your journey becomes, and you will avoid potentially dangerous pitfalls. Once your goals are specific, then write them down!

Measurable Goals

M – Measurable! Now, let's revisit my specific goal of becoming an Obstetrician. The only way to measure this goal is to actually become an Obstetrician. But I also needed a medical degree and then I needed to get board certified to specialize in Obstetrics. The problem at five years old is that you don't know how to gauge whether or not you are on the right path to success. So, while my goal technically had a measure "Are you an Obstetrician, yes or no?", there needed to me more opportunities for measurement along the way.

Let's go back to the weight loss example. The specific goal was to lose 20 pounds. That's measurable. If you know your starting weight, you can simply go on the scale, determine your existing weight, and then subtract your existing weight from your starting weight to see if the difference is 20 pounds or more. If the difference is 20 or more pounds, then you've accomplished that goal. If not, then you haven't. But like the goal of becoming an Obstetrician, "measurable" becomes more meaningful and more useful when you build in measurement opportunities along the way. To do this, you must think of "sub-goals". Let's use weight loss as an example again, but this time, let's move the goal from 20 pounds to 100 pounds. At this higher goal, it's a little easier to see why and how sub-goals might become more useful. An example of a sub-goal in this scenario would be "I would like to lose 1-2 pounds per week". This sub-goal has become your opportunity to measure your progress along the way. For my Obstetrician goal, as an elementary school student, I probably had enough sense to know that doctors were smart. So maybe the sub-goal in that scenario would be, "I will get all As and Bs on each report card". This would give me the opportunity to measure my progress toward being an Obstetrician.

Measurement is also useful in helping you to map your journey. It does no good in our weight loss example to say I want to lose 100 pounds and do so by losing 1-2 pounds per week if there is nothing done about our diet and exercise habits. Hopefully, a rational person would at least ask the question, "So how will I get there?" Enter the *"How will I get there?"* test. In the weight loss example, we would need to create more sub-goals. Asking, "How will I get there?" can help identify several sub-goals. One sub-goal could be: "I would like to do cardiovascular training at three times per week and strength training two times per week". Another related sub-goal could be: "I would like to consume 1500-1800 calories a day". Another related sub-goal could be: "I would like to drink at least one gallon of water per day". Each of these sub-goals is related and should lead to the weekly goal of losing 1-2 pounds, and the main goal of losing 100 pounds.

For my Obstetrician goal, I was smart enough to know that math and science were extremely crucial to becoming an Obstetrician. Therefore, although one sub-goal would be to get all As and Bs on my report card, another sub-goal could be to make sure I got all As in math and science classes. I could even drill it down further to state that my goal was to get all As and Bs on each assignment in class. The main goal then becomes the As and Bs on the report card and the sub-goal is now As and Bs on the assignments. This gives even more opportunities to measure progress. This is the power of measurement – feedback on progress. If along the way, the scale doesn't move or goes in the wrong direction, or if I were to get a C, D or F on an assignment, it serves as a re-evaluation trigger. It's a trigger that something is going wrong and maybe a sub-goal should be modified or added to the journey, such as hiring a tutor or completing longer cardio sessions. Measurement is crucial on your journey. It is the reason why when I use a GPS device, I like to be able to see how many miles are remaining and how much time before I get there. It's feedback on my progress and not only lets me know that I'm headed in the right direction, but also lets me know about delays on my journey. Are your goals measurable? Do you have enough opportunities for feedback along the way? Is there an opportunity for sub-goals that will help you measure your progress? Once you have your measurement criteria and any sub-goals, write them down!

Attainable Goals

A – Attainable! So now that our goal is specific enough, meaning it is actually a goal and not a dream, and it's also measurable with enough opportunities for feedback along the way, the question now becomes, "Is it attainable?" Let's go back to our faithful weight loss example of losing 100 pounds. If your goal is to lose 100 pounds, but you only weigh 105, this is not considered to be an attainable goal. You WILL die before you hit 100 pounds of weight loss. The goal of losing 100 pounds by tomorrow isn't considered attainable. This goes back to knowing the journey. You need to have at least some familiarity with what is necessary to accomplish the goal to determine if it's attainable. In general, anyone who is dedicated to the journey and willing to work hard to do what it takes can accomplish nearly anything. I would love to write "anything", without the qualifier "nearly" as technology and scientific advances make so many things possible. However, there are many things that remain impossible. No matter how hard I try, I could never trade places with my Yorkie, become 10 years old again, or marry Jesus. Some of these goals defy science, time, rules, and access.

Enter the *"What would need to happen for me to do that?"* test. State your goal and then ask, "What would need to happen for me to do that?" In general, if you need a time machine, or if major scientific changes are necessary to accomplish a goal like being able to live as a woman weighing only five pounds, or transforming into a Yorkie, the goal is unattainable. Literally, these are goals that are physically unattainable. To achieve these goals, you would need a God-given miracle. As a faith-based woman, I don't want to say that they are impossible, but they are possible ONLY if God intervenes and just does it for you. These are goals that if you were to state them out loud, your family may want to have you committed for a psychiatric evaluation. Think about your goals. What would need to happen for you to achieve them? Are they attainable? Are they even physically possible for you to reach? If so, keep them. If not, re-evaluate them so that they become attainable.

Realistic Goals

R – Realistic! I have a different spin on realistic. There is an important difference between attainable and realistic. To really appreciate the difference, I want you to think "dream killer". No one wants to be considered a "dream killer". These are people who always find a reason why someone can't do something – why it's impossible. At the attainable state, you are not a dream killer if someone wants to turn into a Yorkie and you tell them they can't. They physically cannot. This is not dream killing. This is simply telling the person that the dream is unattainable. On the other hand, you could be considered a dream killer if you told a 40-year-old man who wants to now become an NBA star that he couldn't. Now, we all know that in the era of Steph Curry and Lebron James and 19-year-olds in tip top condition who have been playing and conditioning for basketball their entire lives, that a 40-year-old man who suddenly wants to get into the basketball game does not have a realistic goal. However, is it impossible? Not necessarily. He could work extremely hard, establish the right training regimen, the right connections, be trained by the best, become the best, and then get drafted! Not realistic, but not impossible. This is where dream killing comes in. If there is even a chance that it could happen, but the odds say that it won't, this puts it in the "unrealistic column".

Unrealistic can also be rule-based. There are just rules that prevent some goals from being realistic. Take this example. Someone dropped out of high school, has absolutely no intentions of wanting to finish, no intentions of going to college, let alone medical school, and has a goal of becoming an Obstetrician. This is unrealistic. Unless the rules of becoming a certified physician change, or this person does a whole slew of illegal things successfully, this is not a realistic goal.

The fact of the matter is this. I wouldn't be writing this book if I didn't believe in unrealistic goals. I do realize that having a baby at 16, not only finishing high school and college, but also obtaining four degrees and then going on to earn six figures before the age of 30, all while raising a child is an unrealistic goal. But since I did accomplish every single one of those things, it is an attainable goal. Were there people along the way who believed that it was impossible? Sure. Were there people along the way who tried to be dream killers – with both good and bad intentions? Sure. Therefore, I want to be cautious about how I give instructions about realistic goals. I never want to be a dream killer. My instructions are that you just need to "get real" about what it will take for you to do what you aspire to do.

While statistics and odds and resources may deem the goal as unrealistic, it doesn't mean it's unattainable. If you are willing to go down the path of most resistance, work hard, do what it takes, stay focused, and put in the blood sweat and tears, then I say do it. However, your goal will never become realistic if you don't get real about your journey. Therefore, for the realistic element of SMART goals, there is a two-part test.

Part one is the *"What do I need to get real about?"* test. Figure out the journey ahead, be honest about your current state. Figure out *everything* that stands between your current state and your desired state. The second part is the *"Am I all in?"* test. Once you have figured out everything that stands between your current state and your desired state, you must determine if you are fully committed to the journey. What are your goals? Are you *really* sure about what it would take you to get from your current state to your desired state? Are you fully committed to the journey? If no, re-evaluate your goals. If yes, write down not only the goal, but also your journey. Also write down the potential pitfalls. What will be so challenging along the way that if you succumb to the pitfalls, your goal becomes unrealistic? What is your plan to overcome those barriers? What support do you have around you to help you if you do face those barriers? Realistic goals are attainable, but you just need to get real and be REALLY committed.

Timebound Goals

T – Timebound! A goal not only should be specific, measurable, attainable, and realistic, but it must also be timebound. Like the measurable component of goal setting, having a deadline or time parameter around the goal is an opportunity for feedback. By what date do you hope to have accomplished your goal? Let's go back to our weight loss example. The goal is to lose 100 pounds by losing 1-2 pounds per week. Well, if we still want our goal to be attainable and realistic, we must also set a time parameter that matches the goal. Based on this, we can do it as fast as 50 weeks (2 pounds per week) or as long as 100 weeks (1 pound per week). Setting this for four weeks gives it a time parameter but makes it unrealistic. That would mean a weight loss of 25 pounds per week. Likewise, one can see how not setting a time parameter on the goal could lead to a lack of focus or a lack of commitment to your goal. This is why so many New Year's resolutions fail. If you think about it, these resolutions are set as something you want to accomplish in the year. But when in the year? By what time? Most people who don't make their goals timebound get all the way to the end of the year and realize they hadn't accomplished what they set out to do 365 days ago! This is why it's important that you not only apply time parameters to the main goal, but also apply time parameters to the sub-goals. Our sub-goal of losing 1-2 pounds per week has a time parameter built in. Each week or every seven days, there should be a 1 to 2 pound weight loss. For my goal of becoming an Obstetrician, the time parameter to the all As and Bs on report cards occurred each time a report card was issued (about four times per year). Enter the *"By When?"* test. For each goal and sub-goal, ask yourself, "By When"? Your answer should yield a reasonable time parameter. Do your goals have a time parameter? Does the time parameter make sense for your goals? Having timebound goals not only is SMART, but also motivates you to accomplish the goal as the time will come for you to answer the question – "Did I accomplish my goal?"

Questions to Consider

Throughout this section, we primarily used two examples to help us understand the importance of dreams and goals and how to develop SMART goals. One example was focused on physical health, losing weight, and the other around a professional goal, becoming an Obstetrician. Each of us have many other areas of our lives for which we should form dreams and goals. In his book "Grounded", Bob Rosen identifies six important areas of health – physical, emotional, intellectual, social, vocational (could also be called professional), and spiritual. I find it useful to think of these six areas in the context of dreams and goals. Consider the following questions for each of the six areas – physical, emotional, intellectual, social, vocational, and spiritual – as you assess your own dreams and goals:

1. What are my dreams?
2. What can I do today to create a visual representation of my dreams?
3. How can I make my goals SMART?
4. What modifications must I make to ensure my goals pass the following tests:
    a. What does that look like?
    b. How will I get there?
    c. What would need to happen for me to do that?
    d. Am I all in?
    e. By When?

5. Where have I written down my dreams and goals?

   Where there is no vision, the people perish... ~Proverbs 29:18
   (King James Version)

DR. ANGELA D. THOMAS

CHAPTER 5

<u>O</u>ptimism & an <u>O</u>pen Mind

I know for sure that what we dwell on is who we become. ~Oprah Winfrey

Remember the time you were so convinced that something would work out, only to be let down when it didn't? Maybe you even told several people about how confident that you were that it would in fact work out, only to have to go back with your tail between your legs and admit that it didn't work. Has someone ever been hopeful that something would work out, but *you* told them that it *wouldn't*? And you only told them this to protect them because there was actually a chance that it *wouldn't* work out? Have you ever had someone say this to you?

Let's consider the reversed situation. Remember the time you were so convinced that something *would* work out despite many reasons why it possibly could not, and you were RIGHT? It actually *did* work out! You were able to prove your naysayers wrong! You were able to rejoice with those who believed *with* you. Have you ever encouraged someone that something that they were hoping would work out would *indeed* work out because there was actually a chance that it *could*? Have you ever had someone say this to you?

The difference in these two sets of scenarios boils down to a difference between optimism and open-mindedness as opposed to pessimism and close-mindedness. These are two extremes of a spectrum. We all have operated at some point along the continuum of the spectrum, but in general, it's most beneficial on your success journey to have a healthy sense of optimism and open-mindedness, than to operate most often as a close-minded pessimist.

Optimists versus Pessimists

According to the Merriam-Webster Dictionary, an *optimist* is "a person who is inclined to be hopeful and to expect good outcomes" and a *pessimist* is "a person who is inclined to expect poor outcomes". Several sources in spiritual, academic, and leadership genres speak to the power of positive thinking, the power of positive speaking, or both. Napoleon Hill made a successful career through several writings on the power of thinking positively. Some examples of his books include, "Think and Grow Rich", "Success through a Positive Mental Attitude", and "Think your way to Wealth". The oldest book on the planet, the Bible, speaks to the power of words through scripture such as *"Death and life are in the power of the tongue..." (Proverbs 18:21 King James Version).* Many other leadership gurus such as David Schwartz, John Maxwell, and Tony Robins all give examples of the power of thinking and speaking positively on your journey to success. If you believe that these principles are true (and if you don't, I'm hoping to convince you) then you should also believe that the optimist who, by definition has an open mind, is likely to become more successful than the pessimist who has a closed-minded view of the world. Let's explore why.

I recall a time when I received a text from a good friend who let me know that he had something to tell me about work. I gave him a call and he proceeded to tell me about how he was recommended for a very important program at work – a program that was in an area where he was believing for an open door. He was recommended by his boss's boss for this program and received the recommendation via email. Several people were cc'd on the email. He went on to explain how so many people who were cc'd congratulated him and said how well-deserved the recommendation was and how amazing an opportunity this was for him. I was excited! My optimistic and open-minded self was overjoyed! But I waited before expressing my excitement. I kept listening. As I was listening, I kept waiting for him to give me, "Oh my gosh! Isn't this so exciting?" I kept waiting with bated breath to rejoice with my friend and instead, at the end of the story he complained that *one* person who was cc'd on the email said nothing to him. "Nothing, Angela. He said nothing!" After all of that, that's what I heard my friend say.

I sat there thinking, "Are you kidding me? You focus on the one person who said nothing when this door opened for you? When you got recommended by your *boss's boss*? When all these other people congratulated you? And you're upset because this person who was cc'd on this email said nothing?" I was floored, and I called him on his attitude. After I called him on it, he did not automatically go into an overjoyed and rejoicing mindset. He just said, "You know what? I guess you're right. I guess so...I guess. Alright...I guess." It was so disheartening to hear that someone who I cared about, who was a self-proclaimed pessimist still in this moment chose to highlight what was negative instead of focusing on the positive. The optimist (me) saw the email recommendation as a beautiful moment, while the pessimist (him) saw it as a frustrating moment. Let's take another example.

There was a candidate who we flew in from California to come to DC to interview for a position. All her interviews were fantastic. Everyone absolutely loved her. It was great until the snow started. She completely unraveled on us. She got over-the-top nervous about the flight, nervous about the car arriving on time, made an unreasonable number of phone calls to high-level leaders, and overall made the situation sound much bigger than it needed to be. She reacted as if she never traveled before and never knew that delays in travel could happen for factors beyond her control. It was a bad situation, but we wanted to make sure she was comfortable, so we accommodated her by paying whatever we needed to pay to ensure her comfort. However, we made the decision that it was clear she was not our candidate. We needed someone who would have seen that situation a bit differently and would have been a bit more resilient (more on "Resilience" later). While a pessimist could've looked at that situation as overwhelmingly negative and a waste of time and resources, our team focused on the snow. We thanked God for the snow because without the snow, we would not have realized early in the process how she would unravel under pressure. We were thankful and grateful and saw the snow as a positive factor that allowed us to learn how to better gauge resilience and fortitude in our interview process.

These two examples highlight how a pessimist can take an overwhelmingly positive situation and focus on the negative, while optimists can take an overwhelmingly negative situation and find the positive. That's the difference between an optimist and a pessimist. In this section we'll further explore the benefits of an optimistic and open-minded perception on your journey to success.

The Power of Belief

I believe, without a doubt, that to successfully accomplish your goals and dreams it is so important to be optimistic and open-minded. You must be able to believe in your ability to accomplish your goals to achieve them. It's belief that keeps you motivated and keeps you going. It's belief in your ability to accomplish your goals that allows you to push through barriers, push through haters, and stay on course. I truly believe that pessimists stay pessimists because they actively seek reasons to validate their position. Likewise, optimists remain optimists because they actively seek reasons to validate their position. Which of these two paradigms are most likely to yield success? The optimist! Think about it, if an optimist is constantly seeking ways to validate their ability to achieve their goals, this validation comes in the form of continuing to work hard, celebrating successes along the way, and pointing out the good throughout the journey. When barriers come, instead of having the attitude of why they *can't*, they find ways to figure out why they *can*. In other words, they figure out ways to overcome the barrier. Let's take the pessimist in contrast. The pessimist is always looking for ways to validate why accomplishing the goal is impossible. Each barrier that presents itself validates this point. Instead of asking why they can, they always see the barrier as a reason why they cannot. For this reason, pessimists are less likely to have success in accomplishing goals when compared to optimists.

While I was in college, there were absolutely days where I felt like being a mom, a student, and an employee were just impossible. There were days I was tired, or my son was sick, or I didn't get the best grade in the class. There were clear reasons to quit along the way. Some days felt like absolutely nothing went right. Some semesters even felt like I was just in over my head. I remember having one semester when I got my first D – ever! I was crushed. I questioned whether or not I was cut out for college. I questioned whether any kind of graduate school was even possible since the D was not the most favorable for my GPA. I wanted to give up! However, I looked at the glass as half full. All the other grades I had achieved up to that point were good. I still had an entire year of college left. I knew that I could buckle down, get good grades moving forward, and the overall picture of my scholastic achievement would outweigh the one D I received. Sure enough, I had nearly straight As my senior year and my GPA skyrocketed. It turned out that I didn't even need to explain the D on my transcript to graduate school. Because I believed in myself and saw myself as still accomplishing my goals, I remained motivated and did exactly what I set out to do. A pessimist in my situation may have viewed the D as a reflection of their aptitude. They may have even gone as far as to say they weren't smart enough for college. Typically, when this is the viewpoint, it becomes a self-fulfilling prophecy. The pessimist doesn't push as hard and doesn't stay as motivated. Before they know it, they fail out of college. You must stay positive!

The Power of Vision and Affirmation

You must view yourself as accomplishing your goal. You must envision it. It is this principle that is behind the "dream boards" and affirmations used in many circles. Dream boards are the activity of going through magazines and other print media to cut out and paste pictures of those items that represent something that you set out to achieve. Usually dream boards are filled with pictures of dream houses, dream cars, dream vacations, clothing, and other tangible items that represent success. These dream boards are to be visited often so that they serve as a reminder of those goals that you set out to achieve. This is the same type of thought that is behind the recommendation that someone who wants to lose weight find a picture of themselves at their goal weight or find a picture of someone else at that weight. Affirmations serve a similar purpose as a statement or series of statements that affirm goals and dreams. Once written, affirmations should be committed to memory and recited daily. Again, this serves as a reminder of those goals that you set out to achieve.

While in my doctoral program, everyone knew what I was working toward, including my church family. During this time, our church welcomed a new pastor and we as leaders began to work diligently to build the church and the ministry. One of the tactics we used to keep open and consistent communication was a Facebook messenger feed with all the key leaders. We would use this feed as a fast source of communication. This was prior to the Facebook feature when you could mention someone using the "@" symbol. Back then, if you wanted to mention someone, you had to type their name. In lieu of typing out their entire name, we'd use initials like the three initials for someone's first, middle, and last name, or if they had a title like "Pastor" or "Elder", we would use the initials of their title plus the initial of their first name. So "Pastor Troy" became "PT", and "Elder Donnie" became "ED".

With this model, people would simply call me "A" on Facebook messenger. This was the first time anyone ever called me "A". I got used to it though. Then something interesting happened. As I progressed further into my doctoral program, the leaders began to call me "Dr. A". It felt weird for two reasons. One, no one ever called me "A" let alone "Dr. A". Two, I hadn't yet earned a doctorate. Therefore, when I first started hearing "Dr. A", "Dr. A", "Dr. A", I would laugh it off. But they never stopped. They kept calling me "Dr. A". Over time, I started to see myself as "Dr. A". I started to respond naturally to "Dr. A" the same way I responded to "Angela" or responded to "Angie". It started to become real to me. It became something I could see – a vision! I started seeing myself successfully defending my doctoral work to my doctoral committee. I started to see myself with my doctoral cap (called a tam) on my head, being hooded by my professor as I walked across the stage. I began to see it all! It became so real – so tangible! Dr. A was imminent and eventually I *became* "Dr. A". It was the power of the vision and the constant affirmation by others who believed in me (we'll talk about "Creating Champions" later), followed by the power of me affirming myself and creating a visual picture of what being "Dr. A" looked like. I already knew what "Dr. A" *sounded* like, but then I created a vision, so I could *see* what "Dr. A" *looked* like. These forces became constant motivators to ensure that I actually *became* "Dr. A". That's the power of vision and affirmation. When you build vision and affirmation around your goals and dreams, you activate and often accelerate your success journey.

An Internal Locus of Control

Optimists and pessimists often differ by their sense of locus of control. An *internal* locus of control means that you believe that *you* have control over those things in life that occur. An *external* locus of control means that you believe that factors *outside* of your control dictate the direction of your life. I've always tried to operate with an internal locus of control. One of the most frustrating feelings for me comes when there is truly something that I cannot control that can ultimately impact my life. Even in that space, I try to find a way to control it! While being controlling isn't always healthy, for goal setting, it is very useful. When you believe that your ability to achieve a goal is influenced by your own efforts, you will give 100% and readjust *your* behavior when things don't go as planned. If you continue to ask yourself, what *you* need to do to make sure you accomplish your goals, and ensure those goals are SMART goals, if you continue to believe in your own efforts, you can get there. Even if outside factors influence the goal, you can simply "reset" the goal and figure out how to overcome those outside influences. This forces you to ask what *you* need to do to make sure *you* accomplish your goals. It's in this space that you can either *choose* to let outside influences dictate your life or you can *choose* to overcome the challenges anyway.

Once I was speaking with my executive coach about someone in the organization who clearly lacks integrity. That person's boss sometimes enables this person's behavior. We were speaking about a specific incident and if something were to come to light about that incident, that person's boss would probably only point to the person on their team's behavior and not take any ownership for their part in enabling that behavior. We went on to discuss how great leaders, no matter if the leader was directly involved or not, would stand up and take ownership for the behavior and even be willing to take the fall. The great leader would be willing to be fired because they recognize that the incident happened on *their* team, on *their* watch, and they ultimately take responsibility.

I began to think about that conversation and how strong of an internal locus of control a leader must have to take such a stance. Such a stance essentially declares, "Even though it wasn't me, I had the ability as a leader to control what happened on my team and I missed the mark. So, take me. It's my fault. I apologize. I can do better. There is a behavior change that I can make as a leader that could have prevented this situation and will prevent it from happening again". What a strong internal locus of control! For many, something goes wrong in our lives and around us and our families, on our jobs, and we're quick to point to something else and to some other factor. It's a very victim-focused mindset and represents an external locus of control. When we constantly point to factors that are external to us, it forces us to live a victim-focused lifestyle where we're walking around constantly subject to external factors that will dictate the direction of our lives. I personally don't want to live that way.

I want to live in a space of empowerment where *my* actions dictate how I live and where I go daily, and how far I go. I don't say this to imply that I'm not guided by spirituality. This couldn't be further from the truth (more on this in the "Spirituality" chapter). I am absolutely guided by my Lord and Savior, but *"...faith without works is dead..." (James 2:26 New King James Version)*. I believe that my works, things that I can control, are part of the faith equation that allows God to orchestrate on my behalf, to lead me to a purposeful and divine destination.

The Charge to Shift

Now what about you? Are you an optimist who most often sees the glass as half full? Do you have a mindset where you set out to figure out why you *can* instead of why you *can't*? Are you someone who not only motivates yourself, but others? Do you truly believe in yourself and your abilities to accomplish your goals? Or are you the reverse? Do you have a mindset of the glass is half empty? Do you have a mindset where you look at barriers as *proof* of why you can't? Do you question your abilities? Do people consider you a "Debbie Downer"? Be honest with who you are. Think back on your goals and your dreams. Have you stood in your *own* way or were you your biggest champion? If you find yourself being more of a pessimist than an optimist, then shift! Often pessimists use this strategy as a defense mechanism. Often there is a fear of failure, a fear of success, or both. The pessimist often believes that if they identify why it won't work ahead of time, when it doesn't work out, they have protected themselves from being let down. The problem with this strategy is the self-fulfilling prophecy – they have "protected" themselves from something that probably *would not* have happened had they had a more optimistic outlook. It's so important to shift from pessimism to optimism. Open your mind and believe that you can accomplish anything you set your mind to!

Choosing an optimistic and open-minded way of thinking is why I love my dad. When you look at my relationship with my dad, it's no secret – no secret to my dad, no secret to my brothers, no secret to my mother, and no secret to me that my dad and I have a different relationship than my brothers have with him. I won't call it better, but I'll just call it different in a positive way. The secret to our relationship is that I simply let my dad be my dad. He even says every now and then "I love you because you just let me be me".

I just absolutely adore my dad for who he truly is. Many girls love their dads. I'm no different. It's possible that I just simply love my dad because I'm a girl, but I believe it's because I *choose* to be optimistic. I *choose* to look at my dad in a positive light. I *choose* to focus on all his great attributes versus the not-so-great attributes, which are all mostly in his past. Am I blinded to the things that he's done in the past? No, but I'm also not blinded to the things that I have done that aren't so great in my life either. Therefore, because I *choose* to forgive myself, I also *choose* to forgive my dad. I also *choose* to focus on those things that are great in me while I work on a few not-so-great attributes. Therefore, I *choose* to focus on the great things that my dad brings to the table, knowing he has a few not-so-great things to work on – and when the opportunities arise from me to help him through those, I do; but I *choose* to focus overwhelmingly on the things that my dad does extremely well. That's why I love my dad, and that's why I have such a great relationship with my dad, and that's how I *choose* to let him be him. It's a choice!

I could have chosen the other way and shifted my mind to only focus on the things that he's done wrong. Why would I? I would be miserable, and he would be miserable. We would find ourselves in a relationship of negativity with negative energy. We wouldn't be able to move forward. I don't want to have a relationship with anyone, let alone my father, that's built on negativity all the time. That's the shift that you need to make. If you find yourself in a chronic mental state of negativity, looking at the glass half empty all the time, then you will always seek to find the reasons that validate all the negativity you're focusing on. In his book "The Magic of Thinking Big", David Schwartz describes it as the self-fulfilling prophecy in your mind. If you're a positive person, you will always choose to look for the positive in a situation to validate your positive outlook. If you're a negative person, you will always look for the negative in a situation to validate your negative outlook. When you choose to look for the negative, you'll find the negative. When you choose to look for the positive, you'll find the positive. Therefore, it boils down to a choice of the type of lifestyle and the type of energy you prefer. Positive energy, by far, is more productive at moving forward on a success journey than negative energy. You must change your mindset. You must shift.

Questions to Consider

1. How can I ensure that I primarily view the world from a lens of "glass half full" versus "glass half empty"?
2. Who knows my goals and dreams and has heard me declare out loud that I will succeed in accomplishing those goals and dreams?

3. What reasons did I (or do I) use to justify why I no longer chase a dream I once chased?
4. How can I begin to find the reasons *why* my goals and dreams are possible instead of focusing on the reasons why not?
5. What can I do *today* to stop holding my dreams and goals to myself and not sharing with others "just in case" it doesn't work out?

I can do all things through Christ who strengthens me.
~Philippians 4:13 (New King James Version)

CHAPTER 6

Determination

The surest way not to fail is to determine to succeed.
~ Richard Brinsley Sheridan

Have you been determined to accomplish something one week, only to find yourself not doing anything toward that accomplishment the next week? Sometimes you go longer than a week, sometimes even months, then life happens, and you find yourself back at square one? Does it frustrate you? Do you feel like a failure? Do you feel like everyone has managed to figure this out but you? How firm is your determination? How do you avoid the pitfalls of being determined in one moment and then not so much in the next? How do you make this determination "stick" long enough to accomplish your goals? Determination is a key element to success. Without determination, you're not as likely to succeed. Let's find out how to not only have determination, but also have what I call *"sustainable determination"*.

Dictionary.com defines *determination* as "the firm or fixed intention to achieve a desired end" and defines sustainable as "able to be maintained or kept going, as an action or process". If we put these two together, *sustainable determination* is the ability to maintain and keep going the firmness of purpose. My experience tells me that it isn't the firmness of purpose or sheer determination that most people struggle with. It's the sustainability piece. There are five key elements that I want to discuss that should help you transition from one who has temporary determination to one who has *sustainable* determination. The previous statement can lead one to believe that it's an all or nothing phenomenon. It isn't. The truth is that most of us have sustainable determination in many areas of our lives. For me, sustainable determination shows itself strong in going to work every day. It also shows itself strong in attending church, attending praise team rehearsal, going on date nights with my husband, eating, showering, grooming myself, feeding the dog, putting gas in my car, paying my cell phone bill, paying for shelter over my head, keeping the utilities on, and much more. Where it doesn't show up – yes, I'm a success work in progress in some of the areas of my life too – is in nutrition, sleep, saving money, cutting down on shopping, calling friends and family more often, working on my business more, and the list goes on and on. See, I don't have it all figured out! But there are some things I do know. There are fundamental reasons why some determination is sustained, and others are temporary.

To introduce the five elements of sustainable determination, I want to begin with a story. In June 2013, my husband and I planned our seven-year anniversary trip to Puerto Rico. I wanted to lose 15 pounds so that I could get into a bikini and have a fantastic bikini body! My husband, who is a personal trainer by the way, just wanted to be "more cut up"—whatever that meant! It was enough for us to decide to have a contest. We were in February when we made the decision, and the trip was in June. So, we decided that we each had to accomplish our goal. What was on the line? Bragging rights! You must understand that each of us like to talk "smack" to each other, so bragging rights is a *big* deal in our relationship. I honestly didn't know and still don't know how to measure "more cut up" (definitely wasn't a SMART goal), but for me, since my goal *was* SMART (15 pounds by June) I *needed* to pull this off. So, I changed my eating. I bought a new workout series called TurboFire by Chalene Johnson – a Beachbody product. This workout required six days of high intensity workouts up to one hour each. I sat down and mapped out the workout calendar indicating which dates corresponded to which workouts. I mapped out when I was going to move from the regular workout series to the advanced workout series and when it was time to order those DVDs. I also planned every meal every day. Each week on Sunday, I would plan the meals, plan a grocery shopping list, and every evening make the meals that were on the list. I was dedicated. Were there times I didn't want to work out? Sure! What made me keep going? BRAGGING RIGHTS! I couldn't let him have bragging rights and I not have them. He also was working out every day and eating right. To him, this wasn't a stretch though. HE'S A PERSONAL TRAINER REMEMBER??? But I couldn't see him doing all of what he was doing, knowing he was one step closer to bragging rights than I was, and I not do them. I also found me a workout buddy! My sister-in-love – Dawntoya! Even though she lived in Michigan and I lived in Virginia, we would text each other every day to ensure we got our workouts in. She also had an exercise goal and program she was working toward.

By June you know what happened? I hit my goal – actually I hit it weeks before then and just worked to maintain. I had to buy new clothes and yes, new bikinis. I was HOT both physically and temperature-wise in Puerto Rico. I was even asked by strangers if I was an athlete! BOOM! Bragging rights!!! After Puerto Rico, I sustained it until September because I needed to look hot at a wedding. I wasn't as intense because I wasn't competing with my husband, but still got in about four days a week of exercise. Ask me could I wear that same bikini two years later and the answer would be NO! What happened? That's where the breakdown of the five elements of sustainable determination comes in.

A Burning Reason

The first element of sustainable determination is "Find a Burning Reason *that Lasts*". Motivational speaker Eric Thomas says, "When the need to succeed is as bad as the need to breathe, then you'll be successful". I absolutely agree! For the Puerto Rico weight loss contest with my husband, there were several reasons – one was I wanted to look good on the beach. The truth is, I would still look good in a one piece, so I always had that as a fall back if I needed it, so to be honest, I wouldn't consider this my BURNING reason. The other reason is that losing 15 extra pounds is just healthier to do. To be honest, I was pretty healthy anyway. At the time, I led a decently active lifestyle. In general, I watched what I ate, but my lifestyle wasn't enough for bikini strutting. It was good, but it was not *that* great. So, since I was already healthy, that wasn't a *burning* reason. For me – I repeat, for *me* – it was the bragging rights! Now that might not be enough to fan other folks' flame, but it definitely was enough for me. That was my *burning* reason. I couldn't let him win! I couldn't let him have the bragging rights and I not have them as well. I *had* to accomplish my goal! The thought of not accomplishing the goal was *worse* than the thought of the hard work and sacrifices that I would need to put into accomplishing the goal. It is precisely the lack of a burning reason after the trip was over why I ultimately gained much of the weight back. I had a burning reason, but it went away. It somewhat transitioned to the wedding, but after that, nothing.

When setting out to accomplish your goals, you *must* find not just a reason to accomplish those goals, but a *burning* reason. The thought of *not* accomplishing the goals *has* to be worse than the sacrifices and hard work that it will take to get you there. Some goals, like earning a degree, or saving up for a specific purpose are goals that once achieved, there is no sustainability element. Finding a burning reason for these goals once is usually enough. For me, as a teen mom, it was "earn a degree or potentially raise your son on welfare". The thought of living my life on welfare was *not* an option for me. I saw a life of struggle ahead of me and a potential cycle of poverty in my son's life as well. For me, that was enough to at LEAST get a bachelor's degree. Once I accomplished that goal, I simply transitioned to another goal. There was nothing I needed to do to sustain that particular goal. Other goals, however, like weight loss have a sustainability element. Once you accomplish it, you must maintain it. You need burning reasons – one to lose and then another to maintain. Sometimes this is the same reason. For example, someone with a history of heart disease and heart attacks in their family who has small children at home find the prospect of dying prematurely and leaving their children without one of their parents quite dismal. For them, that is enough to not only lose the weight, but keep it off. For others, like me, the thought of having to buy a whole new wardrobe of fantastic clothes because I can no longer fit them is *worse* than the thought of working hard to stay within a 10 to 15 pound range of size medium. Side note: the 15-pound weight loss got me to small/medium so there were some smalls I couldn't wear anymore – like that darned bikini ☺. The point is, while I didn't maintain the Puerto Rico weight, I will never become larger than my wardrobe – NEVER! That's a burning reason. If you want sustainable determination, find your burning reason. Is it temporary? Find the next burning reason. Find one that will sustain the test of time!

Connecting to Purpose

The second element of sustainable determination is "Connecting it to a purpose". We'll get more into purpose in the next section "Spirituality", but let's touch on it here as it relates to determination. Purpose and determination are very closely related to the burning reason concept just described, but slightly different in an important way. In my weight loss example, as superficial as it may appear, the purpose was so that I could have bragging rights. But along the way, it became much deeper than that. I really wanted to prove to myself that I could be so determined and disciplined that I could accomplish a goal that took lots of effort and hard work. I'd done this academically, but not in fitness to the level that it would take to accomplish this bikini body. I wanted to prove to myself that I had what it took to do this. I would have disappointed myself if I hadn't accomplished that goal. I knew that if I could do this, I could apply that same rigorous discipline to other areas of my life. I had to show myself that I still "had it". Connecting the goal to a purpose spins the reason more toward the reason "why" versus the reason "why not". If you take my bachelor's degree example, the greater purpose was to better myself, set an example for my son, and show others that you *don't* have to be a statistic. Your life does *not* have to be defined by bad decisions. You *can* overcome obstacles and still accomplish your dreams. Connect your goals and dreams to the greater good! Connect them to a positive purpose for your life, the lives of others around you, and the lives of those who you may never even meet. The more you can make your dream less about you and about money (a common mistake people make) and more about a greater purpose, the more sustainable it becomes. You feel a sense of stewardship over the purpose connected to your goals and dreams. Again, we'll discuss purpose more in the next section on Spirituality.

Schedule It

The third element of sustainable determination is "Scheduling It". In one of Beachbody's TurboFire workout videos, which I can now recite word for word, Chalene Johnson says "You have to schedule your workouts! They have to be as non-negotiable as anything else in your life". Remember how I listed several areas in my life where I do well in sustainable determination? Most of them are scheduled! Going to work every day – Scheduled! Attending church – Scheduled! Attending praise team rehearsal – Scheduled! Going on date nights with my husband – Scheduled! Several of the other items listed are either scheduled or have a "schedule trigger", such as getting a paycheck or hunger pangs or a dog that stalks me because it's hungry, that forces me to make these a regular part of my life. This is how we must be with our goals and dreams. When on my bikini journey, I had to schedule those workouts. As soon as I got home from work, I hopped in my workout clothes no matter what, put the video in and got to work! They were non-negotiable. What about your goals and dreams? What activities do they require of you? Are you actively putting in the work necessary to get you there? Are you scheduling time to strategize? Are you scheduling time to plan? Are you scheduling time to make those phone calls? Are you scheduling time to write? Whatever your goals and dreams require of you, you must schedule the time. Scheduling the time will also help expedite your ability to make these tasks habitual.

Make it Habitual

This brings me to the fourth element of sustainable determination – it needs to "Become Habitual". Habits don't happen overnight. Many say that it takes 21 days to create a habit! The thought behind this is that once you begin to consistently work on your goals and dreams in a scheduled, non-negotiable fashion, the first three weeks will take more focused effort. It will feel unnatural. It will feel like you altered your usual way of being, your usual routine, your typical day to accommodate a new activity. That's because it isn't a habit yet. It hasn't become second nature. You are still adjusting to this new way of being.

This certainly happened for me in the first three weeks of eating and exercising. There were days I felt famished because the new way of eating was not what my body was accustomed to. There were days where my muscles were sore from working out because my body wasn't used to that type of activity that often. There were days I was flat out tired and burned out. There were days I felt a little frustrated because I had to alter the times of other negotiable elements of my life – like watching television or saying "no" instead of "yes" to the extra butter on the popcorn at the movies on date night or relaxing after work to accommodate the new workout schedule. I even found myself running to the bathroom all the time, at the least convenient times, because I was drinking a gallon of water a day! It was an adjustment. But somewhere around the three-week mark, I got used to it. I wasn't as hungry, as tired, as frustrated, as incontinent ☺. I didn't miss TV or buttered popcorn as much as I thought. In fact, I found myself craving healthy foods, looking forward to the workout, and drinking even a bit more water than usual. It became a habit! It became part of my routine. It became part of who I was. Often the reason for the many stops and starts that we see when people have an enthusiastic start to a goal and then they stop, is the failure to hang in there long enough, in a scheduled, disciplined, non-negotiable way. Where do your goals fit into your life? Are you taking the time to schedule dedicated, non-negotiable time toward your goals? Have you been doing this long enough for it to become a habit? If you're still in the habit-forming phase, usually the first three weeks, then push through. Keep going. Stay with it. Eventually, you will see this become a regular part of your routine.

Become Accountable

The last element of sustainable determination is "Become Accountable". In the section on optimism and pessimism, I discussed the phenomenon of people not sharing their goals and dreams out of fear – fear that if they don't accomplish them, then what will people say. Again, as promised, we will discuss the appropriate ways of sharing when we discuss "Creating Champions" in the "Phase II: Babies" section of the book. For this section, sharing your goals and dreams with someone for accountability is an important piece of determination. Accountability is derived from the word *accountable* which Dictionary.com defines as "subject to the obligation to report, explain, or justify something; responsible; answerable". I would argue that the fear previously described can often stem from a fear of accountability. You see, it's one thing to be fearful that after you put in all the work you needed to, exhausted everything, stayed positive, and had determination, that for some reason you still couldn't accomplish your goals and dreams – that's a more manageable fear. You're able to say, I did all I could do, all I was supposed to do, and for some reason, it still didn't click. It's another thing to say to someone that it didn't happen because you didn't do the work necessary to make it happen. Let's go back to my bikini example. If I had done everything that I told you I did to make that goal possible, but I still hadn't lost the 15 pounds; yes, my husband would have still had the bragging rights, but I would have still felt somewhat proud because I proved to myself that I could put in the hard work necessary and hold myself to that. My guess is that I still would have seen results, but not those that I wanted to see. My husband would have also encouraged me and made me feel proud about what I accomplished. But what if I didn't do the work, thus didn't accomplish the goals, then my husband would have bragged hard and felt no sympathy for me whatsoever. That's a spot I just didn't want to be in – I didn't reach my goal because I simply didn't do the work.

What's the point of this when it comes to accountability? In my story, I had one person I was actively accountable to and that was my sister-in-love. I reported to her daily via text about my exercise progress. Passively, I was accountable to my husband. Let's face it. We live together. He sees many of my meals. He's able to witness many times when I'm working out and vice versa. For me, I didn't want to come off as lazy and not doing what I was supposed to do. Also, since my sister-in-love had her own exercise goals, I didn't want my laziness to somehow give her a pass at working out too. I wouldn't want my laziness to indirectly stand in the way of her goals. So, I did the work because I was accountable to someone. I had to actively report and was passively being watched. Accountability drives determination and results.

Let's look at it another way. In the book, "The 12 Week Year" by Brian P. Moran he talks about how the end of the year is one of the most productive times in most organizations. Often the end of the year represents the time that organizations must report on whether they accomplished the goals they set out to accomplish that year – accountability. Do you find yourself most productive when there's an actual deadline you're working toward? Deadlines often mean, either get it done by this time, or don't get it done at all – you're accountable for your work. When your work is linked to having to answer to someone – either you will be able to say you got the work done or you didn't – you are more likely to get the work done. The fear of saying, "I didn't do the work" is often greater than the fear of doing the work and not accomplishing your goal. Find someone to whom you can be accountable. Make sure it's someone who truly will hold you accountable. Be sure to meet regularly. For example, by phone, in person, or via FaceTime could work. This must be someone you respect enough so that saying "I didn't do the work" will feel like you truly disappointed that individual. Be determined not to disappoint your accountability partner!

Questions to Consider

There you have it, the five elements to sustainable determination! Now that you know them and understand them, put them to work. Take your goals and dreams that you've written down in the first section and ask yourself the following questions:

1. How can I ensure that each of these dreams and goals have a burning reason to accomplish them?
2. How can I ensure that each of these dreams and goals are connected to a higher purpose?
3. How can I arrange my schedule so that I have dedicated, scheduled, non-negotiable time to work toward each of these dreams and goals?
4. How can I ensure that working on my dreams and goals becomes a regular, habitual part of my life?
5. Who is that person in my life who I respect and do not want to disappoint who can meet with me regularly to hold me accountable for accomplishing my dreams and goals?

And let us not grow weary while doing good, for in due season we shall reap if we do not lose heart. ~Galatians 6:9 (New King James Version).

CHAPTER 7

Spirituality

The two most important days in your life are the day you were born and the day you find out why. ~Mark Twain

Have you ever felt like your day-to-day is filled with tasks that you'd rather not do? Do you feel like your time could be better spent doing more meaningful work? Do feel like there is a greater purpose for your being here, but your daily life doesn't reflect that purpose? Do you feel like you know what your purpose is, but you just need the opportunity to do more with that purpose? Do you have a problem prioritizing or saying "No"? The concept of "Spirituality" can address these issues and help you travel a more purposeful journey toward success.

I present Spirituality last in this section, but it is certainly not least. If I could've figured out an acronym that would bring spirituality to the beginning, I would have certainly used it. Spirituality is such a crucial component for developing a foundational mindset for success. For me, my being able to achieve my educational goals despite having a child at 16 started years before I needed to work toward this goal. It started with an early introduction to spirituality. Before moving on, I want to be clear here that this section is *not* about religion. I repeat. This section is *not* about religion. I personally view religion as a set of ritualistic ways that represent an agreed upon way of conduct – "doing things ritualistically". If any section in this book touches on religion, it would be the section on needing to schedule dedicated, non-negotiable time to work on your dreams and goals (See the "Determination" section in "Phase I: Bullets"). Instead, this section is about spirituality, which for me and for the purposes of this book means a sense that everything is connected to something greater than us all. However you choose to arrive at that viewpoint, through whatever belief system is up to you. Personally, I am a God-fearing Christian woman, and this is how spirituality manifests itself in my life. But again, this section is about a greater sense of connectedness and less about denominations and converting readers to Christianity. I cannot, however, discuss spirituality, without first explaining how it came to be in my life.

Like many parents, including me, my parents didn't do everything right. Surprise, surprise! What they did do was give me a good foundation. Part of that foundation was my church upbringing. We were *always* in church. We were in church so much that friends and family members thought my brothers and I would grow up to become "weird". While most times I just wanted a "normal" life and wanted to stay home and play with friends, my parents forced me to go to church. At the age of seven something sank in. I guess I was listening and paying attention to what was going on in church, because I wanted to know God for myself. I wanted the relationship with God that the adults talked about. At that age I accepted Christ as my Savior and my personal relationship with God began.

Did my behavior change overnight? Of course not, I was seven. But I *did* feel different. I felt like I had a "leg up" on my friends because I truly believed that God now had my back. I believed that I was truly His child and I had access to things that my friends didn't have. I felt special. I felt like I had a new dad – a spiritual father. OK, but I was still seven and life as a child did continue. But the purpose of me sharing this is so that you know that my foundation began with God. It was *this* relationship that opened my mind to the possibilities of being able to accomplish ANYTHING, because I knew *He* was in my corner. I knew *He* had my back. My parents did well for me in this area. I didn't grow up to be weird, but I did grow up with a spiritual Father, and by virtue of that relationship, I began to dream!

Connectedness to a Higher Purpose

This feeling that I could accomplish *anything*, and that I could dream big came from a sense of being connected to God – being connected to something or someone greater than me – being connected to a higher purpose. That's the first element of spirituality that I would like to introduce – connectedness to a higher purpose. When you have a feeling of connectedness to something greater than you, then who you are and what you become transforms to be less about you and more about why you were created.

In Simon Sinek's book and famous TED Talk "Start with Why", he argues that successful companies and successful leaders can achieve success because they don't just understand "what" they do and "how" they do it, but they understand "why" they do it. One of the examples he gives is of the company "Apple, Inc". Apple understands that it is more than a company that creates computers, phones, and music devices. Apple's founders understood its core "why". According to the Economist, Steve Jobs' mission statement for Apple in 1980 was: "To make a contribution to the world by making tools for the mind that advance humankind." Notice, there is no mention of making computers, making phones, or making mp3 players, it is about a connection to a higher purpose – to advance humankind! Simon Sinek argues that this is the core reason behind Apple's tremendous success. Keeping this "why" at the core of every decision about "what" and "how" leads them to cutting edge technology that remains ahead of competitors and creates a devoted following. It's this "why" that hasn't limited Apple to simply a computer making company, but much more with endless possibilities. They simply need to keep finding ways to make tools that advance humankind. No wonder Apple is entering the field of healthcare! How is that for being much more than a computer-making company? Find *your* why! What is your *why* statement? I'll share a story of how finding *my why* steered me away from my original dream of becoming a doctor – a physician, specifically.

If you go back to the introduction of this phase, you'll remember that Heathcliff Huxtable's profession as an Obstetrician greatly influenced my decision to become a doctor. He helped women. That looked exciting to me. A profession that required the aptitude that I had in math and science sounded appealing and in reach for me, so that's the path that I followed. I knew what I wanted to do and how I wanted to do it – so I thought!

As an undergraduate student at the University of Michigan, I was initially a pre-medical student. I did *OK* in the science classes, typically scoring Bs and some As. Then I met my "friends" organic chemistry, biochemistry, and physics. These scores quickly turned into low to mid Cs, which were only possible because of fervent prayer – without prayer those grades would have been deplorable. Those were not medical school grades, and I did not find these classes fulfilling or interesting. After some true soul-searching, which in hindsight was an introspective look at my own "why" for entering the field of medicine, I realized that the actual anatomy piece of medicine didn't interest me at all. That was not *why* I chose the field. I chose the field because of the people element. I wanted to help people. I wanted to empower and encourage them to live better, longer, healthier, and more fulfilling lives. My focus was more on building healthy communities than curing a sick individual. It was then that I realized that being a doctor (in the physician sense) was not the best fit for me, because it didn't tie best with my core *why*; but the healthcare field was very much still relevant.

As an undergraduate student, I switched to Biopsychology and the Cognitive Sciences which is the science of understanding how biological processes influence behaviors, feelings, and thoughts. As a graduate student, I enrolled in public health school with a focus on health behavior and health education, which empowers people to live better, longer, healthier, and more fulfilling lives. If you take my *why* one step further, the heart of this book is to empower individuals to live better and more fulfilling lives, and it has nothing to do with healthcare. Finding your *why* statement opens the doors to many more possibilities of "what" and "how". Can you say multiple streams of income? If you find your *why*, you find your purpose, and you find your sense of connectedness to something greater than you!

Morals and Integrity

We all know the stories of successful businesses and organizations that seemingly had it all and were on top of the world yet came crashing down when the realities of immoral and corrupt behavior and business practices came to light. Think Martha Stewart. Think Enron. Think WorldCom. Unfortunately, the list goes on and on. This book is about sustainable, scalable success. Success based on immoral and corrupt practices is by definition unsustainable and unscalable. It's built on lies that eventually cannot stand the test of time. It's built without integrity.

Dictionary.com provides two definitions of integrity that are important for our purposes: 1) "adherence to moral and ethical principles; soundness of moral character; honesty"; and 2) "a sound, unimpaired, or perfect condition". The first definition speaks to what most of us think of when we think of integrity. C.S. Lewis characterized it quite well when he said that "Integrity is doing the right thing, even when no one is watching". The second definition speaks to the sustainability of integrity. Think of a building that is constructed. You want that building to be able to withstand any weather condition. You want it to have a solid foundation that cannot be easily compromised or destroyed. A building that is constructed in "sound, unimpaired, or perfect condition". That's true integrity. This is why the practices of Martha Stewart, Enron, and WorldCom eventually led to reputations and organizations that eventually came crashing down. The practices were not sound, they were impaired, and they were far from perfect.

Where do people find a sense of moral character and a sense of integrity? For me, this was a combination of my parental upbringing and my spirituality. I'm probably not alone. Many people find their moral compass by having parents who themselves have a strong moral compass or spiritual connectedness or both. Are there other ways? Sure. But most spiritual teachings, regardless of the denomination, teach some basic (and usually very similar) set of moral principles that are wonderful to live by. If you couple these moral principles with a sense of connectedness to a higher purpose, your purpose defines *why* you do what you do, which influences what you choose to do; but it's your moral compass and integrity that influence *how* you do it. Strong morals and integrity keep you grounded in making the best decisions even when there is a compelling fiscal case to go another way. You always want to be proud of the decisions that you made because they simply were the *right* things to do.

The earliest integrity lesson in a business setting for me came at my very first job at TradeWinds video in Detroit, Michigan. I was 14 years old when I started that job and held that job until I went to college at age 17. As employees, we could give free movies to our family, but the policy was clear that we could not give free video game rentals. At 14, I understood what was right and wrong, but I didn't truly appreciate the business decision behind why the manager would allow us to give free videos but not free video games. It didn't matter though; the policy was the policy, but I do now I understand that video games were precious cargo with lower profit margins on each rental. Video games cost substantially more for the store to purchase, so it took more rentals to earn that investment back. Our giving those away free would cut more drastically into the profit margins. Again, regardless of the rationale, I knew the rule. I was crystal clear on the rule. Nevertheless, my brother wanted to rent a video game and I decided, for whatever dumb reason I had at the time, that it was a good idea to give my brother a free video game. It was simple for me to do. The same way I zeroed out a free video in the computer, I zeroed out the video game. My brother took it home to play and kept it moving. Well, that same day my manager came to me with a printout of the zeroed out a video game for my brother and asked me why I did it. I told the truth. I simply wanted to give him a free video game. At least I owned it right? I just knew I was about to get fired, but instead of being fired, he taught me a very important lesson that day that I will never forget. He taught me that I needed to follow the rules because if I was caught not following the rules, I would be let go. That situation showed me that there was always the potential to get caught, so I might as well just follow the rules on the premise that it's the right thing to do. From that moment forward, I realized how important it was to always do the right thing. Even when you think you can get away with it. Even when you think nobody is looking. Even when you think nobody will ever find out. Why not just choose integrity at the end of the day?

Reliving that situation, I can still feel, all these years later, how uncomfortable, guilty, and crummy I felt. It did not feel good to have my manager come to me and bust me like that. I never wanted that feeling again. I never wanted to be in a business where they couldn't trust me. In that moment, I felt like he no longer could *trust* me. He seemed so disappointed in my decisions. From there, I worked so hard to prove that he could trust me again, which he ultimately did. He may not remember that situation, but I still remember it because it was an important lesson for me about integrity – do the right thing because it's the right thing to do, even when no one is looking!

Relationships and Friendship

The journey to success is not a road that you can travel alone. The fact is that you're not an expert in everything necessary to become a success. The beauty of this fact is that you *don't* have to be an expert in everything either. Malcolm Gladwell is credited for pioneering the thought that it takes 10,000 hours on average to become an expert at any one thing. You're foolish to think that you have already put in the 10,000 hours necessary to be an expert at *everything*. Henry Ford learned the value of engaging experts to not only realize his dream of building the automobile, but also to expedite his dream! He surrounded himself with experts from various fields that included steel making, canning, and even brewing. You must be able to rely on others to become successful; likewise, you must show yourself to be reliable.

When asked about my leadership style, I often will give the answer that I lead by relationships. It speaks to that external locus of control that was discussed under optimism and pessimism. While I'd love to be able to control as much as I can, there are and will continue to be many aspects of my success journey for which I must rely on others and their talents, expertise, access, connections, and responsiveness. It is for this reason, that relationships are key. Often, if you've taken the time to forge a relationship – a cordial, business-like, trusting relationship – with others, you can leverage this to get what you need timely and reliably. How do you do that? How do you build trusting relationships with individuals you often don't know or just met? What I'm speaking of is not becoming best friends or "play cousins" with everyone you meet but taking the time to engage the "person" behind the expertise. This is where spirituality comes in.

There is a core principle in many spiritual teachings that sounds something like this – treat others the way you want to be treated. The Bible states it this way, *"Do to others as you would have them do to you."* (Luke 6:31 New International Version). This principle holds true in business. When you show yourself reliable, then others will show themselves reliable in return. When you speak kindly and give good service then you will be spoken to with kindness and will receive good service in return. When you are generous with your expertise, then others will be generous to you with their expertise. Help someone else, mentor them, show them the way and someone else will help you, mentor you, and show you the way. Show someone grace and understanding, and when you need it, grace and understanding will return. These principles tie closely to the principle of sowing and reaping. Others speak of this as "karma" or the law of attraction – to every action, there's an equal and opposite reaction. What do you want to see manifest in your life? Then sow into others that way. Act that way. Give *out* what you want, and it will come back to you. When you consistently behave this way, you will build relationships along the way. No one wants to do business with a self-centered, egotistical jerk. Don't be *that* person! Treat others the way you wish to be treated because, *"A man who has friends must himself be friendly..."* (Proverbs 18:24 New King James Version).

Choosing Faith Despite Fear

One of the major reasons why I've chosen to include spirituality in the "Bullets" phase of this book stems from my mother's choice to live and not die so that she could raise her children. There are so many different directions that I could take just in analyzing that choice – how that choice manifested itself in so many ways – including ways we probably will never even know, but for this section, I'll keep it basic yet powerful. Her choice taught me the power of choices.

Faith is difficult. Faith is the manifestation of those things that we hope will happen, but we don't see. To truly walk in faith, we must believe in what we're hoping for. We must truly believe that the thing we hope for exists and/or will come to pass. We can't see it naturally; we must see it spiritually. If we go back to dreams, often dreams represent the things we hope will happen. Faith is continuing to work toward that dream even when its manifestation hasn't happened yet. Faith requires risk. Anytime you work toward an unknown destination, there's risk. Risks can breed fear. Many times, dreams are deferred, or they die because fear sets in. Fear surrounding the risk. Many times, we let the risks have too much power and thus abandon what we dreamed or hoped for. When my mother made the decision to live, that took some faith. She was laying on a cold ground and bleeding from five bullet wounds to the stomach. It took faith to believe that she would actually live from such traumatic wounds. It took tremendous faith to maintain the positive attitude that she *had* to maintain to get through the recovery process. To be released from the hospital in 12 days after sustaining such injuries is quite miraculous. That's where her faith stood – in the space of miracles! Even after leaving the hospital, I watched my mother through very trying times when we had no money, when it wasn't obvious how we would keep the lights on or eat, I watched her have faith that we would make it. We never had a utility cut off. We never went without food. We never had an unmet need. I'm sure there were times when she was fearful, but she chose to allow her faith to push her forward despite the fear. She refused to let fear hold her back.

Faith, coupled with sustainable determination, is a powerful force! *"Faith without works is dead (James 2:26 New King James Version)."* Consider determination a key element of the "work" that must happen as you're walking toward a dream that has yet to manifest. Imagine working toward a dream with the expectation that it *will* happen, with faith, using determination that is fueled by a burning reason, that is connected to a purpose, that is scheduled, that is habitual, and has an accountability factor. This brings substance to what you're hoping for. Eventually, you *will* see the evidence of things you don't yet see.

Succumbing to fear is what happens when you take your eyes off the destination. In the Bible, Matthew 14:28-30 gives the account of when Peter walked on water. When Peter stepped out of the boat to walk on water toward Jesus, he stepped out in faith. He kept his eyes on Jesus' hand and began to walk on water. But when he began to look at the unsettled waters around him, the wind, and the waves, fear set in, he succumbed to that fear, and he began to sink. He didn't walk in faith long enough. My mother continued to walk in faith. She walked in it long enough so that fear didn't hold her back. She chose faith despite her fear. I learned faith "by proxy" through my mother's actions. It was her actions that gave me the courage to ultimately choose faith despite fear for myself. She helped me to become spiritually grounded in this principle. Learn the principle of faith. Learn how to sustain it long enough so that fear doesn't hold you back from reaching your destination!

Living on Purpose

There are many resources available now to help individuals uncover their purpose. There are books, daily devotionals, blogs, podcasts, workshops, and the list goes on and on aimed at this very thing. There is absolutely nothing wrong with this and I encourage it. It goes back to the *why* element – to finding a sense of connectedness of your dreams to a higher purpose. This element of spirituality of "living on purpose" is key to your success journey because once you uncover your *why* and your sense of connectedness, your sense of purpose, you can begin to "live on purpose". What does this mean?

I started this section on spirituality with the following questions: Have you ever felt like your day-to-day is filled with tasks that you'd rather not do? Do you feel like your time could be better spent doing more meaningful work? Do feel like there is a greater purpose for your being here, but your daily life doesn't reflect that purpose? Do you feel like you know what your purpose is, but you just need the opportunity to do more with that purpose? Do you have a problem prioritizing or saying "No"? Enter living on purpose! Living on purpose is a concept that speaks to being able to prioritize how you spend your time based on whether the task lends itself to your purpose. If it doesn't do this directly or indirectly, then you should consider no longer doing it or saying, "No". Period.

Let's dig deeper into tasks that speak toward purpose directly. These are tasks where you *very clearly* can see the link between the task and your purpose. For example, if your goal is to be a motivational speaker and you're invited to speak, that's a strong, direct link to your purpose. You probably should say "Yes" to that. Not as strong, but still direct – using the same goal, if you're asked to attend an event where you will have the opportunity to network with many event planners, this could lead to future speaking engagements, so you may want to say "Yes" to that. These are direct links to the task and your purpose. How much of your day is spent doing things that directly tie to your purpose?

If you're like many people who work a full-time job that is not their purpose, chances are your time may be spent on tasks that are either unrelated to your purpose or indirectly related. Let's go back to the motivational speaker purpose to further explore the *indirect* linkages to purpose. Let's imagine that you are asked to assist the youth ministry at your church. This requires that you attend each service and do extracurricular activities with the youth. You may want to say "Yes" to this, as this could indirectly be tied to your purpose. Attending every service could lend itself to alternative ways of presenting material that you may find useful as you deliver your speeches. Working with youth could connect you to parents who may have connections in their organizations where speaking opportunities can result. There are often opportunities for youth leaders to speak in front of the youth and empower them to be great in their lives. This could be an opportunity for you to hone your skills as a motivational speaker. You may want to say "Yes" to this opportunity.

Let's try an even more indirect example. You have a weekly date night with your husband. It's usually dinner and a movie. How could this indirectly tie to your purpose? Healthy relationships, especially marriages, are critical when embarking on a success journey. In "Phase II: Babies", we will explore the concept of "Creating Champions". For our purposes now, your spouse is a crucial champion for you on your success journey. You want to be sure that the relationship stays strong, is cultivated, is watered, and is nurtured. Weekly date nights help with this. Dinner with your spouse allows you to keep the communication lines open and even allows you to practice effective communication, which could enhance your communication skills while speaking. You also could use this time to bounce new ideas off your spouse and actively engage him or her in the process.

The words of caution to be mindful of when engaging in activities that are either directly linked to your purpose or indirectly linked is that you *must* have time dedicated to directly linked activities. You cannot progress on your journey without directly engaging in activities that move you one step closer to success. Have you ever been in a space where you have so many great ideas because you've read, attended seminars, Googled, attended workshops, and learned from others (indirect activities), but you never had a chance to put those things in action because you have no scheduled time to do so (direct activities)? This is why just participating in indirectly related activities isn't enough.

Let's think of this concept in the business sector. Many organizations use the term work-life balance quite often. Businessdictionary.com defines this concept as, "A comfortable state of equilibrium achieved between an employee's primary priorities of their employment position and their private lifestyle". Essentially, the concept acknowledges that employees are more than just employees. They have other hats they wear, other demands on their time, and other relationships to consider and cultivate. The concept acknowledges that a healthy employee in the other facets of their life typically translates into a more effective employee at work. However, what you don't see is an organization allowing the employee to focus on the other facets of his or her life *only*. You don't see them saying, "Spend the whole year at PTA meetings, church functions, and family functions. It's all indirectly related. We get it. We know you'll get to the work we pay you for when you get a chance." No. They still expect the employee to show up to work when scheduled and give 100%. They just simply understand that the other demands on the employee's time and energy may require a day off, vacation time, needing to leave early, needing to come in late – and after having a conversation about that, it's factored in and approved. Treat your priorities the same way. Live on purpose by finding scheduled, dedicated time to work on activities directly related to your purpose. Eliminate any activities that aren't related as much as you can. Participate in activities that are indirectly related to your purpose, just don't overdo it. Create balance.

Questions to Consider

1. How do my dreams and goals reflect a connection to a higher purpose?
2. How do I consistently demonstrate that I actively try to pursue a life based on morals and integrity?
3. How do I consistently demonstrate that I treat others the way I want to be treated?
4. How do I consistently walk in faith despite fear?
5. What can I do today to ensure that my life consists mostly of activities that are directly related to my purpose?

Trust in the LORD with all your heart, And lean not on your own understanding; In all your ways acknowledge Him, And He shall direct your paths. ~ Proverbs 3:5-6 (New King James Version)

Conclusion – Phase I: Bullets

It is our choices... that show what we truly are, far more than our abilities.
~J. K. Rowling

Mindset is critical to your journey for success. You must have the right GOODS that speak to who you are and what you believe. Here is a summary of your "must-haves". You must first have a dream. Your dream will represent the destination. Then you must have goals that become the steps you must take to get to your destination. You must have a positive attitude that you will be able to accomplish your goals and arrive at your destination. This positive attitude comes with an overwhelmingly positive outlook via optimism and an open mind. You must have sustainable determination – a strong belief and conviction that no matter what you face along the way, you will get to your destination. Last, but certainly not least, you must have a spiritual foundation – a strong belief that there is a force larger than you with an ordained purpose for your life. Once you have all your must haves, you have the mindset that forms the necessary core foundation to be successful on your journey.

Questions to Consider

1. What can I do today that can make my dreams more concrete?
2. What can I do today to make my goals SMARTer and function as steps toward accomplishing my dreams?
3. What can I do today to change areas of my life where I have a negative outlook?
4. What can I do today to ensure that I have not just determination but sustainable determination?
5. What can I do today to grow spiritually?

And we know that all things work together for good to those who love God, to those who are the called according to His purpose. ~Romans 8:28
(New King James Version)

Phase II: "Babies" – The Resilience Phase

DR. ANGELA D. THOMAS

CHAPTER 8

B.O.U.N.C.E. – How You Deal with Challenges and Adversity

All the adversity I've had in my life, all my troubles and obstacles, have strengthened me... You may not realize it when it happens, but a kick in the teeth may be the best thing in the world for you ~Walt Disney

Introduction

Can you remember a time in your life that was incredibly tough? Was that tough time a pivotal moment in your life that changed you for the better? Or was it a pivotal moment in your life that left you in a space of regret? When you face tough times, do you find that you are resilient and can bounce back, and move forward? Or do you find that tough times paralyze you, keep you from moving forward, and you find it quite difficult to get back on track? This phase, "Babies", is about resilience! It's about how to bounce back from adversity and how to deal with challenges. It's called the "Babies" phase because it was my season of have a baby at the age of 16, that was a major time of challenge and resilience in my life.

When I was 16, I found out I was pregnant with my son Nate. I was in a relationship with his father. I was 16 and he was 19. He was my first partner, and we were *not* careful despite my having taken all the different sex education classes in middle school and high school. In fact, I was able to quote *exactly* what needed to be done in sexual situations. Despite all this, I did not make the smart choices of activating those lessons that I learned. Therefore, in the summer of 1995, my monthly cycle did not come when it was scheduled to come. I was with my girlfriend and our mothers were out of town at a Mary Kay conference. We were at her home and I shared with her that I thought I might be pregnant. So, we went to the drugstore, purchased a pregnancy test, and I took the test at her house. Sure enough, I was pregnant. I shared the news with my girlfriend. Then we went about our business and proceeded as if nothing happened that day. After we hid the test in the garbage and called my boyfriend to let him know, the rest of the day seemed normal. In the following couple of months, I went through this journey of *owning* that I was pregnant, but at the same time *hiding* it, and at the same time trying to be "normal", and at the same time trying to wrestle with what all this meant.

This was the summer between my junior and senior year in high school. I was a great student with college aspirations and thinking about the next chapter of my life in my journey to become a doctor. Having a baby changed that equation quite a bit. It really wasn't until school started again, morning sickness started to set in, college recruiters started to visit to the high school, and my time for having the option to *not* have my child began to dwindle, that it finally hit me that I was in a tough spot – a *really* tough spot. After I made the decision to move forward with the pregnancy, I realized that this tough spot was actually a crossroad. At this crossroad, the choices I would make could potentially lead me on the path of greatness, or on the familiar path of teenage motherhood riddled with poverty and a reliance on support from social services. I realized that I could no longer essentially ignore my situation. I would have to own it, face it, and build a strategy to overcome it, if I wanted the great path and not the familiar path.

It was in the "Babies" phase of my life that I realized just how tough and resilient I could be – to bounce back from a series of *really* bad decisions that led me to become a teen mom; to devising a strategy that would allow me to experience success on the other side. This phase of the book is about resilience and how to deal with challenges and adversity in a healthy way and overcome those challenges. We will explore concepts such as a brave realism, how to identify and become aware of your obstacles, how to devise strategies to overcome those obstacles, develop tools to help stay in the game and not quit, ensure that the right people are in your corner, and how to have a mindset where you expect to be the exception to any statistic or rule. You will learn how to be resilient and bounce back during times of challenge and adversity.

Yet in all these things we are more than conquerors through Him who loved us. ~Romans 8:37 (New King James Version)

CHAPTER 9

Brave Realist

There are two primary choices in life: to accept conditions as they exist or accept the responsibility for changing them. ~Denis Waitley

How are you when adversity comes your way? Are you overly optimistic? What does it mean to be overly optimistic? Is that a bad thing? Are you optimistic to a fault? To the point where you completely ignore the situations around you? Are you the complete opposite? Are you so fixated on your reality that you get stuck in the now and can't see a future? Are you so stuck that you can't figure out how to devise a strategy to overcome the obstacles that you're facing?

I remember when I was pregnant with my son and had just told my mother about the pregnancy. We weren't in the best space of trying to navigate this pregnancy, specifically, what it meant for her as a minister with a daughter who was 16 and pregnant. One primary concern for my mother was about what her church friends and family would say. How would they look at her? This was a *huge deal* for my mother. I had similar challenges. I was considering what my friends would say and how other kids would look at me at school as I started to show. This was our reality. We knew that we would have to face those types of criticisms and judgments.

However, my mother and I differed in how we approached the situation. I knew my friends and others were no different from me. They were having sex, more often, and with more partners than me. They just hadn't been caught up – they didn't get pregnant and if they did, they chose to have abortions. While I had only been with one partner, my son's father, I was clearly careless. I got caught up. I got pregnant, but I chose not to abort my child. My large belly was just clear evidence of my bad decision-making. I had to face the reality that some people would judge me and say some bad things about me. I had to ask myself how I would handle those situations.

There was no benefit to my ignoring that this would be a part of my reality. It was coming. Because I knew it was coming, I made a decision. I decided to be brave. To get to a space of bravery, I developed what I call my "rationale strategy". I rationalized that these people were no different than me. Each person had his or her own vices and issues. Other kids were likely more reckless with sex than I was at the time, so my attitude toward anyone when they stared at my baby bump became, "Get over it! I'm going to continue to walk around with this belly proudly. The baby is coming, and I really don't care what you think". This was the narrative I would play in my head (I wouldn't actually say it out loud). This became my new frame of mind!

My mother, on the other hand, was still struggling. She was still struggling with what my starting to show would mean as we went to church. She even started trying to encourage me to wear clothes that would better hide my belly. At one point I said to my mom, "You know what, the belly is the belly! If people are going to say something, they're going to say something. But the reality of the situation is that your friends have children who are out there having sex too. My belly is just the evidence that I'm just like them. So, they just have to get over it". When I expressed this attitude to my mother, it freed her! We were both able to move on! No hiding! We eventually were able to transition to *excitement* about a new baby coming into the family.

This section, Brave realism, explores the importance of remaining hopeful that things will work out all while owning the situation that you're in. It is important to be aware of the obstacles and barriers that will come your way because of your situation. The more you own your reality, the better you become at devising strategies to help you navigate through challenging times on your journey.

This section shows you how to combine both optimism and realism in a *healthy* way – where you are hopeful and positive about your future, but are brave enough to look at your surroundings, your obstacles, and your challenges to devise a strategy to act.

The Paradox

In his bestselling book, "Good to Great", author Jim Collins describes the incredible feat of a prisoner of war, Admiral James Stockdale, who was captured and forced to live in incredibly cruel conditions for eight years. He wasn't alone. There were other prisoners of war who were captured, but many did not survive. Admiral Stockdale recounts his experience in his book "In Love and War: The Story of a Family's Ordeal and Sacrifice During the Vietnam War", where he explains the difference between his mindset and the others who did not survive. He says that the difference boils down to his being a realist and the others being too optimistic. He explains that the other prisoners of war would set unrealistic expectations to be released by a certain time such as "by Christmas" or "by Easter", but those unrealistic points of time would come and go, and disappointment would set in. That disappointment would transition into hopelessness, thereby decreasing the other prisoners' will to survive. Admiral Stockdale took a different approach. He was hopeful, yet realistic about his circumstances. He did not sugar coat the situation he was in and did not set unrealistic expectations for release. Instead, he used a healthy dose of realism to understand the situation and devise a plan for survival given the circumstances. This is what Jim Collins means by the "Stockdale Paradox" – realistic yet hopeful.

You may be asking at this point, "Doesn't this contradict the earlier principle about being optimistic and open-minded?" The answer is simple. Absolutely not! The two are not mutually exclusive. You can be positive and open-minded and believe that you can achieve success and at the *same time* get real about your situation. Admiral Stockdale didn't lose hope, he was just real about the situation *as* he hoped. Admiral Stockdale's story illustrates that none of the principles discussed thus far stand alone. Having written, SMART goals is important. Being optimistic and open-minded is also important. However, it is extremely important that you be honest with yourself about what it will *really* take to accomplish your goals. You need to be brave enough to face reality and brave enough to find a way to push through *despite* that reality. In her book "The Battlefield of the Mind", Joyce Meyer explains a concept called the "ready mind". This concept speaks to preparing your mind to hear and face whatever it is that God needs to show you. Often, what He needs to show us isn't pleasant, but when we ready our minds to receive it, whatever it is, then that gives us the opportunity to move forward and deal with it accordingly. A brave realist has a ready mind – brave enough to face the situation no matter how good or bad.

I found that I had to operate in this paradox and with a ready mind several times in my life. Initially, I was in denial when I found out I was pregnant. I took a test and went right on about my business as a typical 16-year-old. It was as if nothing happened in my world. It was summer, but when school began, the reality of my situation started to set in as college admissions representatives would visit our school to recruit the senior class. It was then that I began to ask myself questions such as, "How will I ever be able to go to school with a baby? How will I even finish high school?" I was coming to realize that a baby was growing inside of me and was not going away. The further along the pregnancy progressed, the more I realized that I was not going to miscarry, and since I decided not to have an abortion, I needed a plan. To plan, I needed to get real about my situation. I *was* pregnant. I *was* going to have a baby. I *was* going to have this baby before the end of my senior year in high school. I *still* wanted to go to college. But the reality was that most college kids *didn't* have a baby. I needed to figure out how to deal with the reality that *I* was going to have a baby and devise a plan that would allow me to still accomplish my goals. I needed to be realistic, yet hopeful. I needed to operate in my *own* paradox – the "Angela Paradox" I suppose, although the Stockdale Paradox certainly sounds better.

So, I owned it. My next step was to figure out everything that could stand in the way of accomplishing my goal of going to college. Well on the surface, what was standing in the way was, "A BABY!" Hello! Well, it was not quite that simple when I dug deeper. I had to ask myself, what was it about having a baby while in college that could stand in my way of being successful. The first thing I thought of was housing. Where would I live? I clearly could not stay in a dorm with a baby. I thought of an apartment, but I wasn't sure that was an affordable or realistic option for me. My parents didn't have money for college, so everything needed to be covered by grants and student loans.

One option was to stay at home and attend a local school, Wayne State University. It wasn't my preferred setting as I knew many kids who went this route without a baby, and they didn't finish because of the many distractions that came with staying at home. For this reason, my mother always encouraged me to choose a college away from home – although this was before she knew I was pregnant of course. I still wanted to go away to college, but I did keep staying at home on the list as an option. On one college's visit to our school, the recruiter mentioned in passing that the school had something called "family housing" on campus. When I heard that, it was as if a light went off in my head. "That's the key! Family housing! I can stay on campus with my baby and *still* go to school." So, I began to research colleges that had family housing on campus. This was before the Internet and Google were staples of our existence, so I engaged in good old-fashioned calling around. I focused on colleges in Michigan. I found that the University of Michigan, Eastern Michigan University, and Michigan State University all had family housing. I made the decision that I would apply to all three of these schools plus Wayne State University.

The next obstacle I identified was finding someone to watch the baby when I went to school. Under the stay-at-home model, in theory, my mother would have been an option, but I knew she would never agree to watch the baby full-time. I wanted a more independent solution. Childcare! By the time I decided to figure out childcare, my mother already knew I was pregnant, I was accepted into all four colleges, and I had chosen to attend the University of Michigan. So, I decided to call the help line at the University of Michigan to see if they could help me identify childcare. To my surprise, they had a list of childcare providers that they sent me in the mail. I used that list to call several providers about costs and availability and spoke to the most pleasant grandmotherly woman, Ms. Gladys, who was available to watch the baby Monday through Friday from 6:00 a.m. to midnight for $12 a day, including diapers and formula. Yes, you read that right! It was *amazing*! Every time I dropped off my son at her house, it was like dropping him off over his grandmother's house. This removed the barrier of "who will watch my baby" and removed the potential barrier of not feeling comfortable leaving my child with someone else.

The next obstacle I identified was how to make time for studying with a baby. I knew that I would have to be organized and disciplined to make this work. I planned my schedule accordingly. I decided to schedule my classes as early as possible during the day so that I can use the rest of the time until about 5:00 p.m. to study. If I needed longer to study, Ms. Gladys could keep him until midnight. Ms. Gladys was simply heaven sent! Despite having until midnight, my goal would always to be to pick him up by 5:00 p.m. When I started working in addition to being a full-time mom and full-time student, I revisited my schedule to accommodate work hours. I was forced to have a structured schedule to make it all work. I could not go to parties or hang out like the other students because I had a child to take care of. I was forced to stay home. The reality of my situation was that the only way I could make it all work was to stare my responsibilities in the face, design a plan that accommodated each responsibility, make some sacrifices, and be *disciplined* and *organized* in executing that plan. This is how you must approach *your* barriers and challenges.

Be Honest

You *must* be honest about your current state versus your desired state. Being honest about your reality doesn't mean it defines you, but you must acknowledge your starting point in comparison to your destination. If you're broke and you desire to be rich, be honest about your current broke state! If you are overweight and desire to be thin, be honest about your current overweight state! If you are a C and D student, but desire to get straight As, be honest your current grades! If you are in an entry-level position, but desire to be a CEO, be honest about your entry-level state. If you are an addict, but desire to be clean, be honest about your addiction!

Another component of being real is also being honest about things that you can't necessarily change. I can't change the fact that I'm an African American female. I don't plan to have any kind of drastic medical intervention to change either of these characteristics about me, so I am who I am. I also know that my skin is considered dark, my nose is wide, my forehead is big, my bottom lip is bigger than my top lip, I have big cheeks, and big eyes – and as much as I love a great make-up contour, these characteristics are not likely to change either. I was also born and raised in Detroit, went to Cass Technical High school, have two brothers, have parents who are divorced, and I didn't grow up rich. That's my reality! What's your reality?

Try to identify both internal and external factors that have led to your current state. What can you control? What do you have the power to change? For those things you *can* change, being honest allows you to take next steps toward changing that reality. For those things that you *cannot* control, create a plan to overcome the barrier, and be determined not to let that factor deter you. For those things you *cannot* change like being an African American female, identify if these characteristics are a potential asset, potential liability, or both. If an asset, make plans to leverage that asset – morally of course. If a liability, anticipate the barriers, and create a plan to overcome them.

While common barriers may include unchangeable personal characteristics, there are also common barriers that may be specific to your goals. For example, organic chemistry and biochemistry tend to be difficult for many pre-medical students. If your goal is to become a doctor, knowing this potential barrier helps. As a result, you might plan ahead to secure a tutor or plan to attend professor office hours to overcome that barrier. For someone who is aiming to lose weight, the weight loss plateau is a commonly known barrier. This is the phenomenon of initially seeing weight loss and then despite a consistent diet and exercise plan, the weight loss slows or stops. This plateau explains why nutritionists and fitness experts recommend changing your workout schedule often and eating a variety of meals.

This helps to prevent the plateau. Knowing this in advance allows you to anticipate the barrier and plan ahead to schedule a time when you will switch up your workouts and your nutrition. Being honest about your situation is not designed to depress you to the point of quitting, but to *empower* you to make as many proactive, positive decisions that will help you avoid challenges and overcome barriers along the way.

The Stockdale Paradox focuses primarily on the essential role of realism. A failure to be honest about your situation, yields a low likelihood of creating effective strategies for identifying and overcoming obstacles. However, realism with a pessimistic mindset is unfruitful. To be honest about your situation, understand it, and even create effective strategies for identifying and overcoming obstacles does not go far if you do not believe that your efforts will offer any reward in the end – if you have little to no hope for a better outcome. Success begins in the mind. What do you believe? Where do you envision yourself? Can you see yourself completing the goal? Or do you see yourself failing at it? Can you see where your efforts are taking you? Or do you believe that your actions are futile? It's pessimism that aligns most with a quitting mentality. "It won't work anyway". "I don't know why I'm doing all of this". "No one ever makes this work". It's optimism that aligns with a hopeful mentality and a mentality of endurance. "I know if I just keep at it, I will get there soon". "I know I'm not there yet, but if I keep moving in the right direction, I'll get there". "I can see myself at the end". "I've worked too hard to turn around now". "This situation won't always be like this". "It's hard now, but it won't always be".

You *must* pay attention to the narrative in your head because it reflects what's in your heart and who you'll ultimately become. The Bible says, *"For as he thinks in his heart, so is he" (Proverbs 23:7, New King James Version).* It also says that your words have power *(Proverbs 18:21).* These collectively mean that our minds are powerful because what we think and speak will actually come to pass. Negative thoughts and speech yield negative results. Positive thoughts and speech yield positive results. When you pair a realistic mindset of identifying and overcoming obstacles with hope, confidence, and positive affirmation, you are more likely to *achieve* your desired state.

Ignorance is not Bliss, It's Stupid!

We all know people who ignore bills and phone calls as if their ignoring them makes the reality that they have a financial issue untrue. I've been there before. "If I don't own the fact that it exists and just ignore it, then I'm happier because I don't have to face the situation". It's as if the problem doesn't even exist at all! Many people mistakenly call this ignorance since one is "ignoring" the problem, which is why ignorance gets a bad rap. Dictionary.com defines *ignorance* as a "lack of knowledge, [lack of] learning, [lack of] information". This means that ignorance isn't about ignoring important information, it's about not having it at all. It's about not knowing. Teen mothers who don't know that family housing options exist, which can make their college dreams a reality, are ignorant – they don't have the knowledge. They are not ignoring something; they simply don't know.

So, what do we call people who simply ignore information like bills? They are not ignorant, they're stupid! Dictionary.com defines *stupid* as "characterized by or proceeding from mental dullness; foolish; senseless". See, it's foolish and senseless to know you have a situation and then simply ignore it. When you ignore bills that you know are past due, that's stupid. When you ignore the fact that you are in a bad marriage, that's stupid. When you ignore the fact that your body is giving you symptoms of illness, that's stupid. When you ignore the fact that your bank account doesn't have the money to purchase something, yet you do it anyway, that's stupid. When you ignore the fact that your child is misbehaving and failing in school, that's stupid. To me, one key difference between ignorance and stupidity is that ignorance is typically not the fault of the person – they don't know, what they don't know. However, stupidity is a *choice*! You are *choosing* to ignore your situation. You don't *have* to be stupid!

The saying "ignorance is bliss" is often interpreted as "what you don't know can't hurt you". There are two issues that I have with this statement. The first is that the Bible says that people perish for the lack of knowledge *(Hosea 4:6)*, meaning that what you don't know *can* indeed hurt you. Let's go back to the example of the teen mother not knowing that family housing options exist to make college dreams a reality. Because she doesn't know, she believes that college is not in reach for her and settles for a low paying job that does not allow her to reach her full potential. Not knowing about the family housing option does in fact hurt her. The second issue that I have with the statement is that many people use this in the incorrect context. They use it when they are choosing to ignore information – not a lack of knowledge – *choosing* to ignore. Again, this isn't a state of ignorance, it's a state of stupidity, and YES stupidity can also hurt you.

What's the message I'm trying to convey here? To realize your full potential, you *must* be honest about your situation. Don't ignore the facts hoping they will go away. Don't ignore the facts believing that ignoring the facts will make you feel better, and you won't worry. Any relief you feel from ignoring a situation is only temporary. Often, continuing to ignore a situation only makes the situation worse and you'll find yourself in *more pain* than you originally were trying to avoid. I would argue that choosing *not* to ignore the situation actually has the opposite effect. Yes, facing the facts of your reality may be uncomfortable. Heck, you may find yourself having to let out one good cry, but it also allows you to identify the obstacles in that situation and open the path for you to find a strategy to overcome that obstacle. You can't overcome an obstacle if you don't recognize that it's there. This is the reason why Alcoholics Anonymous often says that the first step to recovery is admitting you have a problem. Alcoholics can't get better and implement strategies such as the famous 12-step program if they aren't honest about their alcoholism. The program is designed to give alcoholics strategies for overcoming alcoholism. No admission of alcoholism, no strategies to overcome it. It's just that simple.

For me and my journey, after I stopped being *stupid* by ignoring the very clear fact that I was pregnant, and after I stopped being *stupid* and ignoring the fact that college was in jeopardy because I was pregnant, I decided to be honest. Yes, that period of stupidity did feel pretty bliss. I was hanging out with my friends and going to school in a happy go lucky way. But it was temporary. In the back of my mind, I knew that one day the shoe would drop. I had a *choice*. I could either get ahead of it and be *proactive*, or I could be *reactive* and take whatever happened as a result. The thought of the latter honestly petrified me. Taking whatever happened as a result likely meant no college and a life of living well beneath my potential, with a high likelihood of living on public assistance. I didn't want that for me. I didn't want that for my child. Don't get me wrong, there are many people, including myself, who had to, and still must lean on public assistance to make ends meet, and to allow them to have resources available to them as they work to succeed in this world. That was eventually the case for me when I had to find a way to help pay for daycare while still an undergrad. I wanted to receive the daycare benefit from public assistance, but the only way I could do that was if I also was receiving food stamps. I had to do what I had to do. I used the public assistance for daycare and food stamps to help me get through undergraduate school. But that was a temporary situation.

I knew that ignoring my pregnancy could have led to a more permanent situation. I didn't want that, so I faced the facts of my reality. I was no longer stupid. I no longer ignored my situation. My situation was clear. I was pregnant. I wanted to go to college. A baby makes going to college difficult. That was the situation. Once I was honest about the situation, I was able to move on to strategy. It boiled down to one simple question, "How can I find a way to make going to college with a baby feasible?" My quest to find the answer to that question began my own personal road to "recovery" – recovery from a not so favorable situation, caused by a series of my own bad decisions.

Permission to react

Now that I've given you my soap box of why you shouldn't just ignore a situation, let me take this opportunity to take my own advice and not ignore the fact that many people struggle with this concept of facing the facts of their reality. This can come in a few different "shades" of ignorance. Let's go back to our bills in the mail example. The first shade of ignorance is the one mentioned previously where you simply ignore the bills in the mail. That's what I call a state of "Complete Ignore". The next shade is when you open the bill and ignore it with inactivity. This is what I call a state of "It is what it is". You simply say, "It is what it is", toss the bill to the side and keep it moving. You didn't exactly ignore the bill, but you made absolutely no effort to change the situation. That's stupid too. You might as well have not opened it at all. The third shade of ignorance is when you make excuses and blame others. For example, opening a collections notice and stating "Well, if the company's rates weren't so high, I could have kept up with that bill" or "I don't like how they treated me anyway, so they won't get me to pay this bill" or "If there were some better jobs out there, maybe I would have the resources to pay the bill". This is what I call a state of "Victim Mentality". It's everyone else's fault but your own. There's one common thread that runs through all three of these *shades*, and here's where I make sure I am honest about the situation – ignoring the situation *does* feel good temporarily. Sometimes it feels *really* good, but here's where I want to help you work through falling for the temptation of a temporarily good feeling. Two strategies have worked for me. The first is reminding myself that the "good feeling" is just temporary. The second strategy is giving myself *permission to react*.

When I'm facing the reality of an unfavorable situation, I give myself the permission to *feel* it. Feel the disappointment. Feel the worry. Feel the anxiety. Feel the sadness. Feel the anger. Feel it! For me this usually manifests in a good old-fashioned ugly cry. I must cry it out! My mom is *really* good about getting those tears to flow for me. It's not anything she says or does, it's simply who she is. Moms typically have been that staple to whom you have run to all your life when you get hurt. Fall and scrape your knee? Run to momma, and she'll help clean it up. Feeling sick to your stomach? Run to momma, and she'll give you Pepto Bismol and ginger ale. This has been my mom for me too. When things get too overwhelming and scary, I tend to run to her and when I do, I can't even barely get the words out of my mouth to explain to her what's going on before I just break down and cry – the ugly cry! I *must* get it out! She's a safe space for me to just cry it out. I give myself permission to do this – permission to react!

There are also some things I feel I just can't or shouldn't tell my mom. What do I do then? I go to God and cry, or use worship at church to cry it out, or sometimes just find quiet time alone to just cry it out. For me it's crying the ugly cry. For you it might be something else. Maybe you need to punch it out! I'm not telling you to go find someone to hit – that will land you in jail – but maybe exercise and find a literal punching bag to get it out. Maybe punching on your sofa pillows will do the trick. Others may find that writing it out helps. Some people keep journals as getting their feelings out in written form is their way of reacting to a situation. I've honestly wrote about this before in a blog. When I was rear ended at a red light, I kept cool about it. I didn't cry, panic, or get angry, but I did feel a sense of needing to react to the situation, so I blogged about it. I got it out – how I felt, what it meant, and my rationale for why that may have happened to me at that time. After doing so, I shared it on social media, and it helped me to get it out and move on to the next stage of getting my car repaired. Now one might have looked at that situation and thought I had permission to react in an unhealthy way. An unhealthy reaction would have been cursing out the driver who hit me or acting violently toward him. If my feelings were indeed anger, then finding a friend to vent to would have been the healthy way to react.

You must react in a safe space. In a space where you feel safe to let it out (like crying in your mother's arms) and where you ensure you don't put yourself and others' safety in jeopardy (like binge drinking your sorrows away then driving). Find a healthy space to get it out. Give yourself permission to do that. Don't hold it in. But once you get it out, you can't stay there. I repeat. *You cannot stay there!* You must pick yourself up, pull yourself together, and move from reaction to action. You must figure out how to move from the situation you're currently in, to a resolution. You must begin to strategize. You have a *mandate to act*!

Mandate to Act

What does it mean to have a mandate to act? Well let's summarize where you've been so far. You've been honest about your situation – really honest! You did not ignore it or say "It is what it is" or blame others, but you owned it! You owned your part in it! You owned that it happened to you. You owned that it won't go away on its own. You owned it! Then you've reacted to it. You may have even cried out with some "Yes" statements. Yes, it sucks! Yes, it's unfortunate! Yes, it's unfair. Yes, it's inconvenient. Yes, it's frustrating. Yes, it's challenging. Yes, it won't be a quick road. And now you're ready to act! There are some other "Yes" statements that you must own as well. The first is "Yes, I don't have to be in this situation forever" and the biggest yes of all is "Yes, I'm going to do something about it!" You must move to these latter two "Yes" statements. You have the power to *choose* whether this situation becomes permanent or remains as it was designed to be – temporary. To do something about it, you must act!

Thus far, the discussion has centered around the premise that an unfavorable situation occurred, which has the potential to jeopardize your ability to accomplish your goals. This is often the case. But another scenario often occurs as well – you know where you want to be and your situation isn't bad, but it certainly needs to change for you to accomplish your goals. Let's dig further.

Let's say you want to be a bestselling author. To do that, at a minimum you must write. Well, you're a mother with two small children, working full-time, cooking, cleaning, driving your children around to their activities, active in the church, you work out daily, and take sewing classes on the side. Your credit is good. You live in a nice house. Your bills are paid. Money doesn't concern you. You're healthy. Your friends and family are healthy and thriving. You really can't complain about your life. But your heart's desire is to become a bestselling author. You know you need to write. You have owned that you don't write. You even complain to your friends that you need to find time to write. Yet, you still haven't made that shift to action. Why? I would ask you to consider other areas in your life that you haven't owned yet. What are you ignoring? Have you owned that you have too much on your plate? Have you owned that maybe you feel obligated to take two hours a day to watch your favorite reality television show so your "mind can just relax" from all the hustle and bustle? Have you owned the one hour a day that you spend on the phone talking to your girlfriend about absolutely nothing? If you owned these things, you might be able to find a little extra time in your day to do what – write! Maybe you're bad at procrastination or working when there is no deadline. Own that! Then figure out how to overcome it. Get a strategy. For the mother who watches too much television, maybe the strategy is to write for 30 minutes FIRST then turn on the television as a reward. Do this every day and watch the situation change over time. For the procrastinator, maybe it means joining a writing club that forces you to show up with new writing on a regular basis. Maybe this will help. But to get where you want to go, you must act. You have a mandate to act if you want to change your situation and accomplish your goals.

After I owned the fact that I was pregnant and how it could affect my college reality, first I reacted with major tears, then I began to act. I went into "make it work" mode. Where could I go to school with a baby? Who could watch my baby when I was there? How would I be able to study? I had to figure it out. I needed to ensure that this situation of "college is in jeopardy" became a temporary state. I just needed to strategize. To strategize, I needed to find the right information. The right information then helped me to understand the options that could work. The right information was finding out which schools had family housing, what daycare providers were available, and the time my classes would be scheduled. Armed with that information, I could form a strategy. I owned it, I reacted, and then I acted. You have a mandate to act!

Now I don't want to come off as extra perfect. Like you, I'm flawed in *many* ways and don't always get it right. I find myself taking the "ignore" path and the "it is what it is" path sometimes as well. Like you, in these areas I am likely not seeing the success that I desire to see. In his book "Intentional Living", John Maxwell argues that most people live life with good intentions. They intend to do this, or intend to do that, but intention is not enough. It's been said that the road to hell is paved with good intentions. The world is not lacking people who have good intentions. The world is lacking people who choose to *live* with intention – intentional living. Living on purpose. This premise is similar to "mandate to act". It's not enough to intend to act. You must intentionally act. Act with purpose. Act with strategy. This, in my view, is intentional living – when your actions are purposefully designed to get you closer to your goal.

Questions to consider

1. What can I do *today* to courageously face the realities of my situation?
2. What are some strategies that I can use to navigate the obstacles in my current reality?
3. How can I make my reaction healthier and safer for myself and others?
4. What is holding me back from taking action?
5. What can I do *today* to begin intentional living?

The Lord is my light and my salvation; Whom shall I fear? The Lord is the strength of my life; Of whom shall I be afraid? ~Psalm 27:1 (King James Version)

CHAPTER 10

Obstacle Awareness

Obstacles are those frightful things you see when you take your eyes off the goal. ~Henry Ford

Are you aware of your obstacles? I mean *truly* aware of the things that could potentially stand in your way as you travel on your success journey. Are you familiar with the typical obstacles that come along the path that you desire to travel? Are you aware of the obstacles that are unique to you and your situation? Have you identified obstacles that you perceive as obstacles but really aren't *true* obstacles? Do you know how to accurately identify which obstacles you will face along your success journey?

When I was a junior in college and still a pre-medical student, the reality began to set in that soon I would need to apply to medical school. I knew there were certain requirements that I needed to meet to have my best chance of getting into medical school. One requirement was to take the MCAT test and score well. To score well on the test, I knew that I would need to demonstrate mastery of concepts such as organic chemistry, physics, biochemistry, and genetics. Additionally, I would need to demonstrate on a medical school application that I earned excellent grades in physics, organic chemistry, biochemistry, and genetics. Unfortunately, my transcript did not reflect that mastery. My transcript reflected Cs in those classes and a D in genetics. My obstacles were now obvious for successfully applying to medical school.

As I began to *really* consider those obstacles, I began to brainstorm potential strategies to overcome the obstacles of bad grades and not demonstrating mastery of required concepts on the MCAT. One strategy was to retake the classes. This would involve a high amount of financial resources to cover the cost of the classes. The strategy also involved enrolling in an MCAT preparation course to be able to fully demonstrate mastery of the required concepts. As the reality of this strategy set in, I asked myself, if this was really something I wanted to do. Was I "all in" for this particular goal of going to medical school? The truth was "No". I hadn't been for a while. However, it was this exercise of facing these real obstacles that actually led me down a different path of reevaluating my core "why" behind wanting to go to medical school in the first place. It was this reevaluation that eventually led me to pivot away from medical school, into the direction that aligned with my core "why".

This was a critical fork in the road on my journey. While it was important that I identified the obstacles and created strategies; it was extremely critical that I realized which obstacles were truly obstacles, understand the magnitude of each obstacle, properly assess the resources necessary to overcome each obstacle, and properly vet a strategy for overcoming the obstacles against time, resources, and goals. This section gives you tools to properly identify obstacles and to uncover and devise *effective* strategies for overcoming those obstacles.

Known and Unknown Obstacles

As the reality of suboptimal grades and a low likelihood of a good MCAT score forced a reevaluation of my core "why", I began to ask myself what appealed to me when I saw Heathcliff Huxtable delivering babies and helping women. Was it the medicine aspect? Was it the helping people in a healthcare setting aspect? I eventually landed on the latter – it was helping people improve their health. I discovered that the *science* of medicine – the physics, the chemistry, the biochemistry, and the anatomy – just did not appeal to me. I just wanted to help people. I wanted to get to the point where I was able to help people, understand their behavior, and how that affected their health outcomes. I wanted to understand how their circumstances led them to make certain health-related decisions. With this revelation, I decided to pivot my concentration from a pre-medical concentration to a biopsychology and the cognitive sciences concentration. This concentration studies why people behave the way that they do and understanding the biology behind the behavior.

When I became a senior in college, I knew I didn't want my education to end with a bachelor's degree. I wanted to go to graduate school of some sort. Then, based on the information I knew at the time, the path that seemed to make the most sense for me was to pursue a master's degree in psychology. Therefore, I began to study for the GRE and eventually took the test. Honestly, I still was not sold that this was the path for me. I knew I could help people, and it was related to their health – their mental health, but I just wasn't completely sold. I honestly felt like my dream of helping people with their health was limited by medical school and since that was no longer a reality for me, I needed to find *something*.

I ended up applying for jobs at places that had *nothing* to do with my core "why" such as banks. In the middle of this season of simply "trying to figure it all out", someone asked me (I can't remember who) if I had heard of public health school. They suggested I look into it and consider applying there for graduate school. I did some research and found out that the University of Michigan had a School of Public Health. I learned that public health did indeed fit my core "why". The American Public Health Association states that, *"Public health promotes and protects the health of people and the communities where they live, learn, work and play."* The World Health Organization defines *health* as *"a state of complete physical, mental and social well-being and not merely the absence of disease or infirmity."* Combined, these definitions speak to the reality that people strive for health in multiple areas of their lives. I did not know this field existed. While I knew about the obstacles to medical school – my grades and potentially poor MCAT scores – I did not realize that another obstacle to my living my core "why" was my lack of knowledge about other pathways to help people with their health. I was *ignorant* to these pathways. Uncovering this unknown pathway of public health, that had been blocked by the unknown obstacle of ignorance, proved to be just the ticket I needed to embark down the right path toward my dream.

Dictionary.com defines *obstacle* as *"something that obstructs or hinders progress"*. Some obstacles are obvious and known and others are not so obvious and unknown. Let's talk about the *known* obstacles. Known obstacles are simply those things that you are aware of or can easily identify with very little effort and some thought. The key to building a strategy for overcoming known obstacles is to first write them down. Go into a brainstorming session. To do this, grab a sheet of paper or open a blank Word document on your computer. Write down your goal at the top of the page. Under that goal, now simply jot down (or type) all the obstacles that you can think of that can prevent you from accomplishing your goal. Think about those things that are both internal to you and external to you. Those that are internal to you are your *internal obstacles*. Internal obstacles boil down to *you* getting in your own way. Internal obstacles can include the way you think, the way you act, the way you speak, your emotions, your mindset, your drive, your discipline, and more. To identify internal obstacles, own who you are and write down those characteristics about *you* that cause you to get in your own way. *External obstacles* are those things that are outside of you, including resources, opportunities, personal connections, people, geography, rules, requirements, restrictions, societal norms, and more. Write each of these down. Your ability to write down your internal and external obstacles means that these are obstacles that are *known*.

Now that you've identified the *known* obstacles, you need to uncover the *unknown* obstacles. These are called blind spots. These are things that others know but you don't yet know. These can also be things that not too many people know, including you, but you need to know. The question here becomes, "How do you find out about these unknown obstacles?" First, begin with your brainstorm list. Ask someone you trust and who knows you well to review your internal obstacles list. Let them know about the goal that you are working toward, show them your internal obstacles list, and ask them to be honest and let you know if anything is missing from the list. Be ready and open to receiving that feedback. Do not be offended. Seek to understand. Take ownership of the issue and celebrate the fact that someone you trust told you the truth about yourself before you started on your strategy journey. This helps you to avoid potential pitfalls that *you* will cause. I recommend asking two other people to do this as well. This can help you to identify other areas and to gut check issues that were raised by the others. If all three people mention a certain issue, that's something that you really want to pay attention to.

Now look at your external obstacles list. You can have the same people review this list as well, but you want to make sure they have *some* familiarity with the goal you are seeking to accomplish. If your goal is to become a tenure-track professor, asking someone with no familiarity or insight into that process won't help you much. Find one to three people with familiarity with the goal you are working toward to review your list and add to it. You may not have access to such people. I didn't have access to anyone at that time who was a teen mother who graduated from college. If you find yourself without this type of access, there is something magical that exists that did not exist when I was entering undergraduate school as a teen mother – Google! Take the time to search on the Internet examples of people who have attained what you are aiming to attain. See if you can uncover stories of how they got there. If you can find these stories, you can learn about some of the successes, failures, and obstacles along the way. You can learn more about the process. Depending on your goal, you may find that there is more information about the process and requirements, and fewer stories of real people who have achieved the goal. For example, if your goal is weight loss, you will be able to find lots of information and success stories. If your goal is very niche like becoming a world class fly fisher (I don't even know if that's a thing), then you may have to dig a bit more. Another great source for identifying external obstacles that you're not yet aware of is good old-fashioned books. These can be books on the process or autobiographies and biographies of individuals who have attained what you're trying to achieve. Be sure to write down any information you find throughout this process for both the internal and external obstacles. Add them to your existing list.

Perceived Obstacles

The steps outlined about soliciting the assistance from friends and researching information on the Internet and in books not only helps you to build your list, but it also helps you to gut check your list. In your initial brainstorm, you added items on your list that *you* believed were obstacles to your success. But what if they actually weren't obstacles at all? What if all this time you thought something would stand in your way and it turns out that isn't the case at all? These are called *perceived obstacles* – obstacles that you believe are real, but actually are not.

Before I heard the words "family housing" from the college recruiter, I strongly believed that I would never be able to stay on campus with a baby. My fate had to be an off-campus apartment if I had any hope of making college a reality with a baby. What was the obstacle I saw? "There is nowhere to live on campus". This wasn't true at all. This was a perceived obstacle for me. Not only was it a perceived obstacle, but I also had already begun building a strategy to overcome this perceived obstacle – apartment living. The true reality was that the obstacle was "Living in a dorm with a baby", that was the true obstacle. The strategy then became "family housing living" once I received the real information.

You need to gut check your list against reality. Often you can uncover perceived obstacles in your "Ask a trusted friend" process or your Internet search. Doing this begins to open doors of new information that allows you to cross off obstacles on your list because you've uncovered that they are actually perceived obstacles. Let's take weight loss as an example. Imagine that you have the goal of losing ten pounds in the next three months. On your obstacles list, you have that you hate low-fat foods. This is an obstacle for you because you believe that the key to weight loss is low-fat foods. On your journey to finding more information about weight loss, including uncovering stories of people who successfully lost weight, you discover story after story of people who actually found that a high protein and low carbohydrate diet worked best for them. You also found that low-fat does not necessarily translate into "good-for-you foods" as many low-fat foods are high in sugar and other nutrient-poor ingredients that attempt to recover the taste lost when the fat was removed from the food. You discover that there are many healthy, good-for-you foods, that you can eat, and you enjoy eating. What just happened? Your obstacle of, "I don't like low-fat foods" is actually a perceived obstacle and you can now cross that off your list. This illustrates the importance of research in the process of finalizing your list of obstacles. While it's good to ensure you are aware of obstacles, you must be sure that these are *real* and not perceived obstacles. You will waste time, energy, and even be *counterproductive* if perceived obstacles remain on your obstacles list.

Magnitude & Worthiness

Now that you know what your obstacles are – the real ones, you must now ask yourself some questions. How big are those obstacles? What would it take to overcome each obstacle? What is the magnitude of each obstacle? Is this obstacle worth overcoming? There are some obstacles that are so big that by the time you overcome them, the return you receive isn't worth the time and energy that you put in to overcoming. Likewise, there are some obstacles that are huge, but the payoff is huge as well. When you assess the payoff, don't just look at the tangible things that overcoming the obstacle will bring, also look at the internal rewards. These can include developing muscles of discipline that are transferable to other areas of your life. These can also include connections with others you've met along the way. These can also include valuable life lessons in the successes and failures that you've experienced on your journey. This also can include being an example to others, such as your children, on the importance of completing what you start and overcoming odds to accomplish a goal.

Now let's do the work. I offer two options for assessing the magnitude and worthiness of obstacles. The first puts each of your obstacles in one of four categories and the second puts each of your obstacles in one of six categories. Let's start with the first option. Give each of your obstacles a rating on the amount of effort you believe that it will take to overcome the obstacle. Now for the second step. Give each obstacle a rating on how much you feel the obstacle is worth overcoming. Note: anything that is a showstopper to you achieving your goal – meaning anything that you *must* overcome to achieve your goal – must be rated as "High Worth". There are only two possible ratings for effort: Low or High. Likewise, there are only two possible ratings for worth: Low or High. When you do this, each of your obstacles should land in one of four categories: 1) Low Effort, Low Worth; 2) High Effort, High Worth; 3) Low Effort, High Worth; 4) High Effort, Low Worth (See Table 1: "Effort & Worth; Low and High").

Table 1: Effort & Worth: Low and High

Effort

	Low Effort High Worth	High Effort High Worth
Worth	Low Effort Low Worth	High Effort Low Worth

Once you have given each of your obstacles one of these categories, here's how I recommend you proceed. For obstacles that are "Low Effort, High Worth", these are the easiest obstacles on your list and the ones that have the greatest payoff. Consider yourself. What drives you? Are you the type of person who needs to see quick results to stay motivated to do more? If the answer is yes, then tackle these obstacles first or as early in the process as possible. Some obstacles have an order effect to them where you must overcome one before you can overcome the other. For example, you may need to save a certain amount of money to pay for equipment that you need. You need both money and equipment. Unless someone donates the equipment to you, you must overcome the money obstacle first then overcome the equipment obstacle.

Now, maybe you are a person who likes to get the hard stuff out of the way first. The thought of having something so large continuing to hang over your head will frustrate you, paralyze you from acting, or both. Then I recommend beginning with the obstacle that is "High Effort, High Worth". This is the approach that I take to my daily exercise. Even though it takes about an hour of my day, it requires high effort of me to complete, but the payoff is *huge*. I get to stay in my cute clothes. I maintain my health. I feel good. I feel a sense of accomplishment. It helps me with my energy levels. There are just so many benefits to exercising that it's high worth. However, despite attempting to do this so many other ways, I have landed on the fact that I must exercise first thing in the morning. I can't have it looming over my head all day as something I have to do later when I get home. I usually don't have the maximum energy I need that time of the day and I end up spending the entire day thinking about it and trying to talk myself either into doing it or out of doing it. It's not worth it. That's a task that I need to do first thing in the morning.

For the category, "High Effort, Low Worth", unless one of your other high worth obstacles is dependent on this obstacle (in which case I would argue that this obstacle is actually "High Worth" as well), then I would encourage you to revisit this obstacle. Is it really an obstacle? Is it really something you need to overcome to accomplish the goal? If that answer is yes, then I recommend expending effort to overcome that obstacle *only* after you've overcome your High Worth obstacles. Otherwise, consider removing it from your list. Likewise, for the "Low Effort, Low Worth" obstacles, while you may consider these to be harmless as they take low effort, it's still effort – effort you could be using to overcome your High Worth obstacles. Again, unless one of your other High Worth obstacles is dependent on this obstacle (in which case I would argue that this obstacle is actually "High Worth" as well), then I would encourage you to revisit this obstacle. Is it really an obstacle? Is it really something you need to overcome to accomplish the goal? If that answer is yes, then I recommend expending effort to overcome that obstacle *only* after you've overcome your High Worth obstacles. You can do these before doing the "High Effort, Low Worth" obstacles. Otherwise, consider removing it from your list. Personally, my order would look something like this:

- Low Effort, High Worth
- High Effort, High Worth
- Low Effort, Low Worth (or remove from the list)
- High Effort, Low Worth (or remove from the list)

Moving on to the second option, like the first option, you will give each of your obstacles a rating on the amount of effort you believe that it will take to overcome the obstacle, and a rating on how much you feel the obstacle is worth overcoming. Again, anything that is a showstopper to you achieving your goal, meaning anything that you *must* overcome to achieve your goal, you must rate as High Worth. Unlike the first option, in this second option there are actually three possible ratings for effort: Low, Medium, or High. Likewise, there are now three possible ratings for worth: Low, Medium, or High. When you do this, each of your obstacles should land in one of nine categories versus the four in option one: 1) Low Effort, Low Worth; 2) High Effort, High Worth; 3) Low Effort, High Worth; 4) High Effort, Low Worth; 5) Low Effort, Medium Worth; 6) Medium Effort, Low Worth; 7) Medium Effort, Medium Worth; 8) High Effort, Medium Worth; and 9) Medium Effort, High Worth (See Table 2: "Effort & Worth; Low, Medium, High"). Using this option versus the first option gives you the opportunity to rate something that may be a little "in the middle" when it comes to either effort or worth, but it also gives more options, yielding more decision points.

Table 2: Effort & Worth; Low, Medium, High

Effort

Low Effort High Worth	Medium Effort High Worth	High Effort High Worth
Low Effort Medium Worth	Medium Effort Medium Worth	Hi Effort Medium Worth
Low Effort Low Worth	Medium Effort Low Worth	High Effort Low Worth

Worth

My recommendations for the first four categories remain the same as in the first option. Here are my recommendations for each of the five new categories. Complete your "Medium Effort, High Worth" obstacles with your "Low Effort, High Worth" obstacles and "High Effort, High Worth" obstacles in an order that makes sense for how you work. In other words, if you do better doing Low Effort, then Medium Effort, then High Effort, choose that order. Others may do better with Medium Effort then High Effort then Low Effort. While others may do better with High Effort then Low Effort then Medium Effort. Finally, some may do better with High Effort then Medium Effort then Low Effort. For the "Low Effort, Medium Worth" and "Medium Effort, Medium Worth", do these as your second set of obstacles after you've completed your high worth obstacles. For the "High Effort, Medium Worth", consider doing these before your low worth obstacles, but after your "Low Effort, Medium Worth" obstacles. Personally, my order would look something like this:

- Low Effort, High Worth
- Medium Effort, High Worth
- High Effort, High Worth
- Low Effort, Medium Worth
- Medium Effort, Medium Worth
- High Effort, Medium Worth
- Low Effort, Low Worth (or remove from the list)
- Medium Effort, Low Worth (or remove from the list)
- High Effort, Low Worth (or remove from the list)

Ability & Resources

Now that you've identified the obstacles and assessed their magnitude and worthiness, you must now consider your ability and resources for overcoming that obstacle. When I was in undergraduate school a major source of being able to make ends meet were my student loans and grants that I received through financial aid. At the beginning of every semester, financial aid would disperse the loans and grants on my student account, take care of any charges that were there, and then send me the balance to pay the rest of my expenses for the semester. Unlike my peers who lived in dorms, family housing charges were month to month, like the rent for an apartment. Dorms on the other hand, were one lump charge per semester. Therefore, those who lived in dorms would have not only tuition charges sitting on their student accounts when financial aid was disbursed, but also their room and board charges. In my case, there was usually tuition and *one* month's rent of family housing. This meant that I really needed to be wise about using the financial aid refund to pay the rest of the rent for the semester.

One semester I wasn't so wise. I believe I was in my junior year in college and was working so that I would be able to pay the rent as I went along – month to month. In a *really* stupid decision, I used that financial aid money on clothes, other bills, and other frivolous things. The months went on and on and I fell behind in my rent. Since I was living in family housing, these charges were on my student account. As is customary for many universities, you cannot register for the next semester's classes without your account being paid. The university will place a hold on your account. Low and behold, when it came time to register for the winter semester classes, there was a hold on my account, and I could not register. Not being able register and register early as an upperclassman meant that I was in danger of not getting the classes I needed to stay on target for graduation and even worse, not being able to attend college at all in the winter semester. I was *devastated* and did not know what to do. The balance on the account was over a thousand dollars at that point. *This* was an obstacle. This was an obstacle that *definitely* had high worth. And because I did not have the money, it would be a high effort obstacle to overcome. What was I to do? I knew that if I could just make it to the next semester, two things would help me. One, I could use that semester's refund check to pay off the balance. Two, I would get a pretty sizable tax refund since I was a low-income single mother who qualified for the earned income tax credit. With my financial aid refund and the tax refund I could take care of *both* the previous balance and my winter semester rent. There was still a problem though. Without removing the hold on my account,

I couldn't register and if I couldn't register, there would be no winter financial aid. I had *no* money and *no* way to remove the hold. All the work I had done to that point as a teen mom in college was about to be *ruined* over one stupid decision. I didn't know what to do. I didn't have the ability (I couldn't remove the hold myself) or the resources (no money) to overcome this obstacle. But it *was* high worth. I had to figure out something!

I'm not sure how I ended up talking to my uncle. I think I might have called my mother and she called my uncle, but in any case, I ended up talking to my uncle and explaining to him the issue. He happened to know an Assistant Provost at my school and called in a favor. That's exactly what it ended up being – God's Favor! The Assistant Provost agreed to use her "pull" to get that hold removed from my account, so I could register. Yes, I got scolded *pretty badly* by my uncle – trust and believe I didn't walk out of that unscathed! But I overcame that obstacle and did just as I had planned – paid off the balance when my refund check arrived, used the rest of the money to credit my student account as much as I could for the semester's rent, and used my tax refund to cover the rest. It turns out that I *did* have the ability (I opened my mouth and asked for help) and the resources (my uncle) to help overcome that obstacle. I *never* made such a foolish decision from that moment on. In fact, it's the story I used when I reminded my son of how to be responsible when he received his refund check for school. I made sure that he understood that he needed to put a credit for his rent on his account.

Would you believe that my son ended up doing a similar thing in the fall semester of his junior year in college, despite my having drilled this story into his head? Fortunately, his balance was with an off-campus apartment complex, so it wasn't tied to his student account and registration, but it certainly was tied to my credit. You certainly reap what you sow. He was short his December rent because he chose to spend the money on something else. I ended up having to pay his December rent, scolded him something horrible of course, and he paid me back when he received his winter financial aid refund. That winter, he made sure he had a credit balance on his apartment account for the semester as not to have that issue again.

Why do I share this story? It's important for you to understand that all obstacles depend on ability and resources. Sometimes at face value it doesn't seem as if you have the ability or the resources to overcome an obstacle. Some obstacles just seem way too insurmountable. Most times you will find that you *do* have the ability and you *do* have the resources. You just have to keep looking. Sometimes that comes in the form of asking others for help or advice. Sometimes that comes in the form of you doing a Google search for a solution or to see how others have overcome similar obstacles. Sometimes that comes in the form of you seeking God for wisdom and guidance and resources. But most times, you have the ability to change that situation and you have the resources. Just keep believing and keep seeking and you will find that you do.

Now, let's talk about the obstacles where you may *not* have the ability and the resources. Let's go back to an NBA dream as an example. Let's say your goal is to become an NBA basketball player. In general, is it an achievable goal? Yes, even though it's difficult, but yes achievable overall. Now let's consider that you are a 50-year-old female who has never picked up a basketball. For your goal of becoming an NBA player, you've identified that your obstacles are female gender (the NBA is a male player organization), your age (many basketball players retire before age 40), and lack of experience with the game (most NBA players have been playing since childhood). This obstacle is certainly considered high effort. Worth is subjective, but for the sake of this example, let's just say, for whatever reason, that you consider it to be high worth. The question now becomes, do you have the ability and the resources to overcome this obstacle?

Well, given today's laws, I'm sure you could probably make some kind of inequality and discrimination argument as to why the NBA needs to let a woman play. I'm sure that would take a significant amount of time and money in litigation. Let's say you invest the time and the money, and you win that legal battle. Now, your age might be a factor. Usually, the retirement age for the NBA is so young because the players have been playing a high impact sport nearly all their lives and their bodies have worn out over time. Since you've never played the game, let's assume this is not the case for you and you're in relatively good shape. Now for the last problem, you have no experience with the game. Remember Malcolm Gladwell's 10,000-hour rule. To become an expert at anything, it takes approximately 10,000 hours of practice at that one thing. Let's just say you hire a personal basketball coach who is willing to train you for 10,000 hours. Even if you trained non-stop with no sleep, that would take about 417 days. That's over a year. And guess what, there are guys who have clocked this many hours and more and are really great at basketball yet still haven't made it in the NBA. Could you accomplish your goal? Sure, there might be a path – a far reaching one, but a path, nonetheless. Do you have the resources to pay an attorney for litigation? Do you have 10,000 hours available and the money it would cost to train with a coach? Do you have a perfectly functioning body at age 50? Most people would answer "No" to many of these questions.

You must treat your obstacles in the same way. First, make sure you understand what it would take to overcome the obstacle. Then assess your ability and your resources. If at first pass, it doesn't seem as if you have either, ask others and do some research to *really* make sure that you don't. If it is the case that you don't have the ability and resources, you may want to strategize how to accomplish your goal without overcoming that obstacle or consider setting an entirely different goal if the obstacle must be overcome to achieve the goal.

The "All In" Question

Now that you know your obstacles, you know how much effort it would take you, how much it's worth to you that you overcome them, and you know that you have the ability and resources to overcome them, your question then becomes – "Am I all in?" This is arguably the most important question out of the entire process. Are you all in? Are you fully committed to the process? Being "all in" doesn't mean that you try something, it doesn't work, and then you give up. Being "all in" doesn't mean that you take a 30-day challenge and if things don't change then it wasn't meant to be. Being "all in" doesn't mean that you try as much as you know how and never ask anyone else or even Google it. Being "all in" doesn't mean that *every now and then* you decide to push toward overcoming the obstacle. Being "all in" doesn't mean that you tell yourself at the beginning of your journey that you'll *try and see* what happens. Being "all in" doesn't mean that you tell yourself cop out excuses like "If it's God's Will, it will work" or "If it's meant to be, it will be". Being "all in" doesn't mean that every day you pick up the phone whining and complaining about how hard it is to your friend who you *know* will offer *no* encouragement or assistance but will certainly join your pity party.

Being "all in" means BEING ALL IN! It means having a mindset that you *can* and *will* overcome the obstacle. It means that you have an "I'll make it happen" attitude. It means that when something doesn't work, instead of quitting, you extract the lesson of what didn't work and try something else until you find the thing that works. It means that you are committed to keep trying until you overcome. It means that you tell yourself at the *beginning* of the journey that you *will* overcome the obstacle and continue to affirm this until you do. It means that you guard your mind and heart from naysayers and surround yourself with positivity – even if that means listening to a positive thinking book on Audible. It means that you are committed. 100%. No matter what! It means you will *find* a way. It means that you are ALL IN! Are you all in?

I braid my own hair. Yes, you read that right, I braid my own hair. If you're familiar with braids, it may shock you further that I used to braid my hair in microbraids. This means individual, really small braids throughout my hair. To give you context for what that means in terms of time, when this style is completed at an average braiding salon, the salon will assign at least two braiders who braid at the same time to reduce the total time to complete the style. When I braid this style, it's just me, so naturally it would take me longer to braid my hair myself than if I were to go to a salon to have it braided. First, I'll tell you why I braid my own hair and then I'll tell you how it relates to this concept of "all in".

In undergraduate school I was just like most other undergrads – broke! I needed a side hustle. In high school, my mother would let me be her guinea pig to try out different hairstyles on her and I would do the same on myself. Well, she was my first *human* guinea pig for braiding hair. My first *true* guinea pig was an oversized Raggedy Anne doll with hair made from yarn. Surprisingly, I did well on my mother's hair. I needed to learn to braid a little tighter because braids did end up falling out on the sections where her natural hair was pretty short. When she got a little too "happy" at church braids would fall as she danced. But beyond that, I felt comfortable enough to attempt the style on my own head. When that worked out great, others started asking me where I got my hair braided. When I would say I braided my hair myself, they would ask me to do their hair and that is when my college side hustle began – I braided hair in college. Making an extra $100 or so per head wasn't bad, but it was just me. I didn't have other braiders to help me, so it was time-consuming. I promised myself when I no longer had to braid others' hair, I wouldn't. When I got to that point, I not only decided not to braid others' hair, but also no longer wanted to take the time to do my own. It was worth it to me to pay the money to have someone else do it and benefit from having multiple braiders braid at the same time.

When I started to get my hair braided by others, I noticed that they would pull *way* too tight making my hair subject to breakage and they also wouldn't braid my hair into a style – something that I would always do when I braided my hair. So, I decided that I would no longer spend money to have something done that I wasn't pleased with and could do better for free. All it would cost me was my time and the cost of the hair (which I had to pay for regardless). For years, I just chose non-braided styles, so it wasn't an issue. Then, like many other black women, I decided to transition my hair from being processed and straightened with relaxers and heat, to my natural curls. The transition was harder on me and my hair than I imagined. One thing I knew that could protect my hair during this process was braids. So, I decided that I would do them again on my own.

Before embarking on that journey, I had to ask myself – "Angela, are you all in?" What that meant was, once I started the process of braiding, I had to be committed to sitting there and braiding what feels like hundreds of microbraids for the next 16 hours. On top of that, if I was going to keep this style until my hair transitioned, it meant that I was going to be committed to redoing this every two to three months with monthly touch ups in between. That meant that I still needed to wash my hair regularly, so I wasn't off the hook for regular maintenance. This also meant another six to nine hours when I removed the braids, then another two to three hours washing and conditioning my own hair, then spending another 16 hours to put the braids back in. This would repeat every two to three months. This meant my hands would likely hurt the next day. This meant I *would* get tired during that 16-hour period, but once I started, I couldn't go out of the house until I was finished. Again, I asked myself "Are you all in?"

Once I said I was all in the first time, each time two to three months came back around, I would have to ask myself the same question again before I started the process, "Angela, are you all in?" Braiding my hair had no "take backs" once I started. In theory, there could be. I could spend eight hours braiding half my head then decide I'm too tired and then proceed to spend an additional three hours taking them all out. That's 11 hours and I still would need to figure out what to do with my hair. When I got to that "I wish I could just stop" point, I would tell myself "I know you're tired, I know there are several hours to go, but you *have* to keep going. If you stop, you did all that other work for nothing. Keep going! It will be worth it in the end." So, I kept going. I kept braiding. I braided through the cramps. I braided through the back pain. I braided through the fatigue. I braided through the crooks in my neck. I even would leave with a hat on my head to make an emergency trip to the beauty supply store to get more hair when I underestimated how much I needed. I didn't stop. I kept braiding. I paused to pee. I paused to eat. But I always came back to keep braiding. I stayed focused. I cleared my day. I minimized distractions because I didn't want a 16-hour process to turn into a 24-hour one. I stayed on course because I was ALL IN! I planned when I could set aside the time at least a month in advance and kept that schedule clear because I was ALL IN!!! And when I was done, it's gorgeous. I still would get people asking me, "Who does your hair?" This was the dreaded question because I don't lie. Then the follow up question usually would come – either "Are you serious, you do your own hair?" or "Can you do mine?" The first answer is yes, and the second was and is still now "No". I was *not* all in when it came to braiding others' hair.

My braiding story is a wonderful example of the "All In" question and persevering along the way despite the pain, agony, fatigue, feelings like you're so far away from the goal, and feelings of wanting to quit. I share it, so you can hear the narrative in my head as I'm going to through it. The narrative was certainly playing, but I chose to keep going! I knew when I was braiding, that one braid at a time got me closer to finishing. Be "all in" for your goals! Be "all in" for overcoming your obstacles! You might find yourself having to course correct (like me having to go get more hair in the middle), but that's ok, keep going. BE ALL IN! Don't start then stop. You've then wasted effort and STILL must expend more effort figuring out an alternative. Just keep going. Remember what you're working toward. At the end of it, it will all be worth it. When you overcome one obstacle through perseverance, it builds the muscle and fortitude that you need to be able to get through the next obstacle. BE ALL IN!!! Commit to it, then DO IT!

Questions to Consider

1. Which obstacles are *real* obstacles, and which are obstacles that I *perceive* to be real?
2. What are the obstacles that will take the most *effort* for me to overcome?
3. Which obstacles are most *worth* overcoming?
4. Assuming my goal is realistic, what abilities and resources do I have available to overcome these obstacles?
5. How do I consistently demonstrate that I'm "all in"?

DR. ANGELA D. THOMAS

My brethren, count it all joy when you fall into various trials, knowing that the testing of your faith produces patience. But let patience have its perfect work, that you may be perfect and complete, lacking nothing. ~James 1:2-4 (New King James Version)

CHAPTER 11

Uncovering Strategies

If you want to make your dreams come true, the first thing you have to do is wake up. ~J.M. Power

How can you overcome an obstacle effectively without a strategy? Do you know how to identify and devise effective strategies? Do you know how to assess the efficacy of your strategy? Once I discovered public health school, I was all in. I knew I wanted to apply. There was one problem. The deadline to apply was two weeks away and the requirements included letters of recommendation and a statement of purpose, both of which would take a considerable amount of time to pull together. I had to find a strategy that would work to get all the letters I needed on time, and to find the time to write an effective statement of purpose. I sat down and planned out who I wanted to have write a letter, based on who I knew would give me a strong recommendation, and would impress the admissions department. I planned out how I would convince them to turn the letter around quickly. Next, I mapped out the time in my schedule where I would be able to dedicate time to write the statement of purpose, with enough time available to have one of the professors proofread it and provide critical edits, and still have enough remaining time for me to revise it for my application. Without effectively devising this strategy, I would have either missed the deadline to apply to public health school or I would have submitted an incomplete or a low-quality application. The strategy worked! I met the deadline and was accepted into the University of Michigan's School of Public Health. I knew my obstacles and then uncovered and implemented strategies to overcome those obstacles. This section will help you do the same.

Choosing the most effective strategy is an important activity for success. Many find themselves in a space where an obstacle persists despite many attempts. An effective strategy reduces the possibility that you will be stuck there for an extended period. When it comes to overcoming obstacles, uncovering your most effective strategy comes from devising a strategy, assessing and implementing it, understanding the barriers within that strategy, learning lessons from unsuccessful attempts, and revising the strategy to eventually win!

Devise a Strategy

Staring the obstacle in the face, you must start somewhere. If you don't start, you are sure *not* to overcome it, so just start. That said, you must use wisdom when you start. So first ask yourself, "Where can I start? What makes sense to do first?" Just figuring out the answer to these questions can be difficult for most. When I was at the beginning of my doctoral program, I would often get the question, "What will you do for your doctoral project?" Well, at the beginning of the program, like many of my peers, I didn't have much of a clue. After answering this question with the honest answer of, "I'm not sure yet", I decided that I needed to be more purposeful in figuring out how to ultimately get to an answer to this question. You see, it wasn't just an annoying question that people asked me, it actually was an obstacle in the way of my completing school. How? Let's walk it out.

To complete school, I must defend a doctoral project. To defend a doctoral project, I must complete a written account of my doctoral work. To complete the written account of my doctoral work, I must complete a doctoral project. To complete a doctoral project, I must have a topic for my doctoral work. Without a topic for my doctoral work, no completing school. I knew that the sooner I could figure out the answer to this question, the better. So, I began my journey.

The first thing I asked myself was, "What am I passionate about?" That led me to go back to the statement of purpose that I wrote for my application to the doctoral program. In that statement, I explained my passion for health equity in the healthcare setting. That was my start! The next time people asked me what I was doing for my doctoral project, I was able to turn that "I don't know" into an "I'm not sure, but it will be something that deals with health equity in a healthcare setting". While I was getting closer to an answer, I still didn't have the answer to the doctoral project question. As I was working full-time, I wanted to capitalize on the fact that I was a leader in healthcare and my department did research on how to deliver safer, higher quality, more innovative, more accessible, and more equitable care. My thought was that if I could align what I needed to do for my doctoral project with what we would or should be doing in my department anyway, it would be a win-win.

Patient safety, otherwise known as preventing medical error or harm, was a major initiative in my organization. The patient safety leader also happened to be my male work BFF! I was closer! A quick conversation with him and we were able to brainstorm some ways that we could look at health equity in the realm of patient safety. This allowed me to be able to articulate, "I will be looking at health equity and patient safety". I still did not know what this would actually look like at the time. But I knew that the more that I dove into the data, it would become clearer. So, I decided to do my required field study with the patient safety team. We decided that looking at the patient safety event reporting system to determine if differences in reporting existed for patients by race, language, income, gender, and age would be a great place to start. Then we would let the data tell us the story about what we could potentially do next, and I would then be able to further frame my doctoral project direction. It worked! I ultimately successfully defended my doctoral work on race differences in adverse patient safety events in a healthcare setting. You must start somewhere. My doctoral project journey should illustrate the power of that concept.

Once you start somewhere, the direction or possible directions will begin to become clearer. As these directions become clearer, you will be able to take a purposeful look at your strategy. John Maxwell discusses the importance of asking questions in his book "Good Leaders

Ask Great Questions". Asking questions is critical to strategy development. He stresses in his book that it's more important to ask the question thinking it might be a "stupid" question, than to not ask the question at all. I agree. If you don't know the information, ask the question, and then get the answer. The more you ask questions, the better you will become at asking great questions and increase the clarity of your strategic path.

Give It a S.W.O.T.

What kinds of questions should you ask? Let's use the common acronym used in the business setting, S.W.O.T., which stands for Strengths, Weaknesses, Opportunities, and Threats. Think about the strengths that you bring to the table for overcoming your obstacles. What are those? In my doctoral project example, my strengths were my many years of experience in research, working in a research field, having a passion that aligned with the work of my department, having a strong relationship with the safety leader, and having the support of the leaders in my organization for my doctoral studies. What strengths do *you* have?

Let's imagine your goal is to lose weight. You know that one of your obstacles is that you must get up early in the morning and another obstacle is that you tend to work late nights. Here are some strengths that could help with this goal – being a morning person, having lots of space in your home for working out, having a good sense of how to eat healthy, and having experienced successful weight loss in the past. Now let's think about *your* goal. Keeping your obstacles in mind, identify your strengths that can help you to overcome those obstacles. Your overarching questions for "Strengths" should be:

- What advantages do I have that can help me to overcome the obstacle?
- What do I do better than anyone else that I can use to overcome the obstacle?
- What unique or lowest-cost resources can I tap into that can help me overcome the obstacle?

- What do people in my life see as my strengths that can help me overcome the obstacle?

Now, think about the "Weaknesses" that might affect your ability to overcome your obstacle? For my doctoral example, there really was no one at the time who stood out in my organization as a health equity guru. While there was a major safety initiative, there was no major health equity initiative. In addition, balancing the day-to-day responsibilities of my job with an additional project was a challenge. For the weight loss example, one of your weaknesses could be that you are completely tired after your day and you typically just want to come home and sleep. Another weakness could be that your gym opens at 8:00 a.m. and you are typically at work at 6:00 a.m. Maybe yet another weakness could be that no matter how much you say you have discipline, chips and ice cream always tend to call your name. You find yourself binging on one of these foods when you get home. Now that we've walked through some examples, consider some obstacles *you're* facing for *your* goal. Your overarching questions for "Weaknesses" should be:

- What could I improve about me or my situation that could help me overcome the obstacle?
- What should I avoid about me or my situation that could help me overcome the obstacle?
- What weaknesses are other people likely to highlight about my life that can prevent me from overcoming the obstacles?
- What factors about me or my situation can cause me to lose traction to overcome the obstacle?

Now, let's think about the "Opportunities". These are factors external to you that you can capitalize on. As previously discussed, there was the opportunity to align what my department does with a doctoral topic. Also, we collected lots of safety event data, we had lots of patients, we operated a large healthcare system, and there seemed to be gaps in the literature that we could fill with regards to race and patient safety. What opportunities are out there that you can capitalize

on and help you overcome your obstacle? Let's revisit the weight loss example. There is a gym franchise that just opened in your neighborhood that has a 30-day free trial and a $10 a month membership. The gym is actually only five minutes from your house and open 24-hours a day. In addition, your brother is a personal trainer from whom you've learned over the years, proper form, and proper use of exercise equipment. You have the financial resources to purchase healthier food selections, and next week your job is starting a fitness challenge that may help you to stay motivated with some healthy competition. These are excellent opportunities that you can take advantage of to help you with your weight loss goals. Your overarching questions for "Opportunities" should be:

- What good opportunities can I identify that can help me overcome the obstacle?
- What interesting trends am I aware of that can help me overcome the obstacle?

Finally, let's think about the "Threats". Threats are also external factors, but those that could potentially *hinder* your ability to achieve your goals. Let's go back to my doctoral project example. One threat would be a lack of interest in the topic in the academic field. I might be passionate about my topic, but if no one else is convinced why the topic matters, my doctoral committee may not accept the idea. Also, the project depended on the ability to access several data sources for the project. This required that I lean on other people such as data managers and statisticians to assist me with mining and analyzing the data. If these individuals did not adhere to the timelines that I needed them to adhere to, as they usually have other priorities, this could have set me behind schedule for completing the doctoral project. In the weight loss example, threats could be living in a food desert where there is no access to healthy food options or in a neighborhood without convenient access to fitness facilities. Another threat could be an incompetent trainer who gives you bad health and wellness advice. This could potentially thwart weight loss efforts. Your overarching questions for "Threats" should be:

- What are some factors that are external to me that could potentially hinder my ability to achieve my goals?
- How have others who have accomplished this goal handled this threat?
- How is a changing environment threatening my ability to accomplish this goal?

Now that you've completed the S.W.O.T. analysis, you should now have the information you need to devise an effective strategy. Think about your strengths. Your strategy should play to your strengths. Think about your weaknesses. Your strategy should consider your weaknesses and minimize the potential for those weaknesses to derail your efforts to overcome the obstacle. Think about your opportunities. Your strategy should be devised to take advantage of as many opportunities as possible. Finally, think about your threats. Your strategy should be devised to minimize the impact of the threats that you've identified and to continue to overcome any obstacles. Write down your strategy. Identify the key steps in the strategy when you write it down. What will you do first, second, third, fourth, and so on, until you overcome the obstacle?

Assess and Implement the Strategy

Now that you have a strategy, you want to assess, implement, and re-assess the strategy. What exactly does this mean? First, you want to do a gut check asking yourself the question "Will this strategy work?" You should also ask others who you trust or others who have overcome the obstacle in the past the same question. When I was thinking about my doctoral project topic and had gotten to the point where I thought health equity and patient safety might be a viable area, I gut checked it by looking at the literature to see if there was an interest and a gap in the literature – there was. I also gut checked it with my friend, the patient safety leader, to determine if it was viable, and he agreed. I asked my practice-based mentor who was a health equity expert about it as well, and he also thought it would work. That was my gut check process. For the weight loss example, if your obstacle is finding the time to work out and you have decided that part of your strategy would be to wake up earlier in the morning to workout at home using the home videos you've accumulated, you might want to gut check by doing a Google search of testimonials for the specific workout videos that you have – did they work for others? You may also want to do a Google search for those who successfully workout in the morning. What do they do to ensure they do this every day? Do they set their alarm across the room, forcing them to get up? Do they sleep in workout clothes or simply prepare the clothes the night before? Since your brother is a personal trainer, you may also want to ask him what he thinks of your plan and if it could work.

Now that you have assessed your strategy, you now want to begin to implement your strategy. Get into action. Start moving. When you begin implementation, give yourself permission to learn. Most people don't devise the perfect strategy on the very first try. Your beginning strategy is designed to get you moving in the best direction that you can think of with the information that you have. Once you begin to implement this strategy, this starts the process of giving you feedback on what works and what doesn't work. Going back to the doctoral project example, once I locked down that I would be researching health equity in patient safety, I identified a project that I could start on for my field study experience. The strategy was that I would look at the safety event reporting system to determine if there was a difference in reported safety events in vulnerable populations. The goal was to combine the information in the safety event database with the information in the patient registration system to capture information about race, language, ethnicity, age, disability status, veteran status, correctional facility status, mental health status, and income. When I started, I was initially overwhelmed with where to start, but I knew I had to start. I began by asking questions about the systems. How could we find race? What systems did we have that collected language and ethnicity? How could we define veteran status? And so forth. The more I asked questions, the clearer things became, and the more other questions began to arise. I was able to assess, refine, and then implement my strategy.

Barriers within the Strategy

Have you ever started out with what you thought was the perfect game plan only to realize your game plan wasn't so perfect? Well, this happened to me with my doctoral research. We left off at me having refined, assessed, and implemented my plan. Once I felt like I had a reasonable grasp on the landscape, I started to dig into the data. "Let's pull the data". "Let's run it and see what we see". Originally, I thought this would be the easy part. You design a good strategy, ask some questions to really understand and then modify the strategy, then the rest is just pushing the trigger on "Go". Right? I was wrong! I hit some unforeseen barriers along the way – many of them actually.

I'll spare you many of the nerdy details of the issues with the data, but I'll highlight two. One of the barriers was that while our system was designed to collect language preference for each of our patients, we had thousands of patients with unknown or missing language preferences. In the world of statistics, this number was too large to be able answer the questions we set out to answer about language. I had to re-evaluate *that* strategy. The second barrier that I'll highlight is that simply stated, the manual entry in one dataset resulted in a lot of typos which made our computer-based query either unable to find the patients we needed, or it matched demographic data to the wrong patient. Here's an example of what that meant – a Black Woman on Medicaid was labeled as a White Man on Medicare. Yes, a problem! Guess what? I had to re-evaluate *that* strategy.

For most goals we set out to accomplish, we will run into unforeseen barriers and obstacles no matter how much we plan, ask the right questions, and are disciplined in our implementation. These things happen. The key is to remain steadfast and continue the course. When I ran into these issues with my data, I didn't let that stop me. I continued with the mindset of, "We have to find a way"! And finding a way, we did! For the language issue, a colleague of mine looked at this and manually went through records to look for indications of safety events where language played a role – question answered. For the wrong patient issue, I decided to manually go through each record and manually find the race, ethnicity, language, date of birth, gender, and insurance information for each person. Was it time consuming? Yes! Did I have to change my plans for an entire weekend to put in the over 40 hours of work that it took to do it? Yes! Did I get it done? Yes! Did it work? Yes! There is always a way. You just can't let running into barriers and obstacles stop you from accomplishing your goals.

Learn the Lessons

In 2015, I was singing on the praise team at church, and I suggested to the music director that we sing a song called "Amazing" by Ricky Dillard. He so graciously said yes to the song, but then asked that I lead the song. Now anyone who knows anything about me singing on the praise team knows that I consider my lane to be holding down the soprano section. It is not leading songs. My comfort level is with background. My comfort level is not with solos. But I begrudgingly agreed to lead the song. I practiced, and I practiced, and I practiced. I even called my brother for advice. I took it seriously.

Well, I started to battle a cold that weekend. I started to get the classic scratchy throat, started coughing heavily, and I started to lose my voice. Every Sunday we would practice our song list before the service started. On the Sunday morning when we were supposed to sing this song, I walked in and I told the music director that my voice was not there and that I didn't think we should sing the song. I even asked that he give it to someone else. He's said, "No" and he tried to encourage me by saying "You got it. You got it. You got it." So, we practiced the song and I'm *clearly* starting to *die*! I *clearly* started to fall apart, but he kept reinforcing that I sounded good. So, I begrudgingly agreed to move forward with singing the song.

So now the actual time comes on Sunday morning to sing this song during service, and I begin to sing. It starts out low and then it goes high. The low parts are even a struggle. For a soprano, the low parts *shouldn't* be a struggle! I knew that I was in trouble. I was officially *in trouble*. Everybody was looking at me and I knew this was *not* about to end well. Now here comes the high parts and I go to sing the high parts, and NOTHING COMES OUT!!! No voice, no nothing! There were tons of people there and staring right at me. But the saving grace was that our sound system wasn't all that great. Therefore, some people thought that the microphone just went out and not my voice. The other saving grace was that my girlfriend was singing tenor. I turned around, looked at her, and gave her the, "Please help me, please save me" look and she jumped in and she finished the song!

I tell this story because I have some responsibility in how it all went down. I originally stepped away from that situation being *really* angry at the music director. I felt that as a leader he should have pulled the plug on the song because I said I wasn't feeling well, and I blamed him originally. But then I thought about myself and the role that I played in the situation. I should have been more forceful in saying, "No". I knew it was going to go down the tubes and I should have held the line and said, "No". From there I learned a valuable lesson. Now, when I don't feel comfortable doing something, I am not shy about saying, "No." That's because I don't ever want to be in *that* position again. I learned my lesson on how to speak up for myself, and how to know when I must take a harder line and not put myself out there to die. This next section is all about making sure we learn the lessons.

Not only do you have to avoid letting obstacles stop you from accomplishing your goals, but you must also switch your mindset to looking at obstacles completely different. Often obstacles, especially if you don't exercise the fortitude to overcome them, can be viewed as symbols of failure. This is especially true if the obstacles are misaligned with the strategy you put in place to accomplish your goals. We learned from the previous section to continue to look for a way. Find the path to overcome the obstacle. Learn the lessons from your previous attempts to overcome the obstacle. This is the key to minimizing the time it takes you to overcome the obstacle and minimizing your chances of facing a similar obstacle again.

One of my favorite sayings is, "Extract the lesson and move forward". Always ask when you find yourself in a tough situation or just coming through a tough situation, "What is the lesson I'm supposed to carry away from this?" or "What was the lesson I should have carried away from that?" I approach each tough situation in my life as a test – as something that has a lesson buried in it to help make me better. To help me along my success journey. To help me become a better person. To enhance what I know. To build muscle. To build character. To force me to find the right path. There are so many lessons. The key is to not miss the lesson.

I'm sure you've heard the analogy before of tests and lessons. Think of school. While I love to learn, I'm not a big fan of tests. In fact, I loathe them. But there's a purpose to them. They are there to help you discover how much of the material you've mastered and what you still need to learn. If you use tests correctly, after taking one, you review what you missed, make a conscious effort to understand why you missed it, learn the information you missed, and when another test comes with that same information on it, you will pass. The same is true with your life experiences and your journey toward success. When things are tough or don't turn out right, ask yourself "Why?" Seek to understand the situation. Seek to understand what went well and what didn't. Be honest with yourself. What did you miss? What information did you not have? What tools could have made the situation better? What misinformation did you have? Don't just go through the barrier or the test and not learn the lesson. There are some tests that we're just happy that we passed, and even though we missed some points in that test, because we passed, we're satisfied and move on. What I've found to be true is that another test will come along and because we never learned what we missed on the previous test, we miss it again. Until you figure out those lessons, you are doomed to repeat the same mistakes again. While failure and obstacles are not usually considered fun, they have power that *wise* people leverage to become better and grow. Learn the lesson!

Questions to Consider

1. What are my strengths that I can leverage to devise a strategy?
2. What weakness do I have that can potentially hinder my ability to overcome obstacles?

3. What external opportunities can I take advantage of in my strategy?
4. What external threats can potentially hinder my ability to overcome obstacles?
5. How will I ensure that I learn necessary lessons as I implement my strategy?

The plans of the diligent lead surely to plenty, But those of everyone who is hasty, surely to poverty. ~Proverbs 21:5 (New King James Version)

DR. ANGELA D. THOMAS

CHAPTER 12

Never Quitting

Many of life's failures are experienced by people who did not realize how close they were to success when they gave up. ~Thomas Edison

Have you ever quit? Have you regretted quitting? Do you now realize that had you not quit, you would be closer to accomplishing your dreams and goals? Do you regret not following through? Are you thinking about quitting now? Have you put in a lot of time and energy and resources into chasing your dreams and accomplishing your goals, yet you're getting frustrated and want to give up? I remember a time where I actually gave up and I *do* regret it.

In 2016, my husband David and I were planning to renew our vows in Hawaii. In Hawaii, there are plenty of water activities and I wanted to make sure I could take advantage of them. The problem was that I could not swim. In high school, we were required to take swim lessons. In my swim class, I would always make an excuse of why I couldn't get into the water, often blaming my monthly cycle because I didn't want to get my hair wet. As an African American high school girl, having swim class first or second period and getting your hair wet seemed non-negotiable. So, I ended up not learning how to swim at all. Fast forward, I was then a 37-year-old woman and I still don't know how to swim. My girlfriend who was also going with us on the trip did not know how to swim either. She and I decided that we would overcome our fears of the water and take swim lessons in the months leading up to the trip. We each took classes in locations that were local to us.

I got far along in my swimming journey. I went from being scared of putting my face in the water to being able to dive underwater, grab rings from the bottom of the pool, to swimming with a paddle, and swimming without a paddle doing a few strokes. I didn't get to the point where I could master breathing well, but I got to the point where I felt comfortable enough that if I went underwater, I could get myself back up. I also couldn't tread water but felt comfortable enough that I could partake in the water activities we had planned.

We had arrived at the last couple of swim sessions before the Hawaii trip. During these sessions, my swim coach and I were supposed to do some drills. He was going to teach me how to effectively use the snorkeling equipment so that I would be prepared when I went snorkeling. My instructor got appendicitis and had to cancel the last two sessions. I never got to practice with the snorkeling gear.

Fast forward to Hawaii. I was still quite confident because I had made such progress in my water journey and so did my girlfriend. We went out on the snorkeling trip, which included a boat ride to the location. We got on the boat and things started to take a turn. The boat ride was much further out and much rockier on the waves than any of us anticipated. Knowing I have a problem with motion sickness on boats at times, I took Dramamine in advance. That didn't, however, mean that other people on the boat who also have motion sickness issues took Dramamine, specifically one young boy who was about 12 years old.

To know me, is to know that one thing that I absolutely hate – I hate to see it, I hate to look at it, I hate to be around it any kind of way – is vomit. To make a long story short, this young boy was constantly complaining of motion sickness and his family offered him NOTHING. I got anxious. I didn't want him to vomit! The more he complained, the more my anxiety increased. Sure enough, he vomited on the boat right next to me. My anxiety went through the roof! It was also dark outside. The boat was deep in the middle of the water and I didn't realize this was actually a *nighttime* snorkeling activity *in the middle of the ocean*. Until this moment I had never even *put on* snorkeling equipment. In this moment, I was in borrowed snorkeling equipment, the boy just threw up on the boat, and I was one big bottle of nerves. In the meantime, my girlfriend was breathing calmly, preparing, and probably saying all types of wonderful positive affirmations in her head about how she could do this. Not me! I was panicked. I was freaked out a little bit, but nevertheless, I told myself that I was going to push through.

The time arrived for us to get out of the boat and swim out into the ocean. We had to swim out to the middle of this ocean where there was a plank that we were to all hold on to with our faces in the water, so we could see the manta rays. There are very few manta rays and they only come out at night. This was the way to see them – at night, in the middle of the ocean, holding on to a plank, with our legs kicked out floating behind us. Did I mention it was in the middle of the ocean? Did I mention it was at night? Did I mention this was my first time in snorkeling equipment EVER? Did I mention the boy threw up in the *same water* after he threw up next to me? Did I mention I *hate* vomit? Ok, just making sure you had all the facts. On the bright side, for safety, there were trainers and professional swimmers in the water to make sure everything went well. The captain remained on the boat. At this point, I was *really* starting to freak out.

My husband, who actually *can* swim, went out ahead of me. When he went out first and he got to the plank, I watched him. He couldn't get his breathing under control. So, I started freaking out even more. Surely, if *he* was struggling, I was confident I was going to DIE! The message I was telling myself at this point was, "I'm not going to be able to do this. I'm not going to be able to do this. I'm not going to be able to do this!" Meanwhile, my girlfriend and her guy friend were on the plank doing just fine. She had already accomplished what she set out to accomplish, but me, I was freaking out. I was literally freaking out as I got off the boat. The trainer in the water said, "Don't worry, I've got you. I'm going to swim out there with you. I've got this noodle that I'll put under your legs and it's going to be great. Don't worry about it. It's going to be fine." But to no avail, I was still freaking out! I pushed through and I stepped out of the boat and reached out to him in the water. I held on to him and he swam me out to the plank. I got to the plank and tried to hold on and tried to float. It did not work!

Immediately, I SCREAMED, "I want to go back to the boat!" I was making a scene at this point. All the staff tried to reassure me that I was fine, and I could do it, but I adamantly start yelling "I WANT TO GO BACK TO THE BOAT! PLEASE TAKE ME BACK TO THE BOAT... NOW!".

And there you have it. That was the end of it. They swam me back to the boat I was the *first* person back on the boat and did not see a *single* manta ray! All that hard work, all those finances, all those resources, all that time that I put in on Saturdays to work on swimming, just went down the drain because I freaked out at the snorkeling. Now, I regret not putting on my big girl panties, sucking it up, and figuring it out! While my girlfriend put *her* big girl panties on, she can always say she conquered her fear and saw *several* manta rays that day. That's what happens when you give up. You waste time, you waste energy, you waste resources, and then you sit in a space of regret while you listen to others' happiness when they push through to success. Now, I must figure out when I can go back to Hawaii and finally snorkel. Let's just hope no one vomits on the way!

Pushing Through

I don't know a single person who has been successful and has not failed at some point along the way. When you read autobiographies from the most successful people, you will hear stories of failure and even stories of almost giving up yet pushing through. Chasing your dreams and goals can be downright hard sometimes. You will likely ask yourself questions along the way such as, "Is it worth it?" "Is this what I'm supposed to be doing?" "Will this ever work out the way I hope?" You may even make statements such as "This is too hard!" "I'm not sure I can keep doing this." "No one is even paying attention." "Maybe this just isn't for me". It's because of these moments that your core "why" is absolutely important. It is this *why*, this *burning reason* for chasing your goals, that tends to be activated in these low moments. Without this *why*, you won't be able to flip your mindset over into an answer that is something like, "Yes, but if I don't keep going that means I'll never be able to..." The thought of never being able to do whatever that core *why* speaks to should be so scary, so ethically violating to you, so damning, that despite how you feel, your answer at the end of the day is NOT to stop, NOT to quit, to KEEP moving forward, to KEEP pushing, and to KEEP pressing.

In his interview on the Oprah Winfrey Network's show "Master Class", multi-million-dollar comedian, radio show personality, and television phenomenon Steve Harvey tells of the moment that he almost quit. He was homeless, living out of his car, chasing his dream of becoming a comedian with only $35 in his pocket when he was ready to give it all up. Before giving up, he called into his answering machine at his mother's house and received a message inviting him to perform at the Apollo Theatre in New York in just a few days – it was Thursday, the performance was on Sunday. With only $35 in his pocket, he felt defeated. He did not have enough money to make it to New York from Florida. As he was literally crying in defeat, he decided to call the machine again to make sure the message said it was for the Sunday coming up. He called back, and the message did indeed indicate that the show was in just a few days. When he was about to hang up, he heard a "beep" for a new message. He listened to the message and it was an invitation to do a show the *next* day at a comedy club in Florida that would pay $150. He accepted that invitation. He was so good at that performance that he was invited to do a performance the *next* night, Saturday night, where he earned another $150. With enough money now in hand, Steve Harvey was able to afford to travel to New York. He called and accepted the invitation to the Apollo and ended up receiving a standing ovation for the performance at the Apollo that ultimately launched his comedy career.

Steve Harvey's story isn't unique. Many successful people often speak of a similar low moment and a subsequent, pivotal breakthrough in that low moment! Had they NOT decided to keep pushing, they would have missed out on the break that was so close, but they didn't realize it. What a tragedy to give up when you're so close to success! This is why you should NEVER quit!

Stopping is a Guaranteed "No"

One of my earliest experiences with the "guaranteed no" concept was when I was a junior at the University of Michigan, and I was in between classes. This was the 1990s, so the talk show craze was huge at the time. I decided I was going to take a nap in between classes. I turned on the television to the Ricki Lake talk show and sat on the couch and started to doze off to sleep. As I was getting a little foggy, the show was cutting to a commercial when the question popped up, "Did you have a friend who stopped being your friend when you got pregnant? If that's you, call 1-800-GO-RICKI". In my half alert state, I said, "Oh, that's me!" I decided to call. I thought it was a long shot because I called other talk shows in the past regarding other topics. Note: I was 19. Please don't judge me! I can't tell you how many letters I'd written Oprah with no response. I'm still waiting by the way! I'd never gotten a call back from anyone. I always had the attitude that the worst that could happen was they never called me back, but I knew that if I never called or wrote a letter, then I would never get the opportunity to be on the show – it would be a guaranteed "No". If I tried, I at least had a chance at getting a "Yes". Therefore, I called and left a message on the show's messaging service. I quickly explained my story. The next day, a producer from the show called and I gave more of my story. A few days later, I was on my very first plane ride! I was headed to New York City to be on the Ricki Lake Show to confront a friend who stopped being my friend after I got pregnant. The rest of that story is quite embarrassing, but I *will* say that the show did NOT fix our relationship. We are friends today, but the show didn't help. It was, however, my mindset that NOT trying was equal to receiving a "guaranteed no" that earned me that free trip to New York and a timeless and entertaining story to tell at cocktail parties! If you at least try, you have a chance of getting a "Yes".

I think of the decision to quit or to keep going in a similar way. When I think about what it means to stop and what it means to quit, I remind myself that stopping is a guarantee that I won't accomplish my goals – a "guaranteed no". Guaranteed! If I keep going, there's at least a chance that I will accomplish my goals. I'd rather put in the energy toward something that can materialize, than operate in a place of guaranteed lack of success – moving toward absolutely nothing. Take the chance at achieving your goals. The worse that can happen is that you don't achieve your goals, but you will learn some wonderful and useful lessons along the way. You'll come out stronger, more knowledgeable, and more equipped to chase the next goal.

Who is Depending on Your Success?

There is another way of thinking that can help you to push through during the moments when you want to quit. This requires that you think about who is depending on your success. During his American Idol Interview, 2018 contestant, Marcio Donaldson, told the story of how he became a dad to his six-month-old son. Marcio and his sister were taken by social services from their mother, who was also raised in the social services system, when they were young because the conditions they lived in weren't suitable. This added up to two generations of the social services system. It was in the system that Marcio discovered his passion to sing. Later, drugs impaired his sister's ability to keep her son. When social services arrived at Marcio's house with his one-week-old biological nephew, they explained that he had a choice – to take in his nephew or send him to the social services system. He decided that he did not want his nephew to go through what he went through, so he took him in. He is now "dad" to his nephew. When he further explained what pursuing his passion for singing meant, he said, "I'm not only performing for me, but I'm also performing for my son. I want to show him what a man can really do when you step up to the plate". Singing was no longer just about Marcio, it was about what was necessary to teach his son!

Who is waiting for you to accomplish your dreams? Who on the other end needs your help? Whose life is depending on your getting your act together? This is what I consider the ethical and moral dilemma that you *must* force yourself into. It's a space of thinking where you literally feel like you will have let the world, God, your mother, and your deceased grandmother down if you don't accomplish your dreams and your goals. I personally imagine God shaking His head in disappointment the longer it takes me to do what He asked me to do. I also imagine the teenaged mother who forgoes higher education because she doesn't know it's possible despite her circumstances – and it's my fault! If I would have just done what He asked me to do, she'd know. I imagine the struggling business owner trying to figure out why he or she isn't seeing the success they imagined when they started out. I see the frustration on their face and say to myself, "It's my fault!" If I would have done what God asked *me* to do, they would have the information necessary to succeed. I see the struggling artist with undeniable talent trying this and trying that with absolutely no strategy or plan and not surprisingly, it's not working. And it's my fault! Had I put the information out about how to be strategic in *anything*, maybe, just maybe they would see incredible success in their artistry!

Who is depending on your success? Maybe you're an aspiring hairstylist who wants to focus on healthy hair. You continue to see ladies with damaged hair in your city. That should frustrate you to the point of saying, "I can't quit! Her hair depends on my success". Maybe you're in school to become a licensed counselor. You see broken marriages and relationships all around you. Yes, your classes may be hard and maybe some you're not doing that well in, but you can't quit. Think about those marriages that are waiting on your expertise to help restore the union to its God-designed purpose. Keep pushing! Maybe you're an educator hoping to start a foundation that gives away scholarships to youth who otherwise couldn't afford college. Trying to raise money seems insurmountable. Think about the faces of those extraordinary children who simply need a financial opportunity to make their dreams a reality. Push through! Don't quit! Keep going for THEM!

No matter your dreams, vision, and purpose you need to have the faces of those who you are purposed to help in your mind! It is these faces that will help push you through each time you want to quit! The closer these faces, these hearts, these lives are to your passion and your purpose, the stronger that ethical and moral obligation becomes to you not to quit – not to let haters steer you away from moving toward your goals. Not to let setbacks sit you down. Not to let obstacles be the "end all, be all". Use these faces to motivate you to FIND A WAY!!! If you're not doing well in classes, ask your professor to help you during office hours, get a tutor, and carve out extra time to study! If raising money is a challenge, go on the Internet and Google "proven strategies for fundraising" and see what you find. Go on social media and ask for tips! Find someone who is successful in fundraising and reach out to see if they can mentor you. Volunteer for a not-for-profit that fundraises successfully and learn the inside! FIND A WAY!!! Push through! There are *real* people with *real* challenges waiting on YOU! They are waiting on the real solutions that YOU, yes YOU will offer them. You MUST push through! They are depending on *your* success. It's your ethical and moral obligation to *them* to be successful!

Don't be Wasteful

I like to eat. A LOT! Correction, I don't just like it, I LOVE it. I just love great food! Growing up with two brothers who are giants – one is 6'8" and the other is 6'5" – and in a household where we didn't have a whole lot of money, we couldn't afford to take food for granted. I learned to eat! I learned to eat fast, eat a lot, and to clean my plate. Why would anyone ever waste food? My experiences with food contribute to my disdain for being wasteful. Many people have a similar "clean your plate" upbringing, hence, why many of us struggle with our waistlines. However, this mindset doesn't always translate into other areas of many people's lives. We can be wasteful with our time, our energy, our resources, our relationships, our speech, and many other areas. Just as a "don't waste it" mindset is helpful for you to keep eating to clean your plate despite being full, it can also be important to ensure you do NOT quit on your goals and dreams. Often when people quit, they do so after putting in a lot of time, energy, money, other people's time, thought, and sacrifice into chasing their dreams. When they hit setbacks and roadblocks, they just quit. There are several reasons. They may forget about the time and energy they've already put into the journey or they may even rationalize the value in quitting despite the time and energy.

I personally believe that those who fall into this pattern haven't yet transitioned into a mindset of using every setback as an opportunity to learn. Those with this mindset will never consider a setback or a failure as a waste of time. "I wasted my money, and it didn't work". "I wasted my time on that conversation because nothing came of it". "I wasted all those hours Googling and it still didn't help". What if you flipped your thinking to, "Ok, spending the money in that particular area didn't get me the results I thought I would get, but at least now I know that area *isn't* a smart investment – let me now figure out what *is* a smart investment." "That conversation didn't quite go the way I thought it would go, but now I know that I don't need to talk to that type of person. The type of person I really need to talk to is someone who... let me find that type of person". "So, Googling didn't help me answer that question, but I know I can't be the first person who needed the answer to this question. Let me try finding someone who has been where I'm trying to go and ask them". Those with this mindset truly believe that *nothing* could be considered a waste of time. There is a lesson moment and a learning moment in every experience. A waste of time would only occur if one decided to quit because of the setback. That *would* waste all the time, energy, and resources invested to that moment, because if one quits, they are guaranteed to NEVER see any fruit of those investments.

Why would you be wasteful? Many people fall victim to a wasteful mindset because they live with a "grass is greener" mindset. This mindset says, "Well this didn't work so let me figure out something else to try because that journey seems easier." They move to something else and then they realize that the new journey will also come with challenges. They realize that grass was NOT greener, and they move to something else. This begins an endless cycle of trying something new. The grass seems greener, so you try it. It's cool for a while. It's exciting. It's challenging. You're learning. And then it happens – you don't see the results you were hoping for. You plateau. You begin comparing yourself to other people who seem to be so much further along than you. The journey seems impossible. You get discouraged. You rationalize why this isn't for you any longer, and then it happens – you see something else that seems promising, greener, more appealing, and you decide to stop what you're doing and try that new thing! It's a cycle. A never-ending cycle! Until you learn to push through despite the frustrations, plateaus, and challenges, you will continue to find yourself in the constant loop of trying something new and never succeeding at one thing. This constant loop becomes a waste of time and resources. Don't be wasteful!

Figure it Out

One of my favorite phrases is "We will figure it out!" It's my "go to" phrase whenever an obstacle presents that I did not anticipate, or a challenge occurs to which I have yet to find the solution. My answer is, "We will figure it out!" or more personally, "I will figure it out!" It's my way of ensuring myself that there *is* indeed a solution, it just hasn't surfaced yet. The benefit of such an attitude is that it not only keeps me moving in the right direction, but it turns something that can be perceived as negative into something positive – a motivating challenge.

On one season finale of the NBC show "This is Us", the character Randall and his wife Beth engaged in a dialogue prompted by fear. Randall asked Beth if they could play the game "My Worst Fear". The rules of this game were simple. They would take turns saying out loud their worst fears about a situation, so they can get it out and move on to figuring out the solution to their problem. As parents of three girls, one of their worst scenarios ended with the girls on a stripper pole! While quite the funny moment on a drama-filled show, the game highlighted a healthy practice of anticipating potential challenges and obstacles. Randall and Beth attempted to think of them all – the worst of them. Once they did, they were able to strategize how to address the problem they were facing. They figured it out!

While it's important to plan and be strategic when trying to accomplish your goals, which includes trying to anticipate obstacles and barriers, it's also important to realize *that you can't anticipate every obstacle*. It's impossible to know them all, and let's face it, life happens. Because there are obstacles that you can't anticipate, it is important that you go into your journey with a baseline attitude that you will figure out a way to overcome any obstacles, anticipated or unanticipated, that come your way. You also need to have the baseline attitude that no matter what, you will be ok. You need to trust your reactions to setbacks and obstacles. Trust that you *will* persevere. Trust that you *will* bounce back. Trust that you *will* overcome.

Nick Vujicic was born with no legs and arms but has found a way to "figure it out"! He has accomplished such feats such as climbing Mount Kilimanjaro and playing all kinds of sports, including football. How do you do that when you don't have any arms or any legs? He says that there is *nothing* that people with limbs can do, that he has not *figured out* a way to do without limbs. Just because obstacles arise, and yes, this includes our own bad decisions, it does not mean we cannot rise above those circumstances. Always find a way to approach challenges and unfavorable circumstances as steppingstones toward accomplishing your goals. When you live life with this attitude and outlook, when adversity comes your way, you find yourself never giving up and declaring to yourself along the way, "I will figure it out!"

Questions to Consider

Consider the following questions as you think about your own attitude and behavior toward never quitting.

1. What do I need to "push through" to ensure I accomplish my goals and dreams?
2. What am I saying "No" to if I stop?
3. Who is waiting on me to accomplish my goals?
4. What resources will I have wasted if I stop?
5. What are the challenges that I am facing *right now* that are waiting on me to just "figure it out"?

For you have need of endurance, so that when you have done the will of God you may receive what is promised. ~Hebrews 10:36 (English Standard Version)

DR. ANGELA D. THOMAS

CHAPTER 13

Creating Champions

Keep away from people who try to belittle your ambitions. Small people always do that, but the really great make you feel that you, too, can become great. ~Mark Twain

My son Nate went through what now we call his "chunky Nate" phase. It was in middle school when he was an overweight, chubby kid. When you're overweight and chubby, regardless of age, you tend to have lower energy and lower stamina. My son has never been "the athlete". However, I would always keep him in athletics growing up. He's been in soccer, basketball, football, baseball, tee ball, and swim. He's done a lot of sports but was never really good at anything except swim. But in his chunky Nate phase, he actually signed up to be part of the track meet at his middle school when we were still living in Northville, Michigan. He had to do a full lap around the track with the other students who were running the 400-meter race. The other children completed the race, but poor Nate was in his chunky Nate phase and was significantly behind in getting around that track. He didn't have the stamina or the energy. He couldn't keep up with the other kids.

Despite it all, he never once stopped running! He was running substantially slower than everyone else, which is why he was behind, but he never stopped running! What happened next was amazing! Of course, I was cheering loudly for him to finish the race, but then other people in the stands began cheering him on too. Even though Nate was dead last finishing the race, he finished the race! His refusal to stop running created so many champions for him in that moment. People who were in his corner and wanted to see him finish – wanted to see him succeed. They wanted to see him cross that finish line and accomplish what he set out to accomplish. He created champions for himself in that moment. I have to believe that he heard the voices of his champions as he was running, as he felt tired, as he knew he was the last one getting around. When he heard all those people chanting and cheering for him, it was enough to keep him moving and he ran across the finish line.

Do you have the right people in your corner? Do you realize that the road to success shouldn't be journeyed alone? The statement that "it takes a village" doesn't just apply to raising children, but it also applies to your success journey. Who is around you? To whom are you telling your problems? Who are you confiding in who will help you as you build and grow? Who is helping you? Who is in your cheerleading circle?

While you are trying to accomplish something great in your life, the quality of the individuals who you allow around you will dictate how successful you become. You *must* guard who you allow in your space. You *must* guard who you allow to be privileged to your goals and your dreams. There's a purpose for positive people being around you who want nothing but the best and nothing more than to see you succeed. Champions are not only individuals who come out on top at the end of a race, journey, or challenge, but champions are also those who cheer for others' success.

Biggest Fan

On the NBC television show "This is Us", there is a character named Jack Pearson who is the father of three children – triplets. The triplets are two fraternal twins and another son who was born on the same day whom Jack adopted. Throughout the show we watch Jack do some amazing things as a father. The kids look at him as superman. They are his biggest fans. The kids absolutely adore Jack. They look up to Jack. They want to *be* Jack. Everything is about Jack. Everything is about their dad. He is absolutely their hero. In their eyes, there is nothing that Jack can't do. It's this perception of the Pearson children of their dad that illustrates the first type of champion – the biggest fan.

One of the biggest fans in my life is actually *my* dad. He seems to think that I can do absolutely everything. He calls me "Dr. Daughter". I can't remember many times that he got angry with me and with everything I've accomplished he's been so proud. Even when I told him I was pregnant, he found a positive way to talk about how I'd get through it. The biggest fan is the person who absolutely believes that you are amazing. You can do absolutely everything and can do no wrong. They look up to you, they admire you, and they believe in you. They're cheering for you. Everyone needs a biggest fan in their circle. Often, you can find a biggest fan in the family – moms, dads, brothers, sisters, spouses, and children are often biggest fans. Biggest fans are important because they become the person you can tap into on days where you feel like you're doing everything *wrong*. This person will give you words of encouragement without even knowing that you're going through something on that day. They'll remind you how amazing you are, how fantastic you are, how smart you are, how beautiful you are, and how you make a difference in their lives and in the lives of others. Biggest fans provide a purposeful space where you can go to when you need to be reminded of your good qualities. *Everyone* needs a biggest fan!

Constructive Critic

I was once watching the cable network "Lifetime". Lifetime has many made for television movies that include murder mysteries and "she stole my man, my baby, or my job" movies as well. Lifetime also airs autobiographical and biographical movies. I was watching the Simone Biles story. Simone Biles is a gymnast who is an Olympic champion. The movie told the story of how she became an Olympic gymnast. In her circle she had many different champions. One of the champions was her Olympic coach. She had two coaches. One coach was her local coach who was a woman who had been coaching her since she started gymnastics. As she became an Olympic hopeful, her goal was to join the team of a very specific Olympic coach. Simone tried out several times but just couldn't make the team. It was because this coach was very critical of Simone. She identified very specific areas that Simone needed to work on to make the team – one of which was her attitude. It was this coach's criticism that motivated her to work harder on perfecting those specific areas, try out again, and ultimately make the team.

I have at least two of these in my life – my older brother Aaron and my younger brother Adam. Like my dad, they are very supportive of everything I'm trying to do and every goal and dream and vision that I've had and continued to have. However, along the way, if they see anything that might be beneficial for me to learn, anything for me to correct, anything for me to consider, any new perspective, any new resource that I should check into, they will also give me that feedback. I never feel like it's coming from a place of them not wanting me to succeed. In fact, it's the opposite. I always feel that they really are trying to help get me to where I'm trying to go.

Everyone needs a constructive critic because unlike the biggest fan, the constructive critic will not always tell you that you're amazing. The constructive critic will tell you the areas that you need to improve so that you can get closer to accomplishing your goals. The constructive critic will give you the feedback that isn't always the easiest to hear, but they give that feedback with the same *heart* of the biggest fan. They want you to succeed. They *believe* you can succeed, but they also know you need *real* help along the way. They would rather you learn from them what you need to work on than from others who do not have your best interests at heart. They give you the feedback from a place of love, concern, and a genuine desire to see you succeed. There are many who are only ever told about their greatness and never told about those areas that they could work on. That's how we get the bad auditions on American Idol from people who are *shocked* to hear from the judges for the first time just how bad they sound! No one ever told them they don't sound good! If you are a person who wants to do better, someone must tell you where you need to improve.

There are areas in all our lives that we need to work on, but we just can't see them. Personally, I call those areas my "blind spots". When I first started using an executive coach, my coach asked about my goals for the coaching engagement. My goal then, remains the same now – I want to uncover my blind spots. There are many areas in my life that I cannot see, and I know that if I uncover them, then I can work on them. But if I never see them, I'll never be able to work on them. One way I uncover blind spots is to ensure that I have a constructive critic in my circle. This helps me not only to uncover the blind spots, but also to work on them over time. Today's blind spots will not be the blind spots of tomorrow. Blind spots aren't "one and done". Just because you've identified and worked on blind spots in the past, doesn't mean you've uncovered them all. Therefore, you need someone who's willing to give you constructive criticism, who is not seeking to hurt your feelings, not seeking to discourage you, not seeking to frustrate you, not seeking to derail your success journey, but someone who's giving you the news you *need* to hear to help you improve and to move you closer to your desired end.

The Assister

It's been said that every great leader has a second in command. This is someone who pushes the vision for the visionary – helping to ensure that it comes to pass. They say that Walt Disney was the creative visionary, but Roy Disney ensured that the business operations were effective. Everyone in your circle doesn't desire to take your place. Many are excited about the potential and future success that they see in *you* and are willing to come *alongside you* and help you. This person is called the Assister. This person is willing to assist, willing to push your vision forward, and willing to help however possible.

If you voice an idea, they say, "How can I help you?" If you mention wanting to go in a certain direction, they've already researched that direction for you. If you say, "I wish I knew more about...", before you know it, you will have an email full of results that they've Googled without even asking. These are your Assisters – people who desire so much for you to succeed, that they are willing to roll up their sleeves and get their hands dirty for *you*! Some Assisters may help by rolling up their sleeves, while others help by writing a check, and others help you with other areas of your life that free you up to focus on your goals.

I have a few Assisters in my life. My girlfriend Charita will no matter WHAT I say I'm trying to do will say, "What can I do? How can I help? What can I do to help you Sis?" My good friend Carlice rides the line of both a Biggest Fan and an Assister, but he has been so excited about my future that he always talks about how he would drive me anywhere, be my chauffeur and do whatever I need him to do to help me become successful. My girlfriend Jocelyn always says, "I know I'm not going to *be* you, but I want to help you in whatever way I can. You just let me know what you need me to do". You *need* an Assister in your corner!

The Prayer Warrior

A young minister, Stephanie Slaybaugh, came to minister at our church. She had a powerful testimony of going unconscious and unexplainably remaining in a coma for an extended period of time while seizing over and over again. The doctors were not quite sure why this happened to her. They were baffled. Her testimony was so powerful because despite the doctors not believing she would walk again, she walked. Even when she was in a coma having multiple seizures, she found herself worshiping. She doesn't remember worshipping, but it was captured by her husband on video. Her recovery wasn't easy. She's a mother of four children. While giving her testimony, she showed a picture of her children with her on the stairs around her with their hands on her praying for her. The back story of the picture was that she was trying to learn to walk up the stairs again. She was having a rough day and she wasn't progressing as far as she hoped. She was having trouble with the stairs and sat down on the stairs and began to cry in frustration. Her children surrounded her and began to pray. They prayed for her strength. Her children were her Prayer Warriors in that moment.

Everyone needs a Prayer Warrior. Prayer Warriors are powerful. Like the Slaybaugh children, Prayer Warriors are there for you in a time of frustration. When their mother was not strong enough to pray for herself, the Slaybaugh children prayed *for* her. You must have Prayer Warriors around you because when you can't even pray for yourself, when you're frustrated, when you're down, when you're in a dark spot, you need someone to cover you, they fight for you spiritually.

Prayer Warriors are also amazing because they are often praying for you when you don't even know it. They are praying for you and covering you constantly. They're praying for you in general and praying that God gives you wisdom and direction. They *keep* your name on their lips as they pray to God. They intercede for you. Prayer Warriors have your back spiritually no matter what and don't even need to know what's going on in your life to pray for you. When you *do* share with them what's going on, you can be confident in knowing that they've already added that situation to their prayer list.

Prayer Warriors are also good when you specifically ask for prayer time. There have been times where I've been so frustrated and so down and so discouraged that I needed to *hear* someone praying for me. I needed to physically hear someone going to God for me. Hearing someone pray for me in those moments of frustration and darkness gave me peace because I could feel the peace of God after they prayed. Prayer Warriors will step in when you're so frustrated, hurt, and discouraged, that you are unable to muster the strength to pray for yourself.

A couple of major Prayer Warriors in my life are my mother and my spiritual mothers. My mother's name is Elder Denise Smith, and my spiritual mothers are Prophet Jacqueline Sims and Prophet Adraine Bibbens. These women are always going to God in prayer. No matter what I share with them, no matter what I'm trying to achieve, and no matter what frustrations I have, I know they are always going God on my behalf. They constantly pray even when I don't realize it.

The Overcomer

A woman by the name of Tererai Trent appeared on the Oprah Winfrey Show. Tererai Trent was born in Zimbabwe where she was unable to receive any education because of poverty. However, she had dreams to earn a bachelor's degree, a master's degree, and a PhD. She wrote these dreams on a piece of paper and buried it. While in poverty and unable to attend school, she self-taught from her brother's books who *were* able to go to school. At one point, she was able to attend school, but was pulled out of the school when her father married her off in exchange for a cow. By the age of 18, she had three kids and no high school diploma. Her husband began to physically abuse her after she shared with him her dream of receiving an education. She later moved to Oklahoma with her husband and five children. Three years later, earned a bachelor's degree and then earned a master's degree. Her husband was ultimately deported from the United States for domestic abuse. Tererai Trent remarried and went back to Africa to retrieve the piece of paper that she buried. Once she located the paper, she checked off the goals that she had written down and accomplished. She returned to Michigan to complete and ultimately earn her PhD.

Tererai Trent is an Overcomer. I was 32 when her story was featured on the Oprah Winfrey Show. At the time, I had earned a bachelor's and two master's degrees, and I was feeling pretty good about overcoming teenage pregnancy to earn those degrees, until I saw her story. She wasn't even allowed to go to school and was being abused. To even have a *chance* at education, she had to envision receiving that education in an *entirely* different country. The way she wrote down her dreams and worked hard until they manifested solidified her status in *my* life as an Overcomer.

Often Overcomers are "silent champions" because they are people who we admire and often don't even know. These are people who have stories that we can reflect on when times get challenging and rough for us. If I were to remember Dr. Tererai Trent, every time I face a challenge, her story is enough to pull me out of a defeatist attitude and find a way to figure it out.

While Overcomers can be silent champions that you don't know, they don't always have to be. You may know someone in your life who overcame incredible odds to achieve success. This may be the story that you pull on when you find yourself in a challenge. Therefore, it is so important that we have an Overcomer as one of our champions – even if they are silent champions.

Questions to Consider

1. Who will always tell me positive things about myself?
2. Who will constructively tell me what I need to improve?
3. Who is willing to assist or help me on my journey in any way possible?
4. Who is always praying for me even when I don't realize it?
5. What stories of Overcomers can I draw on when times get tough for me?

Where there is no counsel, the people fall; But in the multitude of counselors there is safety. ~ Proverbs 11:14 (New King James Version)

CHAPTER 14

Expecting the Exception

Do not follow where the path may lead. Go instead where there is no path and leave a trail. ~Horold R. McAlindon

Do you ever wonder why there aren't more successful people in this world? Have you ever wondered how those who *have* found tremendous success found it? There are only a few names you can call in certain categories. When you consider the best basketball player in the world, names like Michael Jordan, Lebron James, and Kobe Bryant may come to mind. When considering the best golf players in the world, names like Tiger Woods and Arnold Palmer may come to mind. When considering the best tennis player in the world, Venus Williams or Serena Williams may come to mind. Even though there are many other people in those categories, these are the names that stand out for many. We tend to remember stories of people who were set apart and who were exceptions to the rule. We tend to marvel at their stories because they seem to have achieved the extraordinary. They achieved what we have not. Are you trying to achieve something that is extraordinary? Something that is "beyond the ordinary"? Something that is literally extra… ordinary? If that is you, then you need to expect to be the exception.

The status quo is *real*. Many people follow a standard path or standard way of living in our society. Day-to-day becomes the same old, same old. The same grind day after day for many people who live in the monotony of the day-to-day. You don't have to be one of the many people who choose to live that life. You're on a success journey because you want to be better. You have big dreams, big goals, and big visions you want to accomplish that require that you put in something more than just the status quo every day. It requires you to do more than what everyone else is doing. Rickey Minor wrote a book called, "There's No Traffic on the Extra Mile...", which essentially means that it's a road less traveled. Most people are fine with the status quo, but few are willing to do what it takes – a bit more extra effort – to become extraordinary.

For most, what does the "every day" look like? It probably looks something like this. You wake up, eat breakfast, go to work a regular nine-to-five job, come home, maybe order takeout, eat dinner, sit on the couch, watch TV, do some Internet surfing, maybe get on the phone, and talk a bit to a friend or family member, go to bed, and repeat the next day. Some days might include picking up the children, going to church, or other regular societal responsibilities, but this is typically what the days of most resemble. There is nothing unique about this life. One person's life looks very similar to another person's life. There is nothing extraordinary for most. This life looks pretty standard. However, to achieve extraordinary success, to accomplish your dreams beyond anything you've imagined could ever happen for you, you need to do more. You need to be more extraordinary! To do this, you must be the exception to "ordinary". There are five key areas where you can expect to be the exception. Let's explore each in detail.

Beating the Odds

Being extraordinary includes overcoming odds. Here are some interesting odds. Two percent of teen mothers finish college before the age of 30. Of people who are diagnosed with pancreatic cancer (one of the most aggressive cancers), there's only a 20% one-year survival rate and only a 7% five-year survival rate. The odds of being diagnosed with cancer are 50% for men and 33% percent for women. There is a 67% chance of being involved in a drunk driving crash. The odds of being drafted by the NBA are pretty low at 1 in almost 7,000,000. The odds of dying in the airplane crash are 1 in almost 10,000. The odds of becoming the president of the United States are 1 in 10,000,000.

Let's just take two of these important statistics. The first is the odds of becoming the President of the United States. I don't know the odds of becoming the first African American President of the United States, but if the odds of becoming the President of the United States are 1 in 10,000,000, then odds of becoming the first African American President of the United States must be even less. Imagine if President Barack Obama looked at the odds of becoming President as 1 in 10,000,000 and said, "You know what? I'm African American so forget it! Let me follow another path!" He would have never become the first African American President of the United States. I believe that President Obama expected to be the exception to that rule. None of the odds that I read were zero. Even though one could argue that his odds of becoming the first African American President of the United States was zero because there was no other African American President of the United States before him. However, since there is no rule against being an African American President of the United States, I can imagine President Obama saying, "You know what? That means that *I* can be the first!" When the odds are stacked against us and not in our favor for accomplishing our dreams and goals, we must resolve that *we* can be the exception to the rule.

The second statistic to explore further was reported by the National Campaign to Prevent Teenage Pregnancy. They report that the odds of graduating college before the age of 30 is 2% for teen mothers. Two percent is extremely low. This means that 98% of teen mothers do not finish college before the age of 30. I expected to be an exception to the rule. Because of that expectation, before the age of 30, I earned three degrees – a Bachelor of Science, a Master of Public Health, and a Master of Business Administration. Not only did I beat the odds of graduating college before age 30, but I crushed those odds with *three* degrees before the age of 30. I entered that journey knowing that the odds were stacked against me. I expected to be the exception to the rule. The statistic wasn't 0% and even if it was 0%, I would have wanted to be the first teenaged mother to graduate college before the age of 30. You must begin your success journey with a mindset that despite the odds and the statistics, you expect to be the exception. If the odds are bleak, expect to fall on the bleak side. If there are no statistics at all, and no one has ever done it, expect to be the *first* and believe in yourself that you can accomplish it.

The More You Do, the More You Get to Do

Very early in my career I was having a conversation with a more senior leader. I was trying to figure out how to get to the next level in my career. He said to me, "The more you do, the more you do." He explained that it was his boss at the time who introduced him to that phrase. Since then, I modified the phrase to say, "The more you do, the more you *get* to do." It simply means that if you're seeking to go higher, then you need to do higher level tasks at your *current* level, and the people who matter can see that you deserve to be at that higher level. How does this relate to expecting the exception? It's about being extraordinary! Those who are at your current level are content on just doing what is are required to remain at that level. However, when you decide to do more, then you become an exception to those people. At your current level, you become extraordinary – *extra* ordinary! You become someone who is different. You become someone who isn't following the traditional path. You become someone who stands out of the crowd. When you stand out of the crowd, that's when other opportunities come along. You become the person that leadership seeks out when they need something done and you get to do "the more". The more you do, the more you get to do. Don't pigeonhole yourself into just being able to do the tasks required at your level. Figure out ways to do *more,* because when the opportunity to advance to the next level comes along, they will consider you *first* because you've already shown that you're the extraordinary one who can handle the next level. Grant Cardone has coined what he calls the "10x Rule". The rule states that whatever effort you think it will take to accomplish something, magnify it 10 times and do it at *that* level. If you take this approach, you certainly will become exceptional and extraordinary. The more you do, the more you get to do.

For those who are building businesses, you know that in the beginning phases trying to get the business off the ground is challenging. It's hard. You're trying to figure it out. You're trying to figure out what resources you have, and the resources you have are quite limited. You're trying to figure out which direction to go. You're trying to build, but there is so much to do, and everything takes time, energy, focus, and hard work. However, the more you do in the building phase, you'll be able to see the pay off when your business grows to the next level. Using the analogy of building a house, you must first lay the foundation and lay bricks. From there you add things like drywall, windows, electric, bathrooms, and a kitchen. When all the required components of the house are constructed, then you have a complete house. Then you can work on building a *home* that you can come to every day and lay your head peacefully and not have to worry about laying bricks ever again. Yes, some maintenance will be required along the way. There will be some necessary repairs every so often, but you won't have to put in the same hard work that went into building the house initially. The more you do in the beginning, the more you get to do when you achieve success. You'll have more freedom to do the things you desire to do.

Be Different!

Expecting to be the exception also means having a mindset of being perfectly fine with being different, and being perfectly fine with not always fitting in. Choosing to fit in means that you're choosing NOT to be an exception to the rule. You fit in with the crowd. You're doing what everyone else is doing. Your hair looks the same. You wear the same styles. When a new way of wearing jeans becomes popular, then you switch to that way of wearing your jeans. I remember when the rap duo "Kris Kross" was popular and started the craze of wearing clothing backward. I also remember when "Damaged" and "Used" jeans were popular. Everyone had a pair of those. I also remember when the singing group "Jodeci" made a certain style of combat boots popular. They were nicknamed "Jodeci boots" and everyone had a pair. Yes, these were all 90s fashion crazes, so I'm dating myself, but the point is clear. When you look like everyone else, you're not an exception to the rule. The reason why fashion crazes are so successful is because society and retailers capitalize on the fact that most people have a desire to fit in. Fitting in doesn't make you unique. It doesn't make you stand out. It doesn't make you special. It just allows you to be in social situations where you don't feel awkward. It allows you to have something in common with your neighbor. It allows you fit in. Most people are fine with that reality, but unfortunately fitting in does not allow you to innovate, set new standards, and land a spot on the ABC television show "Shark Tank". Fitting in doesn't allow you to have the breakthrough success that you're striving to achieve. You need a mindset where you're perfectly fine with *not* fitting in.

I've never felt that I've completely fit in. I won't lie and tell you that I didn't desire to fit in. Oh, I tried! But some things like money and genes just didn't allow it. It was very frustrating to always feel like you never fit in. Many of my friends have never looked like me. Often, I found (and still find) myself being the only chocolate girl. If I wasn't the only chocolate girl, I was the only one with short hair or my hair wasn't done, or I was too skinny. My forehead was too big. My nose was too big. My eyes were too big. My cheeks were too big. My bottom lip was bigger than my top lip. My eczema was a mess. My lips were too chapped. The list goes on and on.

I was always one of the smartest girls in my class, especially in elementary and middle school. Things that interested me didn't seem to interest my peers. Many times, I would find myself trying to dumb down so I could fit in, but it never worked. I remember in sixth grade I tried to fit in, but I had to choose fashions that my parents could afford. My mom bought me this outfit from JC Penney's that had a turquoise skirt that flared and had suspenders that were hot pink and black. I put it on with a black tee shirt and some black patent leather loafer-like flats where the tops of them were black and white puzzle pieces. I was one big bundle of turquoise, pink, black, and white! I thought I was cute until I went into the cafeteria and an eighth grader laughed at me and called me Punky Brewster – after the 80s sitcom character played by Soleil Moon Frye, who was known for a mix matched style and no longer popular at that point. This certainly wasn't a compliment. She laughed at me along with her friends who joined in. So much for fitting in!

I've come to learn over time that not fitting in is actually an *asset*. It makes you the exception to the rule. You stand out! What you thought was a bad thing, is a great thing! Embrace standing out for your uniqueness. Every single thing that makes you unique – your appearance, your circumstances, your achievements, your experience – becomes something that you can present as an asset! When an employer or a potential client is looking for someone who can fight on their behalf, you are able to draw from circumstances from which no one else can draw. You can tie those circumstances to why *you're* the best person for their need. When I'm searching for someone to provide a service such as a cleaning professional, a mechanic, a cosmetologist, or a nail technician, I'm not looking for the one who provides the service just like everyone else. The standard I'm looking for is someone who stands out and will provide the *best* service for *my* needs.

I'm not looking to just be ordinary. I want to be extraordinary. I'm not striving for an "A" on an assignment; I want an "A+". Fitting in is like poison for someone striving for success. When you fit in, you don't get noticed at networking parties. You just blend right in. There's nothing about you that says, "Let me talk to him or her". There's nothing about you that people gravitate towards. There is nothing about you that makes them want to spend their money for a service that you provide. Fitting in is the *enemy* of being successful and accomplishing your goals and dreams. Be different!

The Non-Traditional Path

Those who expect to be the exception also don't typically follow a traditional path. We talked about how a traditional or status quo day typically looks. A traditional *path* looks like going through school – preschool, kindergarten, elementary, middle school or junior high school, high school, college – and then getting a great job. You stay in that job, climb the corporate ladder, become successful, invest in retirement along the way, get to a certain age, and retire. Somewhere along the way you get married, have kids, buy a nice car, a nice house, and enjoy your grandchildren. Many people have chosen this path. There's nothing particularly wrong with this path as many have found tremendous happiness, peace, joy, and success on this path. However, for those who are trying to achieve extraordinary success, you must be open to not following a traditional path. Not following a traditional path doesn't mean you don't go to college. I went to college, so for all intents and purposes, if that is the definition of a traditional path, I guess I followed the traditional path. However, there's nothing about my path that was traditional. They're going to be elements in your life that don't point to that traditional path. This doesn't mean that you won't be successful.

There are three names I want to call out to give you proof that a traditional path does not automatically mean success, and a lack of a traditional path does not mean a lack of success. Those three names are Bill Gates, Steve Jobs, and Mark Zuckerberg. There are two things they all have in common. One, they have achieved extraordinary success – Bill Gates for Microsoft, Steve Jobs for Apple, and Mark Zuckerberg for Facebook. The second thing they all have in common is that they did not complete college, a non-traditional path. You don't have to follow a certain regimented path to be successful.

Again, my path was *not* traditional. You are reading a book called "Bullets, Babies, and Boardrooms". Babies at 16 don't happen to most people. Sixteen-year-olds with babies don't typically earn four degrees including a doctorate. Most college kids live in dorms and not family housing. This was a non-traditional path. Like fitting in, following a traditional path can be the enemy of extraordinary. The traditional path is for ordinary people. You must travel a different path that no one else has traveled to be extraordinary – extra...ordinary. Travel another path – a more innovative path, a more creative path, the path that makes sense for your goals and dreams, the path that goes against the grain, the path that gets you to extraordinary success!

How You View Yourself

Are you comfortable in your own skin? Do you believe that you can do absolutely anything? Do you believe that where there's a will, there's a way? Do you absolutely believe that you can overcome any odd, any challenge, and any obstacle? Do you absolutely believe that the answers to questions and the solutions to problems are right between your own ears? Do you absolutely believe that you can activate the resources necessary to get you where you need to go? Do you believe you're strong? Do you believe you're courageous? Do you believe that you have strength and fortitude? Do you believe that you have what it takes to achieve extraordinary success? If you could not answer "Yes" to these questions, you might view yourself in a way that's *counterproductive* to success. You may even hold the perspective that you're no good, that you always make mistakes, you'll never get things right, things have never clicked for you, and that you don't have what it takes to be successful. Here's the secret. You'll achieve *exactly* what you believe!

How you view yourself also dictates your reaction when people begin to hate on you. People will begin to hate on you when they see things in you that they may not see in themselves. When you lack self-confidence, when the people begin to hate, your first reaction may be to retreat, dumb down, and maybe not express yourself as much. You may even choose to dim your light and not allow the fullness of who you are to shine brightly. You must be comfortable enough in your own skin to know that God made *you*. God is continuing to grow *you*. You are continuing to perfect *your* gifts. God has called you to a higher purpose and you cannot be phased by people who don't like what they see in you. You must be confident enough to keep moving. When people hate, the source of the hate comes from their own insecurities, and you must recognize that.

Do you believe that you are *absolutely* extraordinary? Do you believe that if you push a little harder, you can accomplish things that you never believed that you could accomplish? You *must* view yourself as the exception. You *must* have a "might as well be me" attitude. Revisiting the earlier statistics, with a 20% chance of a one-year survival rate of pancreatic cancer and a 7% four or five year survival rate, a "might as well be me" attitude will help ensure that you end up being the 20% and the 7% who survive. If 7% must survive, it "might as well be me!" If there's a 2% chance of completing college before the age of 30 as a teen mom, 98% didn't do it, but two percent did. I want to be in a 2%. Someone must be in the 2%, so it "might as well be me!" Having a "might as well be me" attitude allows you to view yourself in a light where you literally feel different with every step that you take. You feel good about being different because you expect to be the exception.

Questions to Consider

1. What are the odds that I'm facing right now that aren't necessarily in my favor?
2. What more can I do *now* to get to a season of being able to do *more*?
3. How can *not* fitting in benefit me right now?
4. How am I traveling on a non-traditional path to success?
5. What do I believe about myself on my success journey?

Because narrow is the gate and difficult is the way which leads to life, and there are few who find it. ~Matthew 7:14 (New King James Version)

Conclusion – Phase II: Babies

The ultimate measure of a man is not where he stands in moments of comfort and convenience, but where he stands at times of challenge and controversy. ~Dr. Martin Luther King, Jr.

Now we know that resilience is another critical component on the journey to success. Adversity will come. Challenges will come. Therefore, having the tools necessary to be able to bounce back and make the right choices in those moments is critical. We need to be brave enough to face the reality of our difficult situation. We need to be able to understand what our true obstacles are, whether they are internal and external to us, and understand how we strategize to overcome them with actionable tactics.

The journey will be challenging, so we must use several tools to stay in a mindset of never quitting. In times when we don't have the wherewithal within ourselves to stay strong, we must ensure that we have the right people in our corner, as our champions. Overall, especially when dealing with a challenge where the statistics are not favorable, we must develop a mindset to expect to be the exception to that rule. To be the exception to that rule, we must be extraordinary and have a mindset of going the extra mile and being the one who will stand out from the crowd, and who will do more to get to do more. We must be okay with being different. We must be okay with being an exception, and when we put all of these things together, we then have the resilience that we need to overcome adversity and challenges and to simply bounce back.

Questions to Consider

1. What facts in my current situation have I been avoiding? What internal and external obstacles am I facing?
2. What can I do today to uncover strategies that will help me overcome those obstacles?

3. What tools can I put in place today that will help me to have strength in moments where I want to quit?
4. Which types of champions are in my corner? Which ones am I missing?
5. What more can I do so that I can get to do more?

Blessed is the man who endures temptation; for when he has been approved, he will receive the crown of life which the Lord has promised to those who love Him. ~James 1:12 (New King James Version)

Phase III: "Boardrooms" – The *Action* Phase

DR. ANGELA D. THOMAS

CHAPTER **15**

R.E.S.U.L.T.S. – How You Work and Remain Focused

Excellence is doing ordinary things extraordinarily well. ~ *John W. Gardner*

Introduction

Do you ever wonder how some people are able to get so much done in a day? Do you wonder why many say, "If you want something done, give it to someone who's busy"? It seems a bit counterintuitive, right? Do you ever wonder how you can be more productive with *your* life? Do you wish you could sit under a highly successful person and just have them pour everything that they've ever learned into you? Do you want to know the secrets of getting the most out of the 24 hours that is given to all of us? Do you ever wonder why some people seem to maximize the 24 hours they've been given, while others seem to squander it away? Are you one of those who maximize? Are you one of those who squander? This phase of the book will walk you through the important skills necessary to get the most from your life and achieve results!

"She gets things done!" "She is very self-motivated and very driven!" "She is clearly goal-driven." "She's very solutions driven." "She's very focused on 'fixing it', 'finding it' and 'checking off boxes'". "I don't think there is anything you put in front of her that she says, 'I can't do'." "She's extremely professional." "She always follows through on anything she agrees to put on her to do list." "She's highly capable." "When she takes something on, she will do a great job." "She is exceptionally organized and task-oriented." "She handles many different projects at once and they all somehow manage to find their way to completion." "She's great at time management." "She's great at communication management, by ensuring everyone is on the same page." "She's extremely thorough." These are all quotes from people who were invited to do a 360-degree interview about me with my executive coach. This is all feedback given to highlight my strengths. These centered on my ability to drive results and on my organizational skills. Don't get me wrong, there were many opportunities also highlighted, but I share these strengths because this phase is about how to get results. Therefore, I want to share some tools I've learned to help you achieve such results.

The third phase, "Boardrooms", focuses on action – how you work and remain focused. The acronym for this phase is R.E.S.U.L.T.S.: Relentless grind, Excellence and evaluation, Understanding failures, Listening and learning, Tenacious momentum, and Smart work. This phase takes you on a journey of my professional life and the lessons that I've learned along the way of how to achieve the results that you desire to achieve. You must enter this phase with the correct mindset and an attitude of resilience as learned in Phases I and II, but it's the proper action, how you work and remain focused, that is the catalyzing fuel necessary to achieve desired results. I share my experiences and lessons learned professionally, in leadership, and in business on how to effectively and efficiently translate effort into success.

"Let them do good, that they be rich in good works, ready to give, willing to share, storing up for themselves a good foundation for the time to come, that they may lay hold on eternal life."
~ I Timothy 6:18-19 (New King James Version)

CHAPTER 16

Relentless Grind

The elevator to success is out of order. You'll have to use the stairs... one step at a time. ~Joe Girard.

Does the magnitude of your goals and dreams seem overwhelming? Do you find it difficult to stay focused? Do you know if you're focusing on the most important elements of your goals and dreams? Are you frustrated with the journey? Does your hard work feel in vain at times?

Success isn't something that happens overnight. We live in a society where we are exposed to so many "quick fixes". The apparent overnight star featured on shows like American Idol, The X Factor, or The Voice are part of our culture. Instant gratification and instant success have become expected when in fact, it's not the norm at all. Often, even those who appear to have experienced overnight success on shows like American Idol, have been singing for a very long time. What we actually see is the manifestation of hard work over years. In these cases, we tend to see more sustainable success. There are some cases, however, where some winners disappear shortly after the win. This could be because they haven't learned how to put the work behind what's necessary to maintain and sustain a certain level of success. Both scenarios illustrate that your success journey is not going to be easy. It's going to take a relentless grind to get there. What is relentless grind?

There aren't many television shows that my husband and I enjoy watching together, but one we do enjoy is ABC's "Shark Tank". On the show, there are five individuals called the "sharks". These are highly successful businessmen and women who are waiting to hear "pitches" by entrepreneurs. The entrepreneur's goal is to build a case for their product and convince a shark to invest in their business. One of the sharks on this show is Daymond John who wrote a book called, "Rise and Grind". The book is titled after a phrase that he uses on social media that empowers and admonishes others to get up and get to work – and not just get to work but work hard and grind it out. Rise and grind means getting up every day with a mindset that you're going to put in the hard work necessary for that day that will get you closer to accomplishing your goals. This section focuses on how to be *relentless* in your grind!

One Bite at a Time

In my doctoral program we had to watch an interview of the school's Dean where she discussed the entire publishing process for academic writing, how taxing it can be, and tips on navigating that process. One of her tips was to consistently write every day, just 15 to 30 minutes a day. When trying to accomplish a larger goal of a certain number of publications per semester, taking the approach of writing something every day for a short period of time can be more beneficial. Those who take the approach of consistently writing 15 to 30 minutes a day find that over time, they actually have more written than professors who aim to binge write for hours every now and then. Building a consistent habit of focusing on a smaller task every day will lead to actions that cumulatively come together to accomplish the bigger goal. There's a common phrase that is used to make large goals seem feasible, "How do you eat an elephant? One bite at a time". When you bite a massive goal one bite at a time, it might take longer to get there, but eventually those cumulative consistent bites lead you to having accomplished your goal. This is what I personally call "making turtle moves".

In his book "Rise and Grind", Daymond John interviewed one successful woman who described her approach to success as doing several small things. When I heard the interview, I was personally in a season where I was striving to build a business and I did not have large blocks of time to spend each day on building the business. Finding large holes in my schedule was nearly impossible for many days of the week. I decided that I would take small steps and began "making turtle moves" – small steps to get closer to my larger goal.

While writing this book, I completed a workout program called 80 Day Obsession. The program had three phases. The first phase was a foundational phase where the moves were less complex. The trainer, Autumn Calabrese, used this phase to teach the moves while challenging you at the same time. At the end of the first phase, you mastered those moves. Then you moved on to phase two where she added a little more to each of the moves. Each move became a bit more complex. At the beginning of phase two, you tried to understand the new moves, so they initially felt awkward. By the end of phase two, you mastered those moves as well. She added even more complexity in phase three.

For example, one of the moves in phase three was called a "Half Turkish Get-Up into a push-up". In phase one, you were introduced to a regular "Half Turkish Get-Up". Throughout phases one and two, you were also mastering other individual exercises such as pushups, bridges, and renegade rows. When you got to the Half Turkish Getups into a push-up in phase three, Autumn Calabrese put all those exercises together. While each of those individual moves felt very challenging in phases one and two, had Autumn put them together in phases one and two the way she did in phase three you wouldn't have mastered the complex move as easily. Autumn Calabrese implemented small incremental changes that led to a larger goal of getting stronger, building muscle, and building the endurance necessary to handle the more complex move. When you implement small, incremental moves, you learn lessons along the way. These lessons can ultimately be applied to other situations and compounded together to handle complex situations, catalyze innovation, and take your journey to success to the next level.

Hard Work and Hustle

Remember the 10,000-hour rule mentioned earlier, that was coined by Malcolm Gladwell? As a reminder, the premise of this rule is that no one is born naturally gifted. Each person's success can be traced back to that person having put in 10,000 hours of work or practice to master a certain skill. Therefore, mastery requires hard work. To get to the top of his golf game, Tiger Woods put in more than 10,000 hours of practice. To become computer coding geniuses, Bill Gates, Steve Jobs, and Mark Zuckerberg put in more than 10,000 hours of coding. For Lebron James and Kobe Bryant to master basketball, they put in at least 10,000 hours of practice. For acting genius Viola Davis to master her craft, she put in at least 10,000 hours of acting.

I put in over 10,000 hours in research, science, and administration thus an expert in those areas. I can type quite fast because I asked for a typewriter in the third grade to type my math homework and haven't stopped typing. I put in over 10,000 hours typing. I'm able to easily draw from many critical leadership principles because I put in over 10,000 hours reading leadership material. The 10,000 hours isn't just 10,000 hours. The 10,000 hours is 10,000 hours of *hard work*. If you find yourself admiring a great pianist, a great songstress, a great rapper, a great producer, or a gymnast, chances are, they are putting in the 10,000 hours of hard work. For you to be the best, you must put in the necessary work to perfect your craft – 10,000 hours of hard work.

If you are aiming to be an expert in your field, or trying to be the best at a particular talent or gift, then ask yourself, "Where's my 10,000 hours?" Where is your hustle to get those 10,000 hours? Often, we find ourselves striving to achieve a goal that we did not begin when we were children like Lebron James, Kobe Bryant or Tiger Woods. Many are trying to achieve a goal that is new in their lives. Maybe you're just entering a career. Maybe you've just been introduced to a subject that you have become passionate about. Maybe you've just started building a business. In any of these cases, you don't have the time to squander. You need to find the opportunities to build 10,000 hours under your belt. Therefore, you have entered a season of needing to hustle by putting your nose to the grind and doing whatever is necessary to find the space in your schedule to clock 10,000 hours. How do you do that?

10,000 hours can come in many forms. It can come in the form of reading or listening to audio books. It can come in the form of attending a conference that lasts several days where you immerse yourself in a particular topic. You must find ways to immerse yourself into the very thing for which you are trying to build your own expertise. At the time of this writing, there is a new area in my portfolio at work that for many is essentially a new field altogether. As I took on this new field, I began to seek out opportunities to immerse myself in that world. What classes can I take? What podcast can I listen to? Who can I sit down with? What can I read? What webinars can I attend? How can I get more and more hours of experience so that I can be well-versed in this field?

In this case, I don't desire to become an expert, but I do want to be well-versed enough to be strategic and communicate clearly about the topic. Immersion requires hustle because I must find ways to immerse while maintaining my other professional and personal responsibilities. So, where is your hustle? The more you hustle, the more experienced you become. Likewise, the more experience you have, the more failures you face. But the more failures that you face, the more lessons you learn. The more lessons you learn, the smarter you become. The smarter you become, the more strategic you can be. The more strategic you become, the more wins you will have and the more results you will get. Get your hustle on!

Deep Work

Deep work is a concept coined by Georgetown University author Cal Newport in his book "Deep Work: Rules for Focused Success in a Distracted World". The premise of the book is that you need to focus on the task at hand. Text messages, email alerts, phone calls, and other interruptions are distractions that prevent us from arriving at a space called "flow". It's in flow where ideas and creativity abound. They emerge from us in a deep state of work. Cal Newport argues that many of us find ourselves standing in a perpetual state of shallow, unmeaningful, and uncreative work. We follow a traditional path of work. In the office setting it typically looks like checking email when you arrive in the morning, creating a "to do" list for the day, beginning to work on the list, checking emails periodically or as they come in, expanding or modifying the "to do" list based on the requests in those emails or from phone calls that come in, and a slew of in-person interruptions. By the end of the day, you find that you did not accomplish some of the things on the list. The other things that were added took precedent or the distraction decreased the amount of time and attention you could devote to completing everything on your list. You never entered a space of flow or deep focus. The next day, you repeat.

The inability to get into deep work translates into an inability to have a "Relentless Grind". We've talked about the grind, but not the *relentless* grind. You must be relentless about your focus. You must be deeply focused on your goals and your dreams. You must minimize distractions, turn off the television, put your phone on "do not disturb", eliminate or disable any email alerts, and sit down in a quiet space and begin to focus deeply on the work. If you are really chasing your core "why", your passion, and your purpose, it should not be very difficult to get into a zone of deep flow and focus on your work. You should be so focused that you lose track of time. You forget to eat. You have several missed calls on your phone. In this space, you feel good about the work that you accomplished. You feel like you moved closer to your goals and dreams. To find this space of deep work, you must have intense, focused, uninterrupted concentration leading to ideas and creativity flowing from you.

Focus on the Important Stuff

As the last section demonstrated, focus is extremely critical. However, it's also critical to focus on what's most important. This can be difficult as there are many different things grappling for your attention. Even surrounding your specific dreams and goals, there are many different tasks from which you could choose, distractions that can derail your focus, and paths that can lead you in the wrong direction.

You must ensure you stay focused on what's important for your specific goals and dreams.

I often tell others to "look for the reasons *why* instead of the reasons *why not*". When in a relentless grind, you must focus on positive thinking. This is not an instruction to ignore barriers and the challenges. As we learned, you must give barriers and challenges your attention to design strategies for moving through them and over them. However, as you're addressing these barriers and challenges, it's important that you focus on the reasons *why* you can overcome those barriers and challenges. Do not focus on negative thoughts. These are unimportant and become distractions that will prevent you from highlighting reasons *why* you can actually overcome.

Many fields have several paths, services, products, technology, certifications, resources, and tools to choose from. When there are so many options, it becomes increasingly critical to focus on your core "why" and the one or two things that you aim to do extremely well in your field. It's important that you focus on what will set you apart from others. Without this level of focus, you risk opening the proverbial Pandora's Box of trying to be all things to all people. In his book, "Good to Great", Jim Collins presents the "Hedgehog Concept". He explains that the hedgehog has these spiny hairs on its body. When threatened, the hedgehog will roll up into a ball and stiffen the hairs, causing the hairs to become pointy to keep the predator from attacking. This is what the hedgehog does well and better than any other animal. What do you do better than anyone else? Focus on what you do well and become laser focused on that versus the other options that don't play to your strengths. When you identify something that speaks to your core "why", is what you do best, and is something that could ultimately benefit you economically, you've identified your critical area of necessary focus.

Professionally, I have identified what makes me unique in the boardroom. During interviews or while I'm introducing myself, I'll often say, "I'm this funky blend of science and administration". Usually, I go on to explain I have a science side and I have an administrative side. These sides of me work together in tandem to make me very unique.

Many of my peers don't have this blend. I'm able to talk science with scientists and use my administrative side to assist them with figuring out ways to accomplish their scientific aims most effectively with the necessary administrative considerations. I'm able to talk administration with the administrators and use my science side to help them to proactively design processes and procedures that support the science effectively. I'm able to seamlessly live in both worlds. That's my hedgehog concept. I always consider my ability to use both sides in decisions about my career. My ability to use both science and administration is important. A distraction for me while making career decisions would be to focus on money, title, accolades, or geography. While I ultimately do need consider each of these, what's most important for my career is my passion for science and administration and the ability to blend them together professionally. I've learned that when I focus on what's important, the rest will come.

Keep Going

Earlier, I talked about how I braided my own hair into microbraids, a style that is extremely time-consuming to install. With only one braider (me) installing microbraids, the style took approximately 16 hours to install. To install these braids, you take a very small piece of extension hair and braid the hair into a very small section of the natural hair. You repeat this over and over until all the very small sections of the natural hair have small, micro braided extensions.

The installation is a commitment. It's like being a little pregnant – you can't be a little pregnant. You're either pregnant or not pregnant. With microbraids, you can't consider a partially braided head a complete style. You need to be fully committed to braiding your hair.

When I had to braid my hair, I had to fully commit to braiding for 16 hours. I couldn't get to hour nine with my hair half braided and decide I was done. I had to keep going. I had to keep pushing. Braid after braid, after braid, after braid for the next seven hours to have a completely braided head. The style would be incomplete until I was finished. There is no "almost" to this style. I couldn't leave the house in an "almost" state. I had to be completely committed to the entire 16-hour process unless I was willing to wear a hat. Even that strategy would be temporary and would only work on the weekend because I couldn't wear a hat to work. I had to be fully committed to the style. It's this level of commitment that you need to have with your goals and dreams.

I know people who have gone to college and have six credits remaining to receive their bachelor's degree. On a typical 120 credit hour bachelor's requirement, despite these individuals having completed 114 other credits, they cannot write that they've earned a bachelor's degree on their resumé. The 114 credits they *did* complete don't matter. They must keep going to earn the last six credits and be able to report a bachelor's degree on their resumé. You must keep going. You can't stop because somebody tells you, "No". You can't stop because you get tired. You can't stop because you put in *most* of the work. You must keep going until you complete the work. However, "keep going" isn't just about task completion. It's about pushing yourself to the next level.

When the time comes, and you do achieve your goal, then you must ask yourself "What's next?" There's always more to do! You earned the Bachelor's. What's next? Is it a graduate degree? Is it finding a job? Is it pushing yourself to the next level on your job? You must keep going. There's always another level to push toward. There's always another certification you could earn. There's always another client you could secure. There is always another platform for you. There's always another speech that you can give. There's always another position you can step into. There's always another million dollars out there to fund your idea. There's always another philanthropist waiting to give. There's always another groundbreaking product to discover. When you accomplish one thing, you must ask yourself, "What's next?" It's not productive to sit and wait for the stars to align in a serendipitous way. You must purposefully strive for more. Keep going!

Questions to Consider

1. What big dream or goal do I need to break down into smaller bites?

2. What additional hard work and hustle are necessary for me to become a 10,000-hour expert in my field?
3. How can I eliminate distractions when I work on my goals and dreams so that I can enter flow and deep focus?
4. What are the reasons *why* I can accomplish my goals and dreams?
5. What can I do *next* that will take my success to the next level?

And let the beauty of the Lord our God be upon us, And establish the work of our hands for us; Yes, establish the work of our hands. ~Psalm 90:17 (New King James Version)

DR. ANGELA D. THOMAS

CHAPTER 17

Excellence and Evaluation

Be a yardstick of quality. Some people aren't used to an environment where excellence is expected. ~Steve Jobs

Have you ever visited an establishment where everything seemed in order? Have you ever visited a restaurant and noticed a typo on the menu? Have you stood in an incredibly long line at a retail shop and saw that the staff were not attempting to service the line? Has a hair stylist failed to give you the style you requested? Have you ever been on the phone with customer service and the agent went above and beyond to try to address your issue? Have you worked in an environment where everyone was held accountable for results? What would it mean if restaurants didn't follow food handling guidelines and procedures when they were fixing your food? What would it mean for your health if you went to a hospital and expected a certain quality of service to be delivered, but you didn't get it? Each of these questions speak to the importance of excellence. Being excellence-minded sets you on the right path to getting great results, but you won't know you've achieved those results without evaluation.

What if you swiped your debit card and never looked at your bank account balance? What if you never looked at your pay stubs or direct deposits? What if you never looked to see what expenses were hitting your account? If this is your reality, you probably are either a member of the ultra-wealthy or have another person taking care of the finances for you. Otherwise, I would be very surprised if your account wasn't constantly overdrawn. Have you ever wanted to drive somewhere that you've never gone to before? What if you decided that instead of following GPS or asking someone for directions or looking at a map, you would just hit the road and hope you arrive there successfully? Each of these scenarios highlight the importance of evaluation, which is simply the act of measuring progress along the way. Both excellence and evaluation are critically important on your success journey.

Excellence vs. Perfection

The Merriam Webster Dictionary Online defines *excellence* as "the quality of being excellent" and goes on to define *excellent* as "superior or very good of its kind, imminently good". The Merriam Webster Dictionary Online defines *perfection* as, "the quality or state of being perfect, such as freedom from fault or defect, the quality or state of being saintly". To be perfect, without fault or defect, means that nothing will ever go wrong. This is an unrealistic perception. If you're expecting people to be perfect, you will be disappointed every time. The same is true with businesses and the systems those businesses use for operations. There is always room for error and thus room for improvement. However, if we strive for perfection, we will land at excellence along the way. If our goal is to be without defect and to ensure that nothing goes wrong, then what people will experience from us or our business is excellence – something that's imminently good and first class. To have an excellence mindset is to have a first-class mindset. Those who don't have an excellence mindset settle for mediocre and this mediocre mindset spills over into their goals, their dreams, their businesses, and their organizations.

When I go to a restaurant, I expect my food to be hot and made the way I ordered it. If I ordered mushrooms on my food, I don't expect the waiter to come back and say, "I know you ordered mushrooms, but we didn't have them, so we decided to give you radishes instead". If that restaurant was operating under an excellence mindset, they would always strive to have all options available for their customers. Things could still potentially go wrong. Maybe the mushrooms didn't come in. Maybe the truck was delayed. With an excellence mindset they would proactively communicate the lack of mushrooms to the customer before placing the order.

I loathe mediocrity. I don't prefer to present something that doesn't reflect my best and looks like I did just enough to "get by". I want to do more than just get by. "Getting by" is a mediocre mindset. A mediocre mindset puts you at higher risk for low-quality service, low-quality products, and low-quality results. Keep in mind that there is always someone else willing to work in excellence. Therefore, when you operate under a mediocre mindset, you make it easy for your competition to outperform you. Mediocrity delivers small-portioned, cold food, while excellence delivers large-portioned, hot food. Mediocrity always runs out of food, while excellence always has all menu items stocked. When I visit establishments and see mediocrity in the details, such as typographical errors in written information and lack of cleanliness of base boards, I will assume that same mediocre mindset will surface in the actual service I will receive. For example, if I go into a restaurant and I see that the floors are dirty, the bathroom is filthy, the soda is out, no napkins are available, and utter chaos ensuing in the lobby, then I'm going assume that you also are not using an excellence mindset in the preparation of my food. I'm out of there! Likewise, if I'm a hiring manager sifting through several resumés and yours comes across my desk with awkward formatting and typographical errors, why should I expect that you will have an excellence mindset if I hire you? An excellence mindset is critical, but remember, it doesn't equal perfection.

Revisiting the resumé scenario, if I see one typographical error, I might forgive the error because the rest of the resumé looks phenomenal. The accomplishments demonstrate an excellence mindset, the way the cover letter was written and addressed specifically to me demonstrates an excellence mindset, and the awards and accolades demonstrate an excellence mindset. I probably will not hold one typographical error against the candidate because the rest of the resumé reflects excellence. The resumé isn't perfect, but it is excellent. Perfection is not always achievable, but if you always strive for it, you'll land at excellence along the way. Excellence absolutely matters.

Handling with Care

Regardless of what people may say, they always want you to handle them and their loved ones with care. I remember when my son Nate was about seven years old, and he had a little bump on his arm. He has a lighter complexion, and I could see that the bump was turning blue. I took him to the pediatrician and who diagnosed him with a dermoid cyst. It wasn't cancerous, but if it stayed on his arm, it could get infected. Given the potential for infection, the pediatrician decided to surgically remove it. Because he was so young, he needed to be put under general anesthesia for the surgery. If you're a parent who has ever had to have your child go under general anesthesia, then you know how discomforting it is to watch your child fall asleep instantly. The sleep is more than a regular sleep. The child is so still that they look almost dead. It's very discomforting. But what's worse is that after watching your child fall into a dead sleep, you then must leave the room and trust people who you've known cumulatively a few hours of your life to perform surgery with excellence, so that your child will wake up and whatever issue that they promised that they would fix, would be fixed. There is no room for mediocrity, you need excellence! You also need the surgeons to handle your child with care because you don't have the expertise in this situation to do it yourself.

The way you would expect a surgeon to handle your loved one with care, you need to handle your own goals and dreams with care. If you're providing a business or service, you need to be handling your customers' affairs with care. When you handle your customers' affairs with care, you attract more customers, and make yourself more competitive. Customers don't want to feel that they are just another number vying for your attention. I remember watching a crossover episode between ABC's "Scandal" and "How to Get Away with Murder". Annalise Keating played by Viola Davis, was building a class action lawsuit against the legal system for its inability to adequately defend those who don't have the resources to retain their own lawyers. She was able to show how public defenders consistently don't provide an adequate defense when compared to people with similar charges who were able to afford private attorneys. The outcomes were drastically different. She argued that public defenders work in a system where they are so inundated with cases that they can't handle each situation with care. They can't give a high quality, excellent defense to each case because of the unreasonable workload. In contrast, the private attorney who's being paid to handle the situation with care, gives an excellent defense because he or she can invest more time and resources into each individual case.

Annalise Keating argued that not only are the outcomes of the cases different, but the lives of the defendants are also drastically different. When a father who is defended by a public defender is sent to prison because of a low-quality defense, he leaves his children at home without a father. Without a positive fatherly influence, the children follow a similar path, and ultimately find *themselves* in a situation where they now must rely on a public defender. A generational cycle begins and continues. In contrast, the father who was defended by a private attorney receives a proper defense, avoids prison, continues with his life, learns from the mistake, and raises a healthy family for generations to come. It's clear that excellence matters!

Walmart v. Nordstrom

We all know Walmart as the large retail chain known for its low prices – its "Rollback" prices. I know that if I want to find the best price, I should probably visit Walmart. But I must be honest. Most times when I go to Walmart, I find myself rolling my eyes. I never feel like I'm entering an establishment that has an excellence mindset – aside from excellence in low prices. I remember when my husband and I lived in Alexandria, Virginia. We were frustrated because there were several Walmart stores we could visit in that area, but most of them looked filthy. The lines were often long. When trying to find an item, there was disarray with items scattered everywhere. Some of the employees were friendly and some were not. It often felt like Walmart sacrificed excellent service for low prices.

In contrast, Nordstrom is a major department store that is known for its customer service excellence. It's known for empowering employees to go above and beyond. There are stories about Nordstrom employees personally driving to pick up an item from another store and delivering it to the customer. There are stories about employees allowing items to be returned without questions. Nordstrom is known for making customers feel as if employees genuinely desire to give each person an "above and beyond" experience. The Nordstrom experience is excellent, and the Walmart experience is mediocre.

I would imagine that if I was speaking to a Walmart executive, that they would make a couple of key points. One point would be that not all Walmart stores are mediocre. Walmart has some very clean stores that are well-run and long lines aren't an issue. I personally know people who have run Walmart stores quite well and I have complained to those individuals when I visited Walmart stores that weren't run as well. The problem is that *my* experience with Walmart overwhelmingly tends to be in more stores that are mediocre versus excellent. The second point I would imagine a Walmart executive would make is that Walmart focuses on low prices as its differentiator and not customer service. Walmart's excellence mindset comes through in the low prices. Nordstrom can't claim excellence in low prices because it targets a higher-end customer, but it can claim an excellence mindset in customer service.

This highlights an important point. You must determine where you can be excellent and ensure excellence in that area every single time. If you're running a business, your customer needs to rely on your business being excellent in that area every single time. If you are an individual striving to achieve success, then you must hold yourself accountable for being excellent in the areas you identified as your "excellent areas" every single time. How do you want people to remember you? What kind of brand have you built for yourself? Have you built an excellent brand where every time you're given a task, you exceed expectations? Or have you built a mediocre brand where your supervisor knows any task given to you will involve constant back and forth to identify and correct errors? Are you the person they always ask to handle the best clients or are you the person who seems to always be passed up for such opportunities? It could boil down to your mindset – excellent or mediocre!

Southwest vs. Others

The Walmart versus Nordstrom comparison can lead one to believe that because Walmart targets a lower price customer and Nordstrom targets a higher end customer that excellence is dependent on the price point. This is not the case at all. Excellence has nothing to do with the price point. Walmart has an excellence mindset that is centered around a low pricing strategy. Excellence in manufacturing, inventory management, communication, and other low pricing strategies are all integral to overall excellence in low prices. Let's look at some businesses that have excellence where the price points are flipped. In the airline industry, Southwest Airlines is known as a budget airline. Southwest targets a lower price point using lower priced tickets and open seating. There is no first-class section. The other larger airlines such as Delta, American, and U.S. Airways typically have higher price points. They have first-class seating and assigned seating. Not only are their tickets more expensive, but they also charge for checking bags. Southwest tickets are less expensive, and they don't charge for checking the first *two* bags. Overall Southwest customers tend to spend less with Southwest than when they decide to travel on the other airlines.

If Southwest chose to follow a Walmart model, then it would choose to focus excellence on the pricing strategy alone. However, Southwest has chosen to have excellence in customer service and the flying experience. Southwest is known for its jovial, customer-friendly, relaxed, and humorous flight attendants, on-time flights, and excellence in baggage handling. Former Southwest CEO, Herbert D. Kelleher was known for leading by example, including loading baggage on planes during busy holidays such as Thanksgiving to ensure the best customer experience.

In contrast, the passenger experience is different on other airlines despite the other airlines having a higher price point. Passengers will pay the higher price point for assigned seating, the use of frequent flyer miles, availability of flights, and first-class options. Despite the higher price point, these airlines are known for having more issues with on-time flights, lost baggage, and a lower overall passenger experience. These examples illustrate that a higher price point does not determine excellence. Similarly, at the individual level, education and social class don't determine an excellence mindset. Anyone can deliver high-quality, impeccable, and reliable work, go above and beyond, work with humility, and exhibit respect for others.

I remember the story of one of my girlfriends who moved to Virginia from Atlanta, Georgia. She's in the property management business. When she finally found a job here in Virginia, the other property managers gave her the seat in the office that received the least amount of traffic because she was the person with the lowest seniority. As a result, they expected her to have the lowest close rate for contracts and leases. She surprised them all when she closed on the highest number of contracts and leases. Why? There was something unique about her service, her smile, and her welcoming light that potential lessees always seemed to gravitate to – going past the other property managers and right toward her. She exceeded her quota of leases because of her infectious warmth and friendliness. It did not matter that she didn't have the seniority or a seat with the most traffic. She had an excellence mindset and delivered excellent customer service. Excellence always prevails!

What Gets Measured Gets Done

The word *evaluation* comes from the root word *evaluate*. The Merriam-Webster Dictionary Online defines *evaluate* as "to determine or fix the value of; to determine the significance, worth, or condition of usually by careful appraisal and study". Simply, evaluation is measurement to determine efficacy or value.

As an executive leader of my organization, we create an annual operating plan for initiatives and objectives we'd like to focus on for the year. We engage stakeholders to decide on those initiatives and objectives, but once identified we must determine how we will know if we actually completed those initiatives and objectives. If we identified "increasing revenue" as an objective, how would we know that we increased revenue? One option would be to measure the amount of revenue we had last year and against the revenue that we have this year. How would we know if that's an effective or fair metric? Maybe something unusual happened last year yielding unusually low or unusually high revenue. We should consider this as we determine an effective metric. Maybe another objective is to implement new software. How would we know if we're on target for implementation? Maybe there are some critical steps that we can identify along the way that will help us to determine if we're on the right track. This could be forming a committee, issuing a bid for the software, and piloting the software in a few departments.

Evaluation is measurement and what gets measured, gets done. Personal trainers and nutritionists encourage clients to write down what they're eating and track their workouts. Many people use a Fitbit or other pedometer to track steps throughout the day because it provides feedback and measurement. Many people report achieving higher numbers of steps when they use a pedometer because of the feedback mechanism. I remember when I used a Fitbit regularly and set a goal of 10,000 steps per day. If I came to the end of the day, and was just short of the 10,000 steps goal, I would be more inclined to find a way to accumulate more steps so that I could achieve the 10,000 steps goal. Without that feedback, I would certainly and unknowingly end the day short of 10,000 steps.

Evaluation is important. You must measure your progress toward success. When I was working on my doctorate, I had to complete a plan of study which outlined the courses I planned to take by semester. At the beginning of each semester, I would review the plan of study and would review it again at the end of each semester. When it was time to enroll in classes, I would look at the plan of study to identify which classes I planned to take for that semester and enroll in those. At the end of the semester, I'd check off the classes I completed. If there was a change in our program, I would go back to the plan of study and determine how those changes affected my plan and modify as necessary. I had a goal to complete the program within a specific amount of time and the only way that I could do that effectively was to start planning effectively at the very beginning of the program and regularly check my progress against that plan. You must measure progress toward your goals and dreams. You must measure what matters to you, to your business, and to your organization.

To effectively evaluate, you must also be willing to pivot. A primary purpose for measuring is to have the information necessary to determine if adjustments are necessary or if you're headed in the right direction. If you're on a journey to lose weight and you're not stepping on the scale or not measuring your inches, then how do you know that your low-fat diet is working? How do you know that your exercise program is working? For example, imagine you're doing an exercise program that is heavy on weightlifting and light on cardiovascular training. For the first two months, your weekly weigh-in shows no weight or inches lost. This gives you an opportunity to at least ask, "What's going wrong here? What am I doing wrong?" Maybe this program just isn't the correct program for your body type. Maybe you need to see a personal trainer for advice. But if you're not measuring progress, you'll never know if you're on track or off track and whether you need to adjust. You must measure your progress!

Questions to Consider

1. How do I consistently demonstrate an excellence mindset?
2. How am I handling my goals or my customers' needs with care?
3. What areas of my goals, my business, or my organization are excellence differentiators?
4. How am I achieving excellence despite having lower resources, education, or experience compared to others?
5. How am I regularly evaluating my progress?

But as you excel in everything—in faith, in speech, in knowledge, in all earnestness, and in our love for you—see that you excel in this act of grace also. ~2 Corinthians 8:7 (English Standard Version)

CHAPTER 18

Swift Action

Being the second is to be the first of the ones who lose. ~Ayrton Senna

Have you ever failed to act right away and you regretted it? Did someone else beat you to achieving a goal you had your sights on? Have you ever had an idea and not only did somebody else beat you to executing that idea, but they also reaped the associated financial gain? Did someone beat you to volunteering for something which ultimately led to doors opening for them and not you? The one who jumps at opportunities is the person who never says "No" to those opportunities.

In his book "Black Privilege", Charlamagne the god, a personality on the nationally syndicated radio show "The Breakfast Club", describes how he landed an on-air spot on the Wendy Williams radio show. At the time, he was a struggling radio personality with a family to care for, so money certainly mattered. When the opportunity to co-host the Wendy Williams Show came his way, Wendy Williams and her manager husband explained that they could not pay him. However, they would allow him to sleep in their home when he came to New York to record the show. Charlamagne still had a radio job in South Carolina; therefore, he would have to commute to New York to do the Wendy Williams Show. He took the job. This was a job he wasn't getting paid for, had to commute across states to fulfill, and had to sleep in their guest bedroom for accommodations. Some may think his decision was foolish, but when the opportunity came, Charlamagne didn't think twice. He said yes. He didn't wait. He took swift action. His swift action mindset allowed him to gain vast amounts of exposure because he was part of the widely popular Wendy Williams Show. He also gained lots of experience working side-by-side with a seasoned radio personality turned mentor, Wendy Williams. This experience was pivotal for Charlamagne as it helped him to catapult his career. You must take swift action!

Why Wait?

When I graduated from the University of Michigan School of Public Health with a Master of Public Health, I was working full-time as a vestibular technologist. I was testing patients who were dizzy to see if the dizziness was coming from an inner ear problem. This role was a clinic-based role for me. All my positions in healthcare had been clinic-based to that point. While in the master's program I developed an interest in research, specifically women's health research. When I graduated with my Master's, my goal was to get a job in the research field, preferably women's health. However, something strange happened to me. I turned into a snob after receiving the Master's. I felt that because I had a master's degree the entry-level research position, which was known as a Research Assistant, was below my level of education. I felt that I was entitled to a position that was the next level up, a Research Associate. Never having done research, I simply felt that the master's degree entitled me to a second level position.

Therefore, in my snobby state, I applied for every position that was listed as a Research *Associate* in fields that had nothing to do with women's health. Fields like psychology and engineering. The entire time I'm applying to these positions, I consistently see a Research *Assistant* position in Obstetrics and Gynecology – hello women's health! Again, in my snobby state, I refused to apply because it wasn't a Research *Associate* position. When the Research Associate positions I applied for NEVER called me back, I decided to humble myself and apply to the position that spoke to my passion – the Research Assistant in Obstetrics and Gynecology. Just a couple of days later, the head physician who was hiring, called me and we hit it off right away. He told me that he was about to offer the job to someone else and saw my resumé under a pile on his desk but noticed "Manager at McDonald's" and "Master of Public Health" on the resumé and he needed to at least speak to the person with this background. That was me! Again, we hit it off! In that conversation he noted that the position was classified as a Research *Assistant*, but he believed that I deserved to be a Research *Associate*. I not only ultimately received the title I wanted initially, but by following my passion, that position was also the position that catapulted my career.

Mine and Charlamagne's stories illustrate how taking advantage of opportunities that speak to passion make sense even when title and money don't always make sense. Both of us took a chance on passion, which ultimately catapulted our careers. In each situation we identified the opportunity available and decided not to wait for another one with a better title and more money to come along. We acted on the opportunity in front of us. Why wait?

Often people let money and titles dictate their next step versus letting passion drive the next steps. A "Why wait?" moment doesn't always come in the form of a job opportunity. You might have a dream or a goal that relies on you taking the first step and you might not know exactly what first step to take. You need to figure it out! Why wait? It might not be the perfect step, but it's a step. Many sit and engage in paralysis by analysis before they take a single step, if they even step at all. If Charlamagne analyzed that entire situation, he could have gotten stuck in paralysis and let the fact that the job didn't pay stop him from catapulting his career. If I would've kept my snobbish attitude, I would have never been offered the position that catapulted my career. My situation today could be drastically different had I chosen to wait any longer. It's up to us to take the first step. I didn't know that the position would take me so far in my career, but what I found was as I took one step, another step came along for me to take, and then another step, and then another step. God reveals your path along the way. If you never take that first step, if you always wait, wait for the stars to align perfectly, and wait for God to talk to you audibly and say, "TAKE THAT STEP", you'll never take the first step and never uncover your path.

You're Not the Only One

One summer, my colleague and I were looking for an intern to help us with our race differences in patient safety project. We were looking for someone who was savvy in data analysis and statistics. We targeted our search at the University of Michigan School of Public Health by posting the job opportunity on their internship job board. We also started to receive resumés from colleagues. This is typical as summer approaches because students are looking for summer work and internships and colleagues start to help family and friends who are students to secure such positions. We had a few resumés come our way from this nepotism network and one stood out. I had a great conversation with him by phone. He was really interested in the position and his background and interests seemed like a match for us. Our budget for the position was the market rate for a research intern. However, when we began to discuss the pay for the position, he indicated that he was looking to make almost double what we quoted. I went on to explain that we couldn't meet his salary requirement but reviewed all the benefits of the position and how he would find it to be beneficial for his career long-term. His response was that he needed to think about it and do some research. We scheduled another time to reconnect. In the meantime, he started sending me several emails with tons of questions. He requested to meet with my colleague. We scheduled that conversation. He sent more emails with more questions.

In the meantime, we began to receive resumés from well-qualified University of Michigan students who were excited about the opportunity – students for whom the money wasn't an issue. These students were super engaged, super excited, and didn't bog the process down with a sea of back and forth questions. They saw the opportunity and wanted it! What happened? We found a superstar candidate while the other guy was still asking a gang of questions. By the time the other guy decided that this was indeed the position he wanted for the pay being offered, our position was gone. We moved forward with the other student! The "questions guy" failed to realize that he was not the only one. Many of us fail to recognize this reality. There is *always* someone else – someone more willing, able, and capable of taking a position, taking *your* position, and taking *your* opportunity.

When you're applying for a job, you must take it as seriously as if you're competing against 5,000 people for one spot. You're not the only one. When you are trying to secure a client in your business, you need to approach that client as if they've been approached by 5,000 other people. When you approach with this mindset, you understand that it's important to explain to the client why your business is unique and why they should choose you. When I coach individuals who are applying for grants, I explain to them that while they might think their science and ideas are fantastic, there are a whole lot of other people who also have fantastic science and ideas. They need to determine a way to demonstrate to the reviewers of the proposals that out of all the other proposals, *theirs* is the idea that the reviewers want to fund.

You are not the only one striving for a specific goal. Even if you happen to be the first, someone else will soon come behind you and try to copy you. You must find a way to be the first in line, deliver high-quality results, and take action with the mindset that someone else is always willing to take your spot. Swift action matters!

Kairos Timing/Carpe Diem

The Merriam Webster Dictionary online defines *kairos* as "a time when conditions are right for the accomplishment of a crucial action; the opportune and decisive moment". *Carpe diem* is a Latin phrase that means "seize the day". Each of these concepts speaks to recognizing the right timing. Kairos timing is in direct contrast to *chronos*. Chronos timing focuses on chronology – literal time, such as the time of day, the day of the week, and the calendar day. However, kairos timing is about the conditions for opportunity, crucial action, and decisions. When kairos timing presents, we must carpe diem! We must seize the day – seize the moment! Revisiting the snobby Research Assistant story, it was great that I ultimately humbled myself in that moment. This turned out to be a kairos moment in my life. It was a moment presenting the conditions for crucial action and an opportune, decisive moment in my life that ultimately catapulted my career.

Let me explain a bit further the kairos timing of this decision. As a new Research Associate, I was just learning the ropes and trying to understand research. A big component of what I was trying to learn was the IRB process. IRB stands for Institutional Review Board. In research, the IRB protects human participants and approval by this board is essential for any research involving humans. The board ensures that researchers don't do something crazy or unethical to humans in the name of "research". In addition to learning about the IRB, I was learning how to recruit patients, how to support them through sensitive procedures, how to collect data, how to understand statistics, and so much more. I worked in a small group. I shared an office with two fellows and besides us, it was essentially the head physician and a couple of other key research collaborators. We just focused on conducting the existing research projects. When I took the position, I did not know that the head physician had applied for a program project grant – a VERY large, multi-million-dollar, multi-year grant. The program project grant was the equivalent of five of the projects that we were already managing. The head physician didn't believe his proposal received a score good enough for funding. Once a proposal is scored, one can often determine whether the proposal has a chance of being funded based on the score. His score wasn't a score that would typically lead to funding. He dismissed the proposal as low likelihood of funding and moved on. It turned out that because the proposal was in response to a special funding announcement, the scoring guidelines were a bit more generous than the typical scoring guidelines, and his score was actually favorable. The proposal was funded, and the start date was right around the corner.

Overnight, we had to manage this huge program. This was a campus-wide, multidisciplinary initiative involving many stakeholders. It was huge! Managing this project required many skills that I honestly did not have, but the head physician had no one else besides me to help him manage it. Hello kairos moment! This was my opportunity to show him that I could do what he needed to be done. I could work side-by-side with him as his program manager to get this program off the ground and to establish the necessary infrastructure. To be successful,

I had to learn lots of skills and learn them fast. I needed to learn as much as I could about research administration. I needed to learn as much as I could about the scientific side of the research. I needed to learn as much as I could about all the stakeholders who were involved in the program. I saw the kairos moment and I seized the day! I learned what I needed to learn and executed what I needed to execute. As a result, in a matter of months, I went from a Research Associate who almost didn't even *apply* for the job, to a Program Manager.

I owned my own development. I saw the timing. I saw the conditions. I couldn't afford to let someone else who already had the necessary skills show that they were the right person to do the job. No, I had to show him *fast* that I had exactly what he needed in that moment and for the long-term. I saw that I was right in the middle of a kairos moment and took swift action. I didn't wait. I seized the day!

Preparation for the Opportunity

In his book, "T is for Transformation", fitness superstar Shaun T tells the story of how he found his way to California from the New Jersey area. In college, he was a dancer turned fitness instructor who made his dance-infused workout classes quite popular at local gyms while in college. This ultimately landed him in California where he was also able to successfully make a name in the local fitness community for his dance-infused workouts. He even landed a spot as a cast member in the exercise video of a fitness guru who had achieved national stardom. It was his participation in this video that opened the door to his very first exercise video, "Hip Hop Abs" with the company Beachbody, and became known nationally for his dance-infused workout moves.

Shaun T describes how one of the executives at Beachbody longed to do a program called "Insanity" and was looking for the perfect trainer to lead the program. Shaun T got wind of this and went into swift action by volunteering himself. He explained that the executive did not understand how the guy known as the "dancing guy" could do a program called "Insanity". The executive explained he was looking for a hard core, bootcamp-like, insanely difficult workout and a trainer who could deliver. Shaun T again affirmed that he could execute. Shaun T realized that despite his reassurances, the executive still branded him as the "dancing guy" and he would need to show him what he could do. Shaun T went into swift action. He prepared for the opportunity. He rounded up some friends from his fitness community, booked a studio, and recorded his demo version of the "Insanity" program. He gave the recording to the executive and simply asked him to "take a look". The executive watched it and was blown away! It was exactly what he was looking for and more! Shaun T became the "Insanity" trainer. According to an article in Forbes in 2015, Beachbody sold over 10 million copies of Insanity! Huge!

From Insanity fame, Shaun T was able to release other popular workouts such as "Focus T 25", "Insane Asylum", "Insanity Max 30", "Shaun Week", and "Transformation 20". Not only was Shaun T prepared with his more than 10,000 hours of fitness training, but he also took swift action to prepare something for the opportunity that was within his reach. This was a beautiful example of when kairos moment, meets carpe diem, meets preparation. With many other trainers at Beachbody such as Tony Horton and Chalene Johnson to name just a couple, I'm sure that Shaun T realized that he was not the only one who would be interested in the Insanity opportunity. He had to take swift action.

It's important that we prepare for the opportunities. Seneca says that "luck is when preparation meets opportunity". I like to say that *"favor happens* when preparation meets opportunity". You must prepare for the opportunity, even if preparing for the opportunity means volunteering first and then taking swift action to prepare something that demonstrates that you're the right person for the opportunity.

How are you preparing yourself for the opportunity? Maybe you want to be the best cosmetologist in your area. How are you preparing for that opportunity? Are you taking classes for the hair treatments you want to offer? If you have a business and you're trying to attract a certain type of client, have you done research on the services your target clients are seeking from your type of business? Have you done research on those clients' pain points and what matters to them? If you want to receive funding from a specific sponsor, have you done your research to determine what types of initiatives they are interested in funding? Have you called a program officer or point of contact to discuss your idea to determine if there's interest? You must be prepared for opportunities. Opportunities open the door for favor!

Delays Delay

Delays cause delays and delays lead to more delays. Delays do nothing but delay! On June 9, 2016, my husband David and I celebrated our 10-year anniversary by taking a trip to Hawaii to renew our vows. We had an amazing time. We stayed in a beautiful home. My girlfriend and her friend also came along. This was the same trip where I had my snorkel/freak out/vomit fail! Anyway, on the way home, we had a tight schedule. We would fly from Hawaii to a connection in Los Angeles and then from Los Angeles to Baltimore. David's son was graduating from high school and we planned it such that when we would arrive back home to the Baltimore airport, he would catch another flight to Detroit for the graduation, and I would remain behind as I had to return to work.

We had it all figured out. We drove two cars to the Baltimore airport and left them both there for the entire week we were in Hawaii. I'd have my car when we returned from Hawaii and he'd have his car when he returned from Detroit some days later! We had it all planned out. However, we knew that if there was one delay, we would be in trouble. I checked us in online while on the way to the airport. Everything reported on time and good to go. When we got to the counter, they couldn't find our tickets. They didn't see us on the plane. We couldn't figure out why. Ultimately, they removed us from that flight because that flight was delayed and because the Hawaii flight was delayed, we would miss our Los Angeles connection flight.

In the DC area, there are three major airports to fly to and from – Reagan National, Baltimore-Washington International, and Dulles International. We had to fly into Baltimore because that's where both of our cars were parked. Well, the airline rerouted our entire schedule landing us in one of the other DC area airports. There was no way we could get to the Baltimore airport in time for David to catch his Detroit flight. The delay caused more delays. Making a really long story short, the whole ordeal was a time-consuming and expensive process of cancelling and finding new flights that could work. We ended up having to spend the night at one of the airports too. It wasn't fun. One delay caused other delays and a whole bunch of other issues.

In our case, there was really nothing David and I could have done to prevent any of this from happening besides deciding to leave a day earlier to prevent such a tight schedule. The mechanical issues that caused the plane delay were primarily outside of our control. This ordeal illustrates nicely the downstream impact of how one delay can cause other delays.

Often, we can control delays. When you delay in your actions and don't take swift action, there's a snowball effect. The more you delay, the more you cause other delays in your life. Imagine if Shaun T would have delayed recording his "Insanity" pitch video. Someone else would have gotten the "Insanity" opportunity and his opportunity to reach incredible Beachbody fame would have been delayed even further or worse he would have never reached such fame at all. There would be no subsequent videos because of riding the "Insanity" fame wave. What if I would have delayed in developing myself to show the head physician that I was perfect for the program manager opportunity? Someone else could have shown him that they were best for the position, thus not allowing me to rise so swiftly in my career. My delay would have led to other delays in my career, and I may not be in the position that I am in today. Delays delay, so don't delay!

Questions to Consider

1. What is the next step that I can take *today* toward a goal that's been stalled?
2. Who else is vying for my position, my goals, my dreams, or my customers?
3. What opportunities are on the horizon that I can seize?
4. What can I do *today* to prepare for that opportunity?

5. What are the areas of my life that if I choose to delay would cause the snowball effect of creating additional delays in my life?

So I say to you, ask, and it will be given to you; seek, and you will find; knock, and it will be opened to you. ~Luke 11:9 (New King James Version)

CHAPTER 19

Understanding Failures

We learn wisdom from failure much more than success. We often discover what we will do, by finding out what we will not do. ~Samuel Smiles

Are you afraid of failure? Does the thought of failing give you anxiety? Were you raised to believe that those who don't succeed are losers? Have you ever been ridiculed for failing? Do you believe that anything other than perfection is failure? Or do you understand that failure is part of the process? Do you believe that there is a lesson to extract every time you don't get things exactly right? Have you embraced the trial and error process? Do you boldly take risks because you know that in the risk-taking you will get your biggest payoff or reward? A healthy approach to failure is extremely important for success. No one gets it right every single time, but if you never try, you'll never succeed. It's the *trying* that gets us closer to success!

No One Likes to Fail, but Everyone MUST Do It

I've heard that the audition process for actors and actresses in places like Hollywood and New York is grueling. However, those actors and actresses who are the most successful don't let hearing "No" stop them. They keep going. I imagine the same is true for the music and modeling industries. These aspiring entertainers must hear "No" far more often than "Yes". The successful don't get discouraged, they keep moving.

They use the feedback that accompanies the "No" to improve their craft and improve their chances for a "Yes" the next time around.

The television network ABC rebooted "American Idol". Fox originally aired this famous talent show searching for the next amazing recording artist. After several successful seasons Fox decided to sunset the show and for a few years, American Idol was no longer on the air. In 2018, ABC rebooted the show. On the show, three to four judges decide whether people who auditioned to sing can move on to the next phase of the competition. Ultimately, America decides who they enjoy most and votes on who becomes the next American Idol. In the 2018 season, recording artist Katy Perry was chosen as one of the judges. In one of the commercials for the show, Katy Perry reveals how she failed multiple times while chasing her dream of being a recording artist. She had many failures and many setbacks. She fell on many hard times financially while chasing her dream, but ultimately became a multi-million dollar recording artist. Nobody likes to fail, but everyone MUST do it. Find me a story of a successful person who didn't fail. I just don't believe it exists. Oprah Winfrey had failure. She was told that she wasn't good enough for television. She was even fired from a television job. Einstein was told that he wasn't smart enough and had trouble in school. Michael Jordan didn't make the high school basketball team his sophomore year. Many successful people can share stories of how they were told that they couldn't do what they were destined to do, because at some point they didn't do it well enough. No one likes to fail. It doesn't feel good. But everybody must do it as part of the process, as part of learning.

Choose your Reaction to Failure

In his book, "I Can't Make This Up", Kevin Hart tells many stories of how things didn't quite work out the way he hoped or planned. In one story, he had a great idea for a television series with a premise that was the reverse of "The Fresh Prince of Bel-Air". While the Fresh Prince of Bel-Air was about a nephew from the inner city of Philadelphia going to live with a rich family, Kevin Hart's idea was for a show about a rich boy having to go live with an inner-city family. The show successfully made it through pilot season and got picked up by a network. At the "upfronts" where the show was to be officially added to the network's schedule, right before Kevin Hart was supposed to go out and promote his show, he was told that the show was no longer moving forward. His entire family was there waiting for his big moment and he never got a chance to even go out! He paid for the cast to fly out for the moment and in an instant, the show was over.

Kevin Hart had a choice in that moment. He could have chosen to give up on his dreams. He could have chosen to let the setback end his career. He could've chosen to go into a state of depression, not talk to anyone, and not want to be around anyone. Instead, he left with a positive attitude and chose to keep it moving. He chose to view the situation as an opportunity that simply wasn't meant to be for that time. He chose to move on to planning his next step and next move. But the way he handled it was quite pristine. Kevin Hart realized that he always could choose his reaction to failure. This isn't unique to Kevin Hart. We all have the same choice. We get to choose our reactions. We can choose to wallow in our failure, choose a "woe is me" attitude, give up on our dreams, and give up on our goals. Or we can choose to say, "That didn't work out for me in that moment. What lessons can I learn from the experience? What is my next step?"

I try to apply a 24-hour rule to any anything in my life – great and not so great. I give myself permission to react for 24 hours. This includes rejoicing when something goes well and being upset when something doesn't go so well. After the 24 hours, I must come out of it and figure out my next move. When things don't go your way, give yourself permission to cry, scream, yell, and vent. The key is not to stay there. After 24 hours, figure out your next step. You have a choice in how you react.

There was a time when I was up for a promotion. Going into that process, I didn't realize that I wasn't the only one. I was told I was the only one, but it turns out I wasn't, and I interviewed like I was guaranteed the position. I didn't compete. The other person knew that I was up for the position and competed accordingly. That person was chosen over me for the job. I chose my reaction to that news, and I'm not proud of how I chose to react. Let's just say that my reaction then is not the reaction that I would choose today. My reaction was one of anger, hurt, and tears. My 24-hour rule was certainly not in effect back then. I stayed in that head space for at least a couple of weeks. The way I carried on wasn't productive for my life, my organization, or for the person who ultimately received the job over me. I made it more awkward than it needed to be because of *my* reaction to the situation. It turns out that not getting that job ended up being the best thing for my career because God didn't want me to walk through that door. He had other doors for me to walk through that speak more to my passion and more to where I want to be in my career. Today, I appreciate that door being closed, but I didn't choose the best reaction then. I do believe that my choosing to react the way that I did probably caused unnecessary delays in my growth in the company because other people who were decision-makers saw my unfavorable reaction. I had the power to choose a better reaction. I should have sought out the lessons that I could have extracted and asked myself, "What is my next step?" and move forward with a positive attitude.

Failures are Part of the Success Recipe

Thomas Edison reportedly failed thousands of times before he invented the light bulb. Some accounts say as much as 10,000 times. Assuming that's true, this means that he learned 9,999 ways that didn't work for the light bulb. Each of the 9,999 attempts took him closer to finding the right recipe to the light bulb, illustrating that failures are part of the success recipe. Without attempting the 9,999, Edison wouldn't have gotten to the successful 10,000th attempt. The Wright Brothers tried several times to get the first airplane off the ground. They faced naysayers, drafted many blueprints, tried many types of materials, and endured many failed attempts before they got the first airplane off the ground. Failures are part of the success recipe. Without the attempts that didn't work, they would have not learned which aerodynamics were important, and how to achieve the right balance of the right elements for the plane to fly and stay in the air. Failure is part of the success recipe.

I have always loved to sing in the choir or praise team at church. Rehearsal is an important element for anyone who sings in any capacity. You must rehearse. You must learn the songs, including the proper lyrics and notes. Part of the rehearsal process includes hitting the wrong notes, saying the wrong words, and singing with an improper blend. The goal is to continue to sing the song repeatedly, so you can learn by hearing and feeling the "off notes", words, and parts. You adjust until it sounds and feels right. If there's an individual leading the song, the dynamics of the lead, the background, and the music all need to work together. If you choose not to practice and decide to just "go for it" on Sunday morning for the first time, there's a high probability that the song won't turn out very well. To sing the song in excellence, you must rehearse, and rehearsal involves many failed attempts. Failures are part of the success recipe.

Michael Jordan stated, "I've missed more than 9,000 shots in my career. I've lost almost 300 games. 26 times, I've been trusted to take the game winning shot and missed. I've failed over and repeatedly in my life. And that is why I succeed". He's failed so many times, but it was these failures that led to all his successes. The failures provide the lessons that show you where you need to adjust so that you can then become the expert. You learn what works and what doesn't work. Failure is part of the success recipe, so just learn to embrace it, learn to expect it, and learn to use it in a healthy way.

Best Lessons from Failures

Some of our best lessons come from failures. One of the lessons that I've learned in the boardroom is to be "slow to hire and quick to fire". Hiring people can be fun, but firing people is unpleasant. As a new manager, it is probably one of the most dreaded activities because you understand so intimately what someone's job means for their livelihood. You never want to be the person who tells them they no longer have a job. The "slow to hire" component of this lesson is usually required when there is a vacancy in an organization and that vacancy is causing you or someone else to take on additional work to fill in for that role. You FEEL having to do the extra work, thus, there's a side of you that just wants the position filled to relieve the pressure of the extra work from you and the team. As a result, you may choose to hire someone who you may not ordinarily hire because you're in a haste to fill the seat. It's called "the warm body syndrome". It's actually "the warm body *mistake*" – a mistake that I've made in my career.

There was a time when my Assistant Director resigned. Instead of replacing the Assistant Director position, we decided to repurpose the position to a manager position and promote someone into that position. Let's call the person "Jane". I personally had limited interaction with Jane, who the outgoing Assistant Director recommended that we promote. I went on the Assistant Director's word that Jane was a good fit for the job. I trusted the Assistant Director, she had hands-on, day-to-day interaction with Jane, and I also knew that I would feel the pain of the Assistant Director leaving, as she would leave a gaping hole in our operations. From what I could tell, Jane seemed to have the aptitude, knowledge, and experience to step into that role. On the word of the Assistant Director, I vouched for, lobbied for, and approved the promotion for Jane.

Had I been listening closer and had not been so hasty, I would have paid more attention to the Assistant Director's comments when she briefly noted that Jane had times where she would get stressed out. But she dismissed these comments by reiterating how good Jane was and affirming that Jane would be great in the role. I didn't give her negative comments a lot of credence because she didn't stay on it long and I was under the pressure of feeling like I needed to fill the role because it would cause additional work and stress on the department. We moved forward with Jane's promotion.

Things were good for a while until stress happened in Jane's life. Stress happened on the job, and stress happened personally. The stress completely derailed Jane. She didn't handle it well at all. Jane *did* have the knowledge and expertise, but she was not a good fit for the organization when it came to her stress levels. When things went wrong, Jane did not know how to handle them both professionally and personally. We ultimately had many issues with Jane's performance, attendance, and attitude, and it was my fault. I failed, but I learned. I learned that you have be slow to hire, even if it's a promotion. You must do due diligence for yourself. You must ask the right questions and ask for references. You must dig deep. If you're too close to remain impartial, you must involve others who you trust in the interview process. You must be willing to find the right candidate, even if that means that the seat stays open, and it means additional work for your operations. I did ultimately learn the lesson!

The other side of the phrase is "quick to fire". I learned the slow to hire lesson, but I still needed to learn the quick to fire lesson. When another position opened, I held true to the slow to hire lesson because I also learned along the way to hire for attitude. You can teach the technical skills but can't really teach attitude. Hire for attitude, integrity, and character and teach the rest. There was a situation where we had two candidates who looked good for a job. One clearly had the technical skills, but some people had mixed feelings about her attitude. The other candidate lacked some of the technical skills, but everyone loved her. She had most of the technical skills, the right attitude, and fantastic references. She was extremely engaged, super friendly, and warm. I went in knowing that I would have to invest a lot more resources on the technical side. I gave her *very* detailed training, including step-by-step manuals that I created that spelled out all steps and the rationale for the steps. I soon discovered that the reason why she didn't have some of the technical skills was because of her inability to learn and think critically at a level necessary for that job.

Despite having all the training resources available to her, we couldn't train the necessary critical thinking skills. However, she was such a great person who was liked by so many, and she was clearly trying. She had some successes, but she had a whole lot of misses. The misses were starting to overshadow all the good things about her. I still did not heed to the early signs. I was not quick to fire because I was so confident that I could get her to turn around. I let the 90-day probationary period pass. When that 90-day window passes, it's more difficult to let someone go. The burden for documentation and providing performance improvement plans increases. During the midst of all this, others on the team grew increasingly frustrated, and keeping her on caused more work for me in the long run. My failure to be quick to fire led to a lot of other consequences including lower employee morale.

I chose to extract the lessons from each of these situations – be slow to hire and quick to fire. Later in my career, I kept a position open for over two years because I was slow to hire the right candidate. I refused to compromise on the skills required. I've also had managers who have worked under me who didn't make it past the 90-day probationary period. When I coach other managers on performance problems they're having with associates, I always coach them to identify any issues early in the 90-day process and give the employee the feedback and opportunity to correct the issue. If they don't correct the issue, then don't extend the 90 days. I coach them to cut their losses and move on. I coach them to be quick to fire. Because I chose to learn from my failures, I now know how to hire the best candidates for my team.

When I find myself in a difficult or frustrating situation, I seek to find the lesson. I ask the Lord to please show me the lesson. Why? Because if it's that difficult, that means it's testing me for something, and chances are I don't want to repeat the test. I believe that if I extract the lesson from whatever I'm going through, then either I'll know how to pass the test quickly if I face the same situation again, or I'll pass the test and never have to take it again. When you fail, you must extract the lessons to determine how to move forward.

Fail Fast

Often, when new technology is released, software fixes are released shortly thereafter. Many technology companies, including Apple, use the strategy of releasing the product knowing that once customers begin to use the technology, they will learn more about the software and what needs to be fixed, than if they hold the technology back from release and try to uncover all the bugs on their own. They realize that holding the technology back to identify potential issues still won't uncover everything. Therefore, they release the technology and prepare for the feedback to help them identify the fixes necessary.

This is how we need to approach our goals. This concept of paralysis by analysis is real. Many are so fixated on needing to get things wrapped up and tied up in a nice bow before they decide to make the first step. The problem with this strategy is that they soon figure out that they spent unnecessary time trying to put everything in a neat package and they end up having to modify it anyway. They wasted tons of time trying to get it perfect. They ultimately must fix it anyway and worse, some never move from the perfection stage into actual action. Technology companies have learned to fail fast and so should you. What does this mean? It means that you must take the first step. If it doesn't work, then you learn from it and fix it. Extract the lesson and move forward. The faster you get the lesson, the faster you can move forward. Take the step and actively look for the things to learn along the way. Take the first step knowing that things probably won't turn out the way you desire. That's completely fine. The key is to try *something*. See if it gets you the results that you desire. If not, then pivot, adjust, and keep moving. You must take steps. You must fail fast. You must extract the lessons from those failures and keep it moving.

Questions to Consider

1. How do I let my fear of failure stand in the way of things I need and want to do?
2. What is my typical reaction to failure? How long do I stay in that reaction?
3. What have I accomplished without any failures along the way? What have I accomplished where failure was clearly part of the process?
4. What are some core principles that I live by today that are the result of learning from past failures?
5. What can I do *today or tomorrow* that will allow me to fail fast?

For a righteous man may fall seven times and rise again, But the wicked shall fall by calamity. ~Proverbs 24:16 (New King James Version)

CHAPTER 20

Listening and Learning

People seldom improve when they have no other model but themselves to copy. ~Oliver Goldsmith

Do you actively make professional development a critical part of your success journey? Is active learning an integral part of your personal development? Do you have "go-to" experts from whom you consistently learn? Do you apply what you learn to your success journey? Do you know how to listen for the spoken and unspoken cues in communication? Do you pay attention to your gut when you're making decisions? Do you own your own development?

I love a great story. I find great stories in several forms, including audio books. Audio books are part of my listening and learning experience. I've learned so much from hearing from those who have traveled the path that I'm either on, or desire to travel. I love hearing new principles and different ways of applying familiar concepts. I love hearing personal stories of overcomers. I love personal stories filled with pivotal lifelong lessons. I hear these stories not only through audio books, but also from mentors, people who I know, people who I don't know, and from watching Lifetime movies. Yes, Lifetime movies! It's because I love stories, especially true stories. Many Lifetime movies are based on true stories and I often extract lessons from their lives. Often, we don't surround ourselves with people whose stories, wisdom, and knowledge can benefit our journey. Often, we go at a journey on our own and discount the amount of knowledge and the wealth of that knowledge that we can gain from incorporating others in the process. We must realize that our point of view is just one point of view and it's colored by our own lens of the world and by our own experiences. We don't know what we don't know. Therefore, listening and learning are critical components of the success journey.

Own your Own Development

Throughout my career, many individuals, including junior employees and students have approached me to mentor them or give them advice. I've also been asked to give my professional development story explaining my career journey and the lessons that I've learned along the way. One of the most critical lessons that I share is to "own your own development". I often encounter employees with a mindset that their manager or supervisor is the one responsible for identifying the next steps in their career. This is a very reactive approach to professional development. This approach relies on someone else. Anytime you rely on someone else, you relinquish control over that aspect of your life. If you relied on someone else to pay your bills from your account, then you're always subject to potentially not having that bill paid. If you rely on someone else to always put a plate in front of you to eat, you run the risk of going hungry every now and then. If you rely on someone else to tell you when it is time to use the bathroom, you'd have accidents on yourself. Why would you choose to take the same reactive approach to your own professional development?

One reason people may choose this reactive approach is because they feel like those who have traveled the path ahead of them are the only ones who can tell them the necessary steps on their journey. While it's true that you must look to learn from others who have traveled the path, you still must own the process of extracting the advice and applying the advice. You can't just take the approach of sitting at your desk or at home expecting someone to come to share with you their journey. You must actively seek out individuals who can help. Use a mentor or supervisor as someone who will allow you to pick their brain. They can answer questions such as: "What books should I be reading? What conferences should I be attending? What worked out for you on your journey? What should be my next step?" They can also provide wise counsel on specific situations you're facing.

When you own your own development, you become an information seeker and you become an active participant in that development. You lead it, you own it. Wherever you're trying to go, you are trying to identify the information necessary to get you there. This can come in the form of advice from a mentor or someone who has traveled the path you're on, but in the end, it ultimately needs to be *you* who *owns* your own development. This is exactly what I did when I was proving to the head physician that I was the right person for the program manager role. I decided to uncover all that I needed to know – every conference, workshop, course certification, and anything else I could get my hands on to teach me about research administration and how to effectively build a research team. I owned it! I had to ask around to get started, but along the way one resource would lead to another resource. Many of the resources I found, especially conferences, I would have to ask for permission and funding from the department, but ultimately it was me who owned the process. I needed to develop myself and the more I learned, the more I learned how much more I needed to learn, so I kept learning and my career has become an ongoing daily professional development exercise.

There are many topics I focus on for development, but one consistent topic is leadership. I listen to many audio books about leadership and how to effectively lead teams. As an executive, this is important for my professional development and my career. This development is so critical for me that I don't wait for someone to tell me the name of a book I have to read next. Often, I've made that decision weeks or months before finishing the current book because I'm always looking for my next book. This comes to me when I hear others mention a book that they have read. I'll note it in my phone to make that my next book. Other times I'll be listening to a book and the author speaks about other books that have helped them, and I'll note that book as my next book. In addition, I will often take the approach of researching some of the top books in a particular topic and make a selection. There is one common theme for each of these approaches – I own my own development! You must own your own development. You cannot take a reactive position to something that's so important for you. If you are aiming to be the best at anything, in any field, you should always be striving to learn as much as you can in that field and own the process of learning it!

Find the Experts

In his book "Think and Grow Rich", Napoleon Hill discussed the concept of "masterminds". Masterminds are a group of individuals who are regarded as experts in a variety of fields. These individuals can be living or non-living. These can be individuals you know or don't know. Napoleon Hill explained how he would imagine having a forum or a meeting with all these masterminds. These masterminds, a group he regarded as experts, would give him advice and strategic direction. What I absolutely loved when I first heard this, was that Napoleon Hill was tapping into a "virtual expert" mindset. This mindset holds the viewpoint that advisors don't have to be people you know, but simply people who you regard as your "go to" experts in a particular field. Fortunately, there are so many experts in many fields who are living and non-living who we can tap into. We can uncover their knowledge, their wisdom, and their expertise in many ways with the benefit of the Internet and books.

I personally have so many virtual masterminds that if I try to name them, I will probably leave some out. Some of them include Jesus, John Maxwell, Malcolm Gladwell, Jim Collins, Bishop T.D. Jakes, Daymond John, Grant Cardone, and Oprah Winfrey to name a few. When I'm facing a challenge, I imagine what they would do, or I will pick up one of their books on a particular topic or situation I'm tackling. If I'm thinking about how to market or sell, I might think Grant Cardone. If I'm thinking about how to be more creative and innovative, I might think Daymond John. If I'm thinking about how to be a better leader, I might think John Maxwell. If I'm determining which organization principles to apply to a particular situation, I might think Jim Collins. If I'm trying to think about a concept in a new and creative way, I might think about Malcolm Gladwell. If I'm trying to teach a scripture in a memorable way, I might think about Bishop T.D. Jakes. If I'm thinking about how to make more of a difference in the lives of others, I might think about Oprah Winfrey. These are my virtual experts for many different areas of my life and there are so many more. This section gives you strategies and tools to find those experts – your masterminds who will become your "go to" virtual team to help build you and guide you along the way.

To really GET this – and I'm mean REALLY GET this, you must buy into the reality that you MUST anticipate that you CAN'T anticipate everything! To make that a bit plainer, you need to KNOW that you DO NOT, and you WILL NOT know everything! The sooner you TRULY believe this to be fact, the better your chances of success. This mindset allows you to be open to listening to those who have achieved what you are trying to achieve. As you are likely chartering territory that you've never chartered before, you must learn! You must find someone who has been where you desire to go. You must find this person in-person or by seeking our friend Google to figure out who you can learn from. If you find yourself needing to take the latter approach, proceed with caution. We often hear that we live in the "information age"! Many now say, and I personally believe it to be true, that we live in the "*mis*information age". The oxymoron here is that we have so much information available to us, often for free, but some of this information is considered good information while other information is garbage! You must seek to find high quality information on the topic that you seek to learn more about and identify those thought leaders around that topic as *your* experts! How do you do this?

Depending on your goal, you may find that there is an overwhelming amount of information on the topic – weight loss fits this category. Alternatively, you may find that there is limited information on the topic – getting a college education as a teenage mother fits this category. The trick is cross-referencing. If you find some information, see if you can find it again on another site. Who are the authors of this site? Can you tell? Is it some random blogger? Does this person seem to have expertise on the topic? Has this person been where you're trying to go? Once you deem the information as credible, do a search for the alternative position. Who disagrees with the position or advice that you've just uncovered? Why? Is that person credible? Are they an expert? This will help you to determine which advice you should take, and can help you anticipate barriers you hadn't anticipated.

Another way to leverage the Internet for learning is to find a list of good books to read. Often, Amazon.com will allow you to take a look inside of the book. Look at the table of contents. Does it seem to reflect the information you need? If so, consider purchasing it. If you're not a reader, maybe listen to it on audio. I've found that with my commute to work, I can listen to many audio books and gain lots of information in fields of interest to me. Also, I love reading on my iPad and sometimes even on my iPhone. These are handy when at the salon, or waiting for a meeting to start, or anytime that I find myself in "waiting mode". You can also just do it the old-fashioned way! Set some time aside and just read the darned book! If you are serious about your goals, you will be just a serious about learning. Mastering the information in the field allows you to become more of a critical thinker in that field! Critical thinking is crucial to your ability to navigate your journey. The more you know about the path, the more you can leverage your knowledge to make wise decisions about the turns to take, the stops to make, when to speed up, when to slow down, when to take a detour, and when to coast along. Think critically! You can only do this well when you learn from those who have traveled the same path.

Be an Engaged Listener

In his book "Great Leaders Ask Great Questions", John Maxwell discusses how asking the *right* questions yield a wealth of information that enhances your ability to lead effectively. One of the premises of the book is that often it's the question asking versus the speaking that is most critical. Great leaders ask great questions that are designed to extract the information they need. In his book "The Magic of Thinking Big", David Schwartz discusses how great leaders are the least talkative in a conversation because they're listening for critical information. They are usually asking more questions to get more information. They are not the ones doing the most talking.

I see this dynamic when I'm in a situation when I'm the mentor or coach. I'll start by asking a probing question such as, "What's going on? What can I help you with?" This is a very open-ended question to get the person talking. My goal is to simply listen and jot down critical notes along the way. My points of advice may come out as they're talking, but often I will hold my points of advice because as they speak, I form more questions that allow me to probe a bit more, leading to even more questions. Eventually, I would have asked enough of the right questions to extract all the information that I need to effectively give them advice. That's the point where I then give the advice and the time I take to give the advice is typically much less than the time they took to speak. It's not unusual for a mentee to talk for 30 minutes or more before I ultimately give any advice.

This sheds light on me as an engaged listener. However, there are many times when I'm not so engaged. One of my biggest risk areas for not being an engaged listener is on conference calls and webinars. I'm not alone. Many people fall into the trap of being distracted on conference calls and webinars because it's not a one-on-one interaction, often lending itself to the ability to put yourself on mute, handle other responsibilities, and simply listen for your name while not truly being engaged in a conversation. I'm completely guilty, yet I realize the potential pitfalls that come with such disengagement. When disengaged, you lose a wealth of information. I'll often walk away without any new information and feeling like I wasted my time. This doesn't mean that the call or webinar didn't *provide* new information that was valuable for my time, but because I was disengaged, I missed out!

How do you avoid this pitfall? How do you ensure you stay engaged? One strategy is to take notes. When you take notes, it forces you to reinforce what you're hearing because you're writing those things down. Another strategy is to ask questions. Asking questions is a two-way street. Great leaders aren't the only ones who ask great questions, but great learners do too! When you are seeking advice from someone else, you need to ask great questions. This will keep you engaged in the conversation and keep you learning as well.

Listen for the Spoken and the Unspoken

One my best girlfriends is extremely private. She's one of the busiest people I know, but extremely private. She doesn't tell many people about details in her life, but she will tell me many of those things. Often, she will intentionally leave out important details like having to go to the emergency room or being sick or having received a major award. Yes, it can be very frustrating being her friend because she will literally leave out these critical pieces of information that other people are more prone to just share willingly. Therefore, I've learned that with her, I must listen for what's being said and what's *not* being said.

I have trained myself to know enough about her routines to notice when things are off with her communication or when things don't quite sound right. When I pick up on this, I will often say, "What question am I *not* asking you? What questions should I be asking you? I know you're not telling me something because I find myself having to listen to what's being said *and* what's *not* being said." This isn't unique to just my girlfriend holding back information, as there are many times in business where you must be able to pick up on the nonverbal cues of what's being said and what's not being said. Careful conversations with carefully placed words are telling.

For example, if someone is working from home but doesn't want to reveal that they are working from home, they might say on a call, "I'm not on site today". Another example is if you're talking about revenue being down, and this meaning that if the revenue doesn't increase, they might have to consider layoffs, instead of discussing this head on, they may say "If revenue doesn't increase will have to consider cutting some of our largest expenses". While trying to avoid speaking on personnel cuts (what's not being said), speaking on cutting the largest expenses (what's being said) should tip off a savvy leader that these largest expenses are personnel, since personnel expenses are usually the largest expenses in any organization. Here's another example. If you're having a conversation about professional development and seeking advice on whether to attend a conference, if the person you're asking doesn't want to slam the conference as a bad conference, they might say, "There are some benefits to going to that conference, but it's up to you. I think you could find something valuable to get out of that conference." You should pick up on their not being overjoyed about the conference; ask follow-up questions like, "Is there a reason why I would have to *find* something valuable to get out of the conference?" It reiterates the importance of being a great listener.

When you are a great listener, you can ask great questions because you are able to identify where you may need to push or probe a little bit further. You want to make sure you walk away from the conversation without being forced to make any assumptions. In the space of "what's not being said", the speaker is leading you to assume something. When you pick up on this, you must decide if assuming is benign – meaning that even if you assume, there's not much at risk – or if the opposite is true – the assumption can be detrimental. Sometimes the speaker is purposefully leading you to an assumption because additional clarity can be damaging. For example, in politically charged situations, I will purposefully choose my words so I'm clear, yet worded in such a way where there are some unspoken assumptions that someone who is savvy can properly infer. Learn to listen for the spoken and the unspoken!

Listen to Your Gut

The second component of listening is a bit more abstract. It's simply to listen to your gut! Your "gut" goes by many other names depending on who you ask. It's often referred to as "whispers", "intuition", "God", or the "Holy Spirit". Whatever you call it, there are times when that something is telling you, "Yes, do it!" and there are times when that something is telling you, "Don't do it!" Often when that "something" is speaking to you, you can't explain why, but you just get the *feeling* that you should or should not do it. Listen to that feeling! It's often correct. Don't confuse this with fear or doubt. This is an actual feeling that you cannot explain.

When I was in the field study phase of my doctoral project, we were just beginning to see some of the early data, called preliminary data, around race differences in patient safety events.

The data was now in! I was very excited going into the weekend. With this data, I was now at the point where I could run some statistical analyses to answer the big question for my research. I was excited! I got excited too fast because as I began to look at the data, I noticed that dates of birth were off. For example, someone who was born March 23, 1913, was noted as March 23, 2113. The system was pulling in the last two numbers of the year, but in the wrong century! This was especially happening for the older patients – they were recorded as extremely young (or in some cases not even born yet) when they were actually our *oldest* patients. I noticed this consistently throughout the records but was determined to rationalize that it wasn't a huge deal. These errors were easy to identify and correct. However, my gut wouldn't let me shake the feeling that this was major issue.

My gut started saying, "Angela, if you're seeing these types of errors in the dates of birth, how confident are you that the race is matching correctly with the right patient?" If this was an issue, it would be a *really* big issue, because this error wasn't as easy to catch and fix. There were thousands of records to go through. However, as much as I did not want to, my gut kept telling me that I needed to validate and verify that everything matched. I listened. I conducted some manual searches to do a quick "spot check", and sure enough I found a case where someone who was identified as an African American female on Medicaid was actually a Caucasian male on private insurance. All it took was finding one error for me to know that I couldn't trust the rest of the data. In the end, I was glad that my gut told me to check. In research, you must be able to rely on the quality of the data to answer the questions you seek to answer. Had I not listened to my gut, we would have proceeded down a trail of answering a question based on invalid data.

I was glad that my gut talked, and I was glad that I listened. Any time I'm trying to make a decision in my life, and something is causing me to doubt, I pay attention to it. If something is not sitting well with me, I pay attention to it. If the decision logically makes sense, but something's just not settled in my spirit, I try to delay making that decision. The reverse is also true. Sometimes, decisions don't make sense. If you go back to my example of being so snobby that I wouldn't apply for a Research

Assistant job; or go back to the Charlamagne the God example of his taking a job on the Wendy Williams show that meant travel without pay and sleeping in a guest room, these didn't make logical sense from a title or financial perspective, but ultimately launched our careers. In our guts, we knew they were the right moves to make. You must listen to your gut!

Listen to Learn

We've explored a few avenues for listening for information in this chapter – essentially listening to learn. But before closing this section on listening, I want to stress the importance of being fully present and engaged in what the speaker is saying. Often, we fail as listeners because we are thinking on other matters, anticipating or crafting our response before the speaker can even finish, have already dismissed the speaker's position as unimportant, or we are just flat out distracted. How many times have you asked someone to repeat themselves because you simply "tuned them out"? Parents are good at this.

Have you ever been engaged in a debate with someone where they have one position, and you hold the exact opposite position? Have you found that you either go into that discussion dismissing anything that they say because you've already determined that your position is superior and nothing that they can say has value or will force you to change your position? Many of us enter conversations with the mindset of thinking of our rebuttal before the speaker can finish their point. When you are not listening, you are not learning. Train yourself to LISTEN! Tune in! You may not agree with what the speaker says, but at least you can engage in a conversation and ask questions. This may actually help you to solidify your own beliefs but listening can also offer some insight that can help you on your own journey. Keep the meat and throw away the bones. But if you don't listen, it's harder to identify the meat and identify the bones. If you listen, *really* listen, you'll figure it out!

Questions to Consider

1. Who are the "go to" experts on my success journey? How do I actively learn from those experts?
2. How can I become a more engaged listener?
3. How can I train myself to ask great questions?
4. What are some situations where I have been able to identify the unspoken?
5. In what situations has listening to my gut paid off?

My dear brothers and sisters, take note of this: Everyone should be quick to listen, slow to speak and slow to become angry ~ James 1:19 (New International Version)

CHAPTER 21

Tenacious Momentum

Success is the sum of small efforts, repeated day in and day out. ~ Robert Collier

When you start something new does it feel difficult in the beginning? Do you feel like you'll never ever make it to the "easy part"? Does it feel like there is no easy part at all? Do you feel like you'll be stuck working hard forever? Do you feel like the hard work will never pay off? Does it feel daunting and overwhelming? Does it feel like you have so much to do and will never get it done? On the flip side, do you feel like it's worth it to put in the hard work at the beginning because you know there's a payoff in the end? Do you begin with the end in mind which causes you to push through the initial hard work to get to your desired end?

I shared earlier how my husband and I had a workout contest when we were going on our anniversary trip to Puerto Rico. I shared how my burning reason for wanting to lose 15 pounds was simply to have bragging rights. I didn't want to be in a position where he reached his goals but I didn't because this would mean that he would have bragging rights alone. I also shared how after the trip and the contest were over, I didn't replace my burning reason for working out and eating right with another burning reason, so I gained the weight back.

Later, I realized how much I enjoyed the way I looked and I felt when I constantly led a healthy lifestyle. I began to reflect on those contest days where I worked out six days a week. I wanted that feeling again, but I still did not have another burning reason. I had to find it! One burning reason that I found was that my life was growing increasingly busier, and I needed more energy to sustain that level of activity. Another reason was that I am getting older and illnesses that increase with age could become a factor for me if health did not become a major priority. Certain chronic illnesses such as diabetes and hypertension run in my family and I needed to make sure that I was protected from the risk of developing these illnesses. The last reason was that I wanted to be around for my son and my grandchildren to come and live a long, healthy life. While I didn't stop working out after the contest, I drastically slowed down. I continued to work out, but it was inconsistent. I would always do something, even if it was two days a week, but it was nothing like the six days I was clocking during those contest days. With these new burning reasons of 1) energy, 2) disease prevention, and 3) living for family, I decided to step up my game!

At the suggestion of one of the ladies in the church, we started a Facebook group focused on health called "Sisters on the Move". I decided that I would try to consistently work out every day. It started off as more of the same – 2 to 4 times a week. I had to ask myself, "Why". It was then that I was honest with myself. My consistency in the Puerto Rico days worked because I was disciplined enough to exercise as soon as I got home from work. Post Puerto Rico, my life changed so dramatically that working out this way was no longer a possibility for me. My days became so booked and unpredictable that evening workouts were just impossible. In addition, on days where I had the time to work out in the evenings, my days were so intense and draining that it was too easy for me to use this as an excuse not to work out at all. I knew I had to do something different. The only option for me was to go back to a practice that I used a long time ago – work out in the morning.

This was not an easy decision for me because my days already start so early that the thought of having to wake up even earlier felt like yet another deterrent and barrier to my being able to stick with it. Therefore, I had to figure out a plan that would give me the highest potential for success. I decided to look at workout programs that I could do at home that were shorter in duration. My rationale was that if I do it consistently every day, but in a shorter duration, then over time I will see the results. I started to work out using Shaun T's Insanity Max 30, which is only 30 minutes long. I would switch it up to do Autumn Calabrese's 21 Day Fix and 21 Day Fix Extreme workouts which are also only 30 minutes long. Consistently I would work out every day, six days a week. To stay accountable, I even started posting videos of my workouts every morning on Sisters on the Move. All of this worked! I found myself having consistently worked out six days a week, every single week for an entire year. I felt amazing! It became part of my day. Those first few weeks of getting up early to work out were so hard. Even the workouts themselves seemed hard, but over time, the more I did it, the more it became part of my life. Now, it has become second nature to just wake up, put on my workout clothes, and go downstairs and get a great workout in before I start my day. What was even more incredible was that the more I did it, the stronger I became. The workouts weren't as arduous. I would have to change up the workouts to keep my body from a plateau and overall, I got stronger, leaner, and healthier with a clean bill of health from my physician.

This is the heart of this section – tenacious - momentum. It's all about how to do the work, push through the work, and reap the benefits of that work on the back end! You have to do the hard work in the beginning so that over time you become stronger, your processes become "well-oiled", and your journey doesn't need as much effort from you as it did in the beginning, You can put in the work necessary in the beginning that will land you in a space of just having to maintain momentum, freeing you up to think of more creative ways to take your dreams and goals to the next level. Let's dig into this concept of tenacious momentum and how you can leverage tenacious momentum on your journey to success.

Building a Well-Oiled Machine

In his book "Good to Great", Jim Collins describes the "Flywheel Concept". This concept centers around something called a flywheel. Dictionary.com defines a flywheel as *"a heavy revolving wheel in a machine that is used to increase the machine's momentum and thereby provide greater stability..."* Jim Collins describes the function of the flywheel as something that needs tremendous effort in the beginning to get it moving. In the beginning it takes a lot of hard effort just to push it. However, eventually as you keep exerting the hard energy to push the flywheel to move and the more you push and the more it moves, it eventually reaches a point where it spins mostly on its own, with minimal effort from you. Every now and then you might have to tap the flywheel to keep it moving, but the initial hard work of pushing gives the flywheel the momentum necessary to essentially spin on its own. Hard work in the beginning builds momentum and momentum fuels sustainability with minimal effort in the long run. In short, when done correctly, a lot of effort in the beginning can translate into little effort in the long run.

When I was the Manager of Research Operations with the Department of Obstetrics & Gynecology at the University of Michigan, one of the primary tasks in my role was to increase the infrastructure for research administrative support. I saw tremendous opportunity in areas such as notifications of intent to submit proposals, assistance with budgets, proposal management, and more. There were many processes and procedures that I wanted to implement, and in the beginning, there was so much to accomplish. There were many forms to create, many formulas to automate, many people to interview for feedback and suggestions, and many results to run. The beginning felt very time-consuming and challenging. However, I knew that with every form that I created, it would be the last time I'd have to create that form. I knew that with every formula I built in, there was pay off in the use of that formula as measured by efficiency. I knew that putting in that work in the beginning and doing what needed to be done to build the infrastructure was going to pay off. While I was working hard, day in and day out in the "beginning", I did so with the "end" – infrastructure and efficiencies – in mind.

Begin with the End in Mind

As you are preparing to embark on a new journey of success, you must understand that if done correctly, the journey will include a significant amount of hard work in the beginning. To ensure these initial efforts of hard work in the beginning pay off in efficiencies and effectiveness in the long run, you must build while having the end in mind. A common analogy for this is building a home. To build a home, you must have an architectural blueprint for the home. This represents where you're trying to go – how you want the home to look, function, and feel at the end of the process. To do this effectively, you don't just start laying bricks and foundation without really knowing exactly how the foundation will support the home you've designed. You must first have an architectural plan and design and then begin to build. While you are building that home, things may change along the way. You may begin to see structure and design elements that need to be adjusted because you didn't foresee certain challenges in the beginning. Or maybe your creativity kicked in after seeing a design element in another home that also works for your vision. Or maybe the parts you planned on using were discontinued or there was a change with permits that you didn't know that you needed to obtain. Regardless of these changes along the way, you must still begin with your end in mind. Knowing where you want to go prevents a waste of resources, which include time, money, and raw materials – all critical and expensive in building a home.

This is no different on your success journey. There was a point in my career when I was tasked with growing a research program. The first thing I did was try to determine where the program needed to be. What did "growth" look like? In short, it looked like a nationally recognized research program. This was at a time where the program was bare bones. Viewing the program as a nationally recognized program was a huge end game goal. I needed to break it down and truly dissect what that looked like. I asked myself, what does a nationally recognized program look like? The answer: It looks like millions in research funding, a significant bench of research investigators, several internal and external collaborators, and a sound, well-oiled infrastructure to support ground-breaking science locally and nationally. Therefore, that's where I started! If we were going to have millions of dollars in research funding with many investigators and collaborators, I had to determine and build the type of infrastructure necessary to support something that large. I knew that if I built it with "small" in mind, it wouldn't be sustainable at "large". Therefore, instead of building something that would work for the reality of "today", I thought about the goals of "tomorrow" first, and then figured out something that could work for both today and tomorrow.

You must be smart about how you begin your tenacious momentum. You must plan first and then adjust your work along the way. Revisiting the building a house analogy, if I were to build a house today, I would not attempt to sketch that out without consulting with an architect and contractor. They are experts in areas that I have very limited knowledge. I may have vision, but I don't have all the requisite expertise. Designing a blueprint does not necessarily have to just be you sitting down with your own expertise, mindset, and limited knowledge. Determine who you might want to consult. Consult the experts – those who have been where you're trying to go. Aim to gather diversity of thought around your idea to uncover some additional new ideas! My word of caution here is that you must be willing to be flexible. You must be willing to pivot when necessary. You must be willing to learn from what doesn't go right – what doesn't go as planned or as you envisioned. That is the next principle! You must be willing to learn from failure. The key is to fail *fast* and fail *forward*.

Failing Fast and Failing Forward

When starting out, many of us start from a place of almost nothing. Typically, we have limited resources, limited experts, limited team members, and limited knowledge. What we often have are new, creative ideas that we want to implement, and see come to fruition. Our creative ideas are innovative and, don't quite resemble anything else that has been done before. When we find ourselves at this starting point, it is extremely important we fail fast and fail forward.

This was the case with our church. When we were building our ministry, our mantra was to fail forward. We had so many different areas of ministry we had to build – the women's ministry, the men's ministry, the music ministry, the new members' ministry, and many other areas. With this charge ahead of us, it was important for us to function as a team. The background of the team certainly influenced the dynamics and the culture. Our church was not a "family church" – a church led by a legacy of family members who founded the church. Our church was situated in a neighborhood, a city, an environment, where most who reside there did not grow up in that city. The Washington, DC, Maryland, and Virginia area, affectionately known as the "DMV" is filled with a population of individuals who are very professional, yet very transient. The military and political environment surrounding the area heavily influences its transient nature. This is a very different environment from the environment that many of the leaders of our church grew up in or served previously. Many of us came from family churches led by family members with a congregation of individuals who were not transient. Therefore, when we considered the nature of our leadership team and the needs of the congregation, there were many innovative initiatives that we needed to try without precedent. There were many historical and traditional ways of leading a church that we decided to modify to fit what we believed were the unique needs of our congregation.

To do this was no easy feat. Finances were limited. Human capital resources were limited. As a faith-based, non-profit organization, the human capital we did have were mostly volunteers, forcing us to manage human capital differently than in a traditional, paid scenario.

What we did have was the willingness and the courage to try, even if that meant we failed. There were several areas we needed to just "try and see". The process around visitors was just one example. We needed to ensure each new visitor received a visitor's card. We needed to determine the format and content of a new members' class. Gender ministries were another example. How would we structure the women's ministry and the men's ministry? We even had to figure out where in our worship service we would acknowledge visitors and celebrate birthdays and anniversaries. Along the way, we would try, see how it worked, and then make changes. There were so many changes that we made along the way and we made them fast! We locked into the mindset that we were willing to try and if it didn't work, we would pivot and try something different the next time. We learned many, invaluable lessons from trying it out first. If it did not work, we succeeded in figuring out what didn't work. We extracted the lessons from the experience and applied those lessons to a different approach that would get us one step closer to determining what worked.

One of the reasons our team of leaders took the fail forward approach was that we knew that if we continued to talk it out, attempt to plan it out, and try to come up with the perfect solution first, we would land in the impossible zone of paralysis by analysis. We would be stuck not doing anything because we were so busy analyzing and over analyzing that we wouldn't take a single step forward. Many of our best lessons come in the trying – in the action. I would imagine that a basketball phenom like Lebron James tries a certain basketball move to determine whether that move is effective against his opponent. In the action he determines what was effective and where he needs to correct. He goes back and watches film from games already played. That also helps, but it's the real-life action that really makes a difference in his game. How does it feel? What does the court look like? What does the opposition's formation look like? Live action makes a difference.

Here's the caution. When you have limited resources, you do have to be mindful of how use this approach. You must find the balance between acting and not being wasteful. There are strategies you can incorporate to do this. We discuss these strategies, including how you can leverage "the power of broke" in our next section, "Smart Work". There are ways to fail fast and be wise about your resources. The key here is that you must act despite the limited resources and the fear of wasting those resources. We all have "waste fears". A fear of wasting time and a fear of wasting money are the top "waste fears" that prevent people from failing fast and failing forward. These waste fears are at the root of how we can fall into the trap of paralysis by analysis. Yet, we don't realize that this trap is costly on its own! Yes, when you're in this trap you might not have spent any money, but you waste invaluable amounts of time and time is currency. Wasted time is expensive. You must start! You must take the first step forward. You must be willing to not just fail fast, but to fail forward fast. This will allow you to learn the lesson quickly, figure out what doesn't work, and then figure out what works. It doesn't benefit anyone to just fail. If you're not learning from the failures, then you will not move forward. To move forward, you must learn from the failure. Extract the lessons from the failure and move forward.

Wax On, Wax Off

In the popular movie franchise "The Karate Kid", Mr. Miyagi was attempting to teach the main character, Daniel LaRusso, karate. One of his methods of instruction was to have Daniel wax a car. An iconic line from the movie is "wax on, wax off", where Mr. Miyagi would repeat this over and over to represent the motion of waxing in one direction – let's call that counterclockwise with the left-hand – and then waxing in another direction – let's call that direction clockwise, with the right hand. Daniel was instructed to just keep waxing on and waxing off. He did just that repeatedly. Daniel grew frustrated with Mr. Miyagi because he could not understand how waxing a car was helping him to learn karate. He could not understand why he was wasting time on waxing on and waxing off, when he could have been learning how to kick. He could have been learning how to punch. He could have been learning how to defend. He could have been learning many more effective karate moves, but instead, Mr. Miyagi had him waxing on and waxing off. This wasn't the only unconventional teaching method that Mr. Miyagi used to teach Daniel karate. Another example was teaching him to paint with a certain stroke that engaged his wrist in a precise way. But there came a point in the film when Mr. Miyagi finally begins to show him how all these unconventional methods that he now mastered actually apply to karate. The wax on and wax off motion actually was an extremely effective move for Daniel when he need to block an opponent's strike. The painting motion also contributed to Daniel's becoming an effective martial artist. Eventually, Daniel learned to appreciate how Mr. Miyagi took the time to teach these unconventional methods because during a match when Mr. Miyagi would call to Daniel "Wax on, Wax off", Daniel knew exactly what to do to be effective in the match.

Mr. Miyagi's wax on, wax off highlights how several small movements build into something greater, stronger, and effective. When you're building something – your business, your career, your family, your organization, your finances, your health – take the small steps first. Do the "small stuff"! It's going to be hard initially. It may feel arduous. It might even feel repetitive. You may question why you are even doing the small stuff. You may want to jump right in into the complex stuff right away. The faster you do the complex stuff, the faster you build right? Wrong! There are lessons in strength building. Every single one of the smaller steps are helping to build strength and build knowledge that will support your journey. These smaller steps are building your ability to handle the complexity. When you arrive at the more complex issues in your success journey, you will need the lessons from the smaller steps because they helped to build the critical thinking skills necessary to handle the complexity. The small steps add up, yet so many people rush to get past this necessary phase. This phase is tough, but you must endure it and execute it in a purposeful, strategic way for learning to be used effectively in your upcoming season of complexity. Be willing to take the small steps. Be willing to learn in incremental stages. Along the way, you will begin to pull the lessons together in a systematic fashion.

Systems Thinking

When I was working at the University of Michigan in the Obstetrics and Gynecology department, still very early in my management career, I found myself frustrated with one of the associates on my team. In my frustration, I ran into my mentor's office and complained to him that I felt things had progressed to the point where the associate should be terminated. Being the fantastic mentor and forever calming presence that he is, he very simply said to me, "When a person is having performance issues, I always look at the process first before I look at the person. Often, it's a process issue and not a person issue". That statement arrested me in the moment. It took a minute to understand what he meant. What did he mean that it's a process issue versus a person issue? Eventually I came to understand that if the process is broken and you have a person trying to work within a broken process, by default, they are going to make mistakes. They will be error prone. But none of this is their fault. It's the fault of a broken process – a broken system.

This conversation is where I pinpoint the start of my journey to become a systems thinker. Along the way, I picked up certifications in methods such as Lean and Six Sigma, which look at systems to determine if there are opportunities for quality improvement. Beyond official methods such as these (and there are many more), systems are everywhere and it's important to begin to think in terms of systems to increase sustainability and scalability. Even the example I gave earlier about the Half Turkish Get-ups into a push-up is a form of a system. A system is ultimately a combination of individual components working together to produce a final end product. Breaking down the exercise, you see the smaller components of bridges, push-ups, and renegade rows all working together to produce one thing called a Half Turkish Get-Up into a push-up. Perfecting each individual exercise was necessary to execute the end product effectively – a system of smaller, individual exercises working together.

In his book "The E-Myth Revisited: Why Most Small Businesses Don't Work and What to Do About It", author Michael E. Gerber stresses the importance of systems thinking in the context of entrepreneurship. Specifically, Michael E. Gerber highlights systems thinking as franchise thinking using the example of the McDonald's fast-food franchise. He describes how their model launched the franchise movement, where franchises focus on developing systems and processes that can be duplicated across multiple locations without relying on specific individuals. In theory, when you visit one McDonald's and then visit another McDonald's, you should have a similar experience at each location. The challenges and rewards of implementing such a model was depicted in the major motion picture "The Founder". In this movie, the original McDonald's location, ran by the McDonald's brothers fascinated a guy named Ray Kroc. Ray Kroc paid attention to the systems that the McDonald's brothers put in place even in the very beginning to move customers quickly through the line and deliver consistent food each time. Ray Kroc eventually convinced the brothers that there were even more opportunities for a system. They focused on perfecting the small elements initially, such as how many pickles were the right number of pickles, how much ketchup was the right amount of ketchup, how toasty did the buns need to be, and what was the perfect grease temperature for frying the fries. Then they progressed to determining how to deliver the right amount of ketchup and bun toast each time. Is there a device that could achieve the right ketchup distribution or bun toast? Once they perfected those individual elements, they began to bring them together as a system.

Ray Kroc was the mastermind behind seeing the systematic nature and potential of McDonald's. He realized that the processes they had in place could be duplicated in other areas. He just had to determine how to ensure such duplication. He had to fail fast and fail forward on figuring out how to finalize systems, document those systems, train employees on those systems, implement those systems, and control quality within those systems. Ensuring quality was one of the McDonald's brothers' major concerns, but they not only figured out the quality piece, but also determined how to build, implement, and maintain effective systems. These systems are the foundation for the franchising success of McDonald's.

As demonstrated by the McDonald's story, systems thinking is important if your desire is any of the following: sustainable growth, scalable growth, maximizing time, or maximizing resources. To achieve any of these, you must use systems thinking. To begin developing your ability to systems think, start with you as an individual. At a minimum you should want to maximize your own time and your own resources. Systems thinking can help you improve the way you manage your life. Let's start with simply thinking about something we will call "your day".

Thinking about your typical day of the week, what are all the elements that work together to produce your day? For example, your day can include waking up, brushing your teeth, getting dressed, and determining what to wear. To complete these tasks, you typically set an alarm, have your toothbrush and toothpaste in the bathroom in a specific location, and clothes in a specific location. Then maybe you move on to cooking breakfast. To do this, you need to identify what you're cooking, the ingredients necessary to cook it, and the availability of those ingredients in your home. After eating, you might be ready to head to work. To leave out you must grab your work bag, grab a coat, and hop in the car. Do you know where your bag is in the house? How about your coat? How about your keys? Does your car have the gas it needs? I think you get the picture. There are so many individual elements that work together just for you to get out of the house to go to work. The questions don't end there. Do you know where you're going? Do you need your GPS? Do you know your assignments for the day? Do you know how to complete them? Do you have the right access to the right tools to complete the assignments? When you get off work, do have to pick up the kids? Did the kids have extracurricular activities? Were there any issues with the kids? Do you need to schedule time to speak with their teachers? What will you feed the kids when you pick them up? Will you try to squeeze in a workout? The list goes on and on.

Individuals who are systems thinkers don't get overwhelmed by the number of individual elements at play, but they realize the incredible risk for waste – lots of waste – around each individual element. Here's where waste can occur. What if you didn't set your alarm and got up late? Wasted time. What if you couldn't find your toothbrush and toothpaste? Wasted time. What if you didn't think about what to wear ahead of time? Wasted time. What if you knew what you wanted to wear but couldn't find the pieces of clothing you had in mind? Wasted time. What if you went to cook something, but the ingredients that you needed weren't there? Wasted time. What if you got into your car already late for work given all the other wasted time only to realize you need gas? More wasted time. What if you arrived at work and realized there was a deadline for the day that you didn't effectively plan for, and it will take you 16 hours to complete the assignment that was given to you a week ago and you haven't even started? Wasted time AND a missed deadline if you don't work overtime today. What if you get a call from your kid's school that you must pick them up from school and you're in the middle of trying to meet a deadline that you're already behind on? What if you actually met your deadline, picked up the kids on time, but by the time you get home, you're too exhausted to exercise? What if you're so exhausted, you decide not to do the homework for the degree you're working on, but instead you turn on the television because you want to see what happened on your favorite show? Wasted time.

Systems thinkers look at all this waste as opportunities to build systems that minimize or eliminate the risk for waste. Here are some things to think about as you begin to view your life as a system. Maybe you need to put the toothbrush and toothpaste at the same location every time. Maybe you need to spend the evening prior determining what you're going to wear the next day, pulling out those clothes, ironing them, and making sure they are ready-set-go for tomorrow. Maybe you need to reorganize your closet in a way that suits the way you think about your wardrobe. Maybe the closet should be re-organized by clothing item or by color code or both. Maybe you need to organize your shoes. Maybe you need to come up with a system for grocery shopping to ensure you plan your meals in advance and purchase the right quantity of ingredients for the week. If you find yourself missing deadlines, maybe you need to start a weekly or daily system of writing a list of priorities that you need to do for work. Maybe you need to begin placing important deadlines on your calendar. If you are finding that you keep missing workouts that you plan to complete at the end of your day, maybe the end of the day is not best time for you to schedule those workouts because your days inevitably get crazy. Maybe targeting the beginning of the day might work better for you. Maybe the middle of the day may work if your job has a workout facility or is located near a facility. These are some examples of how systems thinking can help you approach your life in a way that allows you to maximize time, energy, and resources.

This same approach applies to organizations. How do you maximize efficiency, minimize resource utilization, and deliver a high-quality product and excellent customer service? Each time I had the responsibility for building a department's research program, I would begin with the end in mind. Part of beginning with the end in mind was that I knew I could not build an infrastructure that depended on me being the one who had to sit down and perform repetitive work such as data entry. I knew I had to build an infrastructure that automated these processes as much as possible. Budgets and calculations are always a major part of a research program. The need for manual calculations must be reduced to create efficiencies. I had to determine how to minimize data input to maximize the amount of information and product output. This is always an area of focus when I set out to build a system. I also focus on ways to take the human element out of the equation. Strategies to remove the human element is two-fold: 1) remove the likelihood of a person creating an error because they are simply "human"; and 2) automate the process to minimize or eliminate the need for human touch.

One field that focuses on the "human element" is a field called "human factors". I've had the pleasure of working alongside human factors professionals for several years in my career. These experts focus on how the human element in process, design, infrastructure, team dynamics, device use and more, influences how humans interact and perform. One of my favorite examples is the ATM machine. The old design of an ATM was that a person would insert their card in the machine, input their pin number, and tell the ATM how much money they were requesting. The machine would then deliver the cash requested (pending the account had that amount of cash available). In the perfect world, the person would take the cash, wait for the machine to return their card, retrieve the card, and leave the machine. For some people, this was not reality. What actually occurred was that they would take the cash and then leave the machine, thereby leaving their card behind in the machine. The reason for this error is that our brains are hardwired to complete the task that we set out to complete. In the ATM example, the task we set out to complete is "getting cash from the

ATM machine". With that in mind, once we have received the cash, our brains say, "we're done, time to leave" and we leave. In the old ATM process that meant leaving the card behind – forgetting the additional task that occurs after the original task is completed. This is called a "post-completion error" and it occurs when one forgets to complete an additional task that must take place after the completion of the desired task. This was happening to brilliant people everywhere!

It not only happens at the ATM but also happens when you forget to attach an attachment to an email, or when you forget to remove an original after making a copy at the copy machine, or when you forget to take the pump out of your car after filling it up with gas! I've done them all – yes, including the gas! Returning to the ATM example, ATM manufacturers eventually wised up and decided to redesign the ATM to account for how the brain was hardwired instead of trying to train incredibly smart people on how to remember their card. Therefore, most ATMs now will give you your card back FIRST, then give you your cash or they have you swipe your card instead of inserting it. This is a beautiful example of systems thinking because the ATM manufacturers understood where in the system they could correct for the human element and reduce the risk of error.

Remember when my mentor told me that instead of blaming the performance issue on the employee, to look at the process? Imagine if I fired an employee because they kept leaving their card in the ATM. The performance issue wasn't really a performance issue. It was the brain behaving the way the brain is hardwired to behave. I would have fired them for their brain! Therefore, it's important to look at the processes when errors continue to occur. If you can fix a broken process, you can usually eliminate the error.

Here are some questions to ask when you're designing a process using systems thinking. Where does the process rely on someone to remember to do something? Could the process be automated to eliminate reliance on memory? Is this element even necessary in the process? Where does the process rely on manual touch by an individual? Can that manual touch be automated? Where does the process rely on one person's specific knowledge or expertise? Can that knowledge and expertise be built into the system? Does the process rely on someone spending incredible amounts of time with little payoff? Is there a way to minimize the time? These questions are important because relying on memory increases error rates, manual processes increase error rates, relying on one person creates bottlenecks, and time-consuming tasks decrease efficiencies.

How can you apply similar questions to your life? How can you build a system to help you remember birthdays, anniversaries, when bills are due, your kid's baseball schedule, or deadlines at work? Is there something that you look at every day? Maybe your smartphone. Maybe your work calendar. What about your "to do" list? Are you failing to complete items on that list because you're attempting to maintain that list in your head? Do you need to write them down? Is paper better for you? Is electronic better? Is the notes section of your phone better? Or maybe a Word document on your computer is best. Or even Post-It notes on the refrigerator may be the best solution for you. A real example for me is that I had to determine an effective system for ensuring I always have cream for my eczema in my possession. I must be prepared for "the itch"! I change purses and bags very often, but one thing I usually carry is my make-up bag! I have learned to put my eczema cream in my makeup bag because I am rarely without that bag. Systems thinkers are self-reflective enough to identify how to use their habits, characteristics, preferences, and typical environment to maximize time, minimize waste, and maximize productivity.

Questions to Consider

1. Did I begin with the end in mind?
2. What are the small things that I must do now to build a system later?
3. Where will I commit to hard work now so that I can gain momentum at the end?
4. Where can I fail fast and fail forward today that will move me one step closer to success?

5. What can I do now to ensure that I have a system in place that leads to my success?

When you eat the labor of your hands, You shall be happy, and it shall be well with you. ~Psalm 128:2 (New King James Version)

CHAPTER 22

Smart Work

The ability to concentrate and to use your time well is everything if you want to succeed in business or almost anywhere else for that matter.
~ Lee Iacocca

Are you working as smart as you should? Are you maximizing your resources? Are you working efficiently? Have you built adequate systems? Are you appropriately leveraging technology? Are you focusing on those things that you do best? Are you leveraging the expertise and skills of others? What are those things that you don't do well? How much of your time are you spending on activities that will yield 80% or more of your success? How much time are you spending on activities that barely contribute to your ability to accomplish your dreams and your goals?

In his book, "The Power of Broke", Shark Tank's Daymond John explains how having little money can benefit one's success journey. He argues that when you don't have enough money or resources, you're forced to be creative. You're forced to figure out how to leverage the resources that you have, to achieve the outcome that you desire. As a result, you step into a space of innovation. This is the space that allows you to differentiate yourself. When compared to your competition, you're able to identify solutions that no one else has or the paths that are least traveled. This space potentially allows you to build a competitive edge. Daymond John argues that even if you have the resources to invest in multiple technologies or extensive expertise, the condition of being broke is so powerful that even those with resources should act as if they don't have them. Resources could function as an artificial crutch that stifles the type of innovation that is required when resources are limited. When you have exhausted all financial resources, you are forced to harness the power of creativity. An abundance of financial resources can lengthen the time to achieve true success because you haven't been forced to tap into your creative muscle. This principle is at the heart of the concept "smart work". You must approach your work as if every resource you have is not just limited but *very* scarce.

This concept isn't limited to financial resources. If you approach your work with a scarcity mindset or a broke mentality, then you function as if you're broke when it comes to time, you're broke when it comes to money, you're broke in connections, you're broke in expertise, you're broke in number of employees, and more. Your time is precious. Your money is precious. Your time with your family is precious. Your time to be able to do the tasks that only you can do is precious. If everything is so precious, then how do you build a life, a business, or a system around you that's efficient enough to maximize all those resources and allows you to develop innovative ways to successfully accomplish your goals and dreams? Smart work will allow you to do just that!

Inventory of Resources

I worked with a physician who was being a mentored by a scientific researcher. The scientist and I were having a conversation one day about recent research proposals that the physician submitted. He went on to say how he learned while working so closely with her throughout that process, that she didn't leverage the resources that were available to her. As a result, she wasted precious time that she could've been using to write the science. She spent time working on tasks related to the proposal submission that someone else could have handled for her. She wasted time on administrative tasks such as creating a budget, which is a service that the administrative team offered. She wasted time completing forms. Again, another resource that the administrative team offered. He was floored as to why she would do this when it was most crucial that she focus her efforts on writing the science.

The purpose of the story is to highlight how you need to take proper inventory of your resources. You need to know what's available for you to leverage. As an individual, you must know what expertise you bring to the table. Likewise, it is also important to know what others in your life bring to the table. What have others said that they would help you with? What are some resources in your community you can capitalize on? Without taking an adequate inventory of resources, you will waste time unnecessarily.

I believe in leveraging available resources in my life. One resource that is available to me that I leverage all the time is Amazon Prime. I love when Amazon Prime boxes arrive at my house nearly every day. Meal prep services are another resource that I have leveraged. Because I don't have much free time, I know that there are resources available that handle certain tasks for me. I don't have much time to go to the grocery store or to the mall. I don't have much time to shop or cook. My days are packed! Yes, I still need clothes. Yes, I still love clothes. Yes, I still need personal items. Yes, I still need to eat. However, there are services available that will do these tasks for me. This means that with Amazon Prime, I don't have to go the store because with a click of a button, two days later the item arrives on my porch. When I was using the meal preparation service, I didn't need to go to the grocery store because the meal service that I enjoyed used local chefs to make my meals and deliver them every Monday and Thursday. I simply had to go to the gym that was around the corner from my house twice a week, pick up my food, pop it in the microwave for two and a half minutes, and I was good to go. This was me leveraging my resources.

Now, each of these resources cost. There's an annual Amazon Prime membership fee, but when I weigh the value of the time that I save in that year to the amount of money that the membership costs me, it works out to be a great investment. Likewise, with the meal preparation service, the service costs, but when I weigh the amount of the cost of the groceries, the cost of my time to fix the food, the cost of wasting food because I fixed too much, and the cost to my body of fixing unhealthy options, there is a return on investment for using this service. You must take inventory of your resources to build a smarter life, do smarter work, and build a smarter organization. You must know all the resources that are available to you, and you may not be aware of many. Ask friends, ask coworkers, and ask colleagues to help you identify true resources that are available.

What "Only You" Can Do

At one time my best friend from college, Julia, had a regular annual meeting in Washington, DC. When she would come to Washington, DC for that meeting, she and I would always try to get together to have dinner to catch up. During one trip, she and I were having dinner in DC and catching up and I began to share with her how crazy my life was and how much I was having to balance everything. I proceeded to tell her that the cleanliness of my house was suffering as a result. I couldn't find time to take care of the house. I couldn't find time to wash this and clean that. She listened, and then said to me, "You need a cleaning service". When she said this, immediately dollar signs began ringing in my head. My immediate response was, "I can't afford a cleaning service". She countered my protest by saying, "You totally can afford a cleaning service. I know you can. You can't afford not to have one. You need that peace of mind. Every time you come home from your busy life, you don't want to have to worry about the cleanliness of a house." She went on to say, "And that's going to be worth it to you. You need to get a cleaning service."

She convinced me! I conceded and told Julia, "OK, you've convinced me! I'm going to get a cleaning service. I will go home and over the next few days look for a cleaning service. I was serious about finding a cleaning service when I left that dinner. Then, I let the dream go. Fast forward about a year later when I was having lunch with another colleague. She and I were comparing our lives over sushi and explaining how busy we had become. Then she talked about her cleaning service. I said, "Hey! How does that work out for you? Do you find it to be very beneficial?" She said, "It's a life saver! I'd rather my lights be turned off or my gas be turned off than to sacrifice my cleaning service. The service comes every Wednesday, and they are part of the family. I don't know what I would do without my cleaning service". I then proceeded to tell her about the conversation I had with Julia in the past and she said, "Listen honey, you need to get a cleaning service. I don't know what you're waiting on. It's the best investment you can make. There's no way you should be trying to balance everything in your life and not get a cleaning service." Again, I was convinced and just like after the conversation with Julia, I was focused! I went back to my computer and started to research cleaning services, and then let the dream go – again. This time, it wasn't so long before my next reality check about needing a cleaning service kicked in.

On one Saturday I carved out time to clean my house because it was getting out of control yet again. I started to clean the shower, which was way out of control at that point. I started to get mad. Not just mad but really angry because I didn't understand why my husband had not been contributing to helping to clean the shower. I got so upset that I threw down the cleaning supplies, went to my computer, and booked a cleaning service to come in the next couple of days. I was so upset. I literally said out loud to myself, "I'm not wasting my Saturday on this. I have a zillion things I could be doing besides cleaning the shower. On top of that after I clean the shower, there's still a zillion other things to clean in this house". I felt so overwhelmed, and I said, "Enough is enough! I'm booking the cleaning service!"

That Saturday the service came, and in two hours one lady and her assistant did to my house, what I hadn't been able to do in months, maybe even years. I felt exactly like my colleague said. I would prefer my lights go out or my gas go off than to go without my cleaning service. It was in that moment that I realized I needed to pay others to do what they do best, so I could focus on what I do best. I was fortunate enough to have the resources to make this decision. Everybody is not in the position where they can always pay someone to complete certain tasks, but that should always be a goal. You should always identify those areas in your life where there's a service, a technology solution, an expert, or another useful resource that could handle something for you that you don't do best, allowing you to focus on the things that you do best. This will escalate your progress toward your goals, your dreams, and your purpose. When you focus on the things that you do best, you will ultimately realize a return on that investment.

Setting Expectations

As you begin to identify those things that you do best and what others do best, and you begin to collaborate, one important task that you must accomplish at the very beginning is to set expectations effectively. Setting expectations sets the stage for minimizing confusion, minimizing wastes of time, minimizing relationship breakdowns, and minimizing communication breakdowns. Setting expectations has an incredible payoff when done effectively.

I was once asked by a student who I mentored, what I do in seasons where I have several competing priorities and begin to feel overwhelmed. My feeling overwhelmed doesn't happen often despite my being one of the busiest people I know. I still usually find a way to hit all my obligations and deadlines. However, every now and then a season comes in my life where I literally just don't have enough time in the day to complete everything. I try hard to maximize all I can do in a day. I implement all the tips and strategies I've shared with you in this book on how to be efficient and effective but when all my various responsibilities converge in their busy seasons all at the same time, it becomes the perfect storm. This is a season where my personal life is demanding, ministry is demanding, work is demanding, teaching is demanding, business is demanding, and more. The perfect storm. How did I answer my mentee's question? How do I handle it? How do I manage it all? I began to tell her that it boils down to expectations.

As a woman of my word who works with such high integrity, I have built a reputation that when I say I'm going to do something, I do it. This has forged a positive relationship with others that they can count on me. Because of their history with me as a woman of my word, they rarely hear me say that I need an extension on a deadline or a promise that I made. Therefore, when they hear me say, "Hey, can I get this to you on a different day?" They know that I'm asking from a place of *true* overload. This is only a strategy that I use when I know that my not delivering on the original deadline I promised will not cause any harm. Maybe I promised to deliver on Tuesday, but the actual deadline is two weeks later. When I realize, ahead of the Tuesday promise, that I will not likely make the Tuesday deadline, I'll let them know. The conversation usually goes something like this, "Hey, I know I promised this to you by Tuesday. I apologize, but I do have a few urgent deadlines I'm pushing to meet by Tuesday. I know what I promised you isn't due for another couple of weeks. Is there any way I can get this to you *next* Tuesday?" The response 100% of the of the time has been "Yes" or "Not a problem" or "No big deal, if you need more time just let me know".

While I explained this to her as a possibility, I honestly rarely use this approach. Instead, in a season of overload, as new initiatives continue to come my way, saying "Yes" could be the proverbial straw that breaks the camel's back. Therefore, I ensure that I'm incredibly clear about expectations. First, I clarify with the "asker" their preferred deadline. Often, I find they don't have an urgent deadline. If they do mention a deadline that I won't be able to accommodate, I'll respond with a deadline that I *can* accommodate and deliver on that day.

This is another case where excellence matters. When you have a history and reputation for delivering with excellence, then when you must take the rare opportunity to ask for an exception, they'll grant it. Even then you must ensure that your communication sets clear expectations for you and the other party. Then you can use even this situation as an opportunity to under promise and over deliver. When you set the proper expectations, you ultimately find yourself with healthy relationships you have built over time that have been guided by expectations, integrity, and excellence. This allows you to work smarter by eliminating wasted time trying to salvage and mend broken relationships caused by a lack of clear expectations and a failure to deliver.

How Can Technology Help?

When we received a large contract from the federal government, which was a contract model we had never managed before, we did not have the infrastructure built to manage this type of contract effectively. The infrastructure we had was effective for other mechanisms, but not this one. Our existing tools, resources, and technology were all inapplicable, forcing us to determine what would work best for this new model. We knew this new model required a rapid turnaround for proposal submissions, so we had to work quickly. We knew that whatever we put in place had to allow us to move faster than before. Given this reality, I made this one simple statement: "There must be a technology solution that can help us!" We then took an inventory of our existing resources and worked to determine what could work to ensure the rapid turnaround. We didn't go down the path of identifying any "snazzy jazzy" computer software, as that wasn't our goal. We were looking for simple, low-cost ways to leverage the existing computer technology we had available to allow us to enter large volumes of redundant information into a proposal as effectively and efficiently as possible. We ultimately leveraged many automated functions in the Microsoft Office suite. For example, we created several form templates that leveraged the mail merge function in Word, allowing us to auto-populate several documents easily. When we went to submit one of the rapid turnaround proposals, this technology solution was useful allowing us to create many forms with much of the same information without having to manually type in that information several times over, which also minimized the risk for typographical errors.

The technology market today is so vast that there is almost a solution to nearly any problem. When I approach anything that seems to take a long time or seems to be quite manual in nature, I usually take a pause and say, "There must be some kind of technology solution". When you find yourself making a similar assertion, simply Google the issue and you'll be amazed at what you may find. I would also encourage you to revisit Google six months later if your initial search did not yield a technology solution for your issue. Technology is increasing so rapidly that one day there's nothing out there and the next day someone has created the technology solution. Therefore, you want to ensure that you are staying abreast of technology changes that can fast track your work along the way. Just like fashion, when it comes to technology one day you're in and the next day you're out.

Think about the evolution of computing. We began using manual typewriters – that's how I learned to type. The manual keys triggered what was called a "typeball" to hit against the ribbon that had ink on it to press against paper that was rolled into the machine. There was a bell that triggered you to know that you were approaching the end of a line and a manual return you would push to move the typewriter position down to the next line on the paper. THIS was very effective technology then, which advanced from the pen to paper method of writing. The manual typewriter advanced to the electronic typewriter where the return was now a button. The pressing of the keys was less arduous and felt more like the computer keyboards of today. You still had to roll the paper into a machine and it still functioned with the typeball hitting a more advanced ribbon to place the ink on to the paper. The electronic typewriter advanced to word processors which introduced the computer screen and being able to type what you wanted on the screen, backspace to correct, save onto a disc, and tell it to print on to the paper (still having to roll the paper into a machine). That then advanced to computers as we know them today (with advances along the way), which have advanced to laptops, tablets, and smartphones for computing. Other technologies have had and will continue to have similar journeys; therefore, you must stay abreast of these advances. Often there is a technology solution that can help you to work smarter. Working smarter means looking for it!

Remember the 80/20 Rule

What are you spending your time on? The Pareto Principle is named after the Italian economist Vilfredo Pareto, which is also known as the 80/20 rule. The 80/20 rule is simply that, 80% of your results come from 20% of your inputs. For example, in the world of retail, 80% of your revenue is likely to come from 20% of your customers. In the world, 80% of wealth comes from 20% of the population. In summary, a small number of inputs contributes to most of your desired outputs. Now, the principle has been expanded to many different areas and different ways of thinking. This book is no different. Let's apply the principle to "smart work". To work smarter, maximize the amount of effort you are putting into tasks that *really* matter and minimize the amount of effort you put into tasks that have minimal value or pay off toward your goals.

This is a principle I must actively keep top of mind. I am one of those individuals who is considered a "jack of all trades". I do take issue with the latter part of that quote, "master of none", as there are some things that I have mastered, but I do have a variety of skills because I've been a lifelong learner. I LOVE to learn. I'm a researcher. Thus, I feel like I can learn and sometimes master almost anything. Most things I can at least attempt to learn, like sewing or refinishing furniture for example, by watching videos online, reading online, and picking up just enough information to either be dangerous or have an intelligent conversation – depending on the day. My list of interests and skills is quite lengthy, and I can be very easily distracted by activities that bring minimal value to my goals. Therefore, I must take inventory of those activities that I do but don't contribute to my success journey. The Pareto principle (80/20 rule) is invaluable and can be used in many areas of your life. Consider the 80/20 rule in your personal life. Consider the 80/20 rule on your job. Consider the 80/20 rule in your business. Consider the 80/20 rule in your day-to-day schedule. Identify the 20% of activities you engage in that cause you 80% of your frustration. Stop doing those activities! Identify the 80% of activities that are only contributing to 20% of your results. Stop doing those activities! What gives you maximum results? Usually, it's 20% of your activities that are yielding 80% of your results. Find a way to increase the amount of time you can spend on those activities. The more you increase time engaging in those activities, the more you maximize your results.

Questions to Consider

1. What are the resources that are available to me that will help me achieve success?
2. What are those activities that I do best that I shouldn't delegate to others?

3. What are those activities that I am currently doing that I can delegate to others to do?
4. How can technology help me achieve success more effectively and efficiently?
5. How do I minimize the time that I spend on activities that are causing me the most frustration and maximize the time on activities that yield maximum results?

If the ax is dull, And one does not sharpen the edge, Then he must use more strength; But wisdom brings success. ~Ecclesiastes 10:10 (New King James Version)

Conclusion – Phase III: Boardrooms

What you do speaks so loudly that I cannot hear what you say.
~Ralph Waldo Emerson

Now it should be crystal clear that our three-legged stool just cannot stand without "Action". Action is necessary to achieve results. Yes, having the other two legs – mindset and resilience are critical, but having a relentless grind, operating in excellence, evaluating our progress, understanding and learning from failures, being engaged listeners, asking the right questions, doing the hard-work in the beginning, setting up the right systems, and working smarter not harder are all critical to effectively and efficiently translate effort into success.

Questions to Consider

1. What can I do today to become more relentless in my grind?
2. What metrics must I implement now to begin evaluating my progress?
3. What failures have I had in the past that I need to revisit today to extract the lessons that will help me moving forward?
4. How can I become a more engaged listener who asks great questions?
5. What systems can I develop and implement that will allow me to work smarter and not harder?

For if anyone is a hearer of the word and not a doer, he is like a man observing his natural face in a mirror; for he observes himself, goes away, and immediately forgets what kind of man he was. But he who looks into the perfect law of liberty and continues in it, and is not a forgetful hearer but a doer of the work, this one will be blessed in what he does. ~James 1:23-25 (New King James Version)

CHAPTER 23

Conclusion

So, there you have it! You *can* have it "all". You *can* achieve "balance". While each of our definitions of "all" and "balance" may differ, exercising the mindset, resilience, and action principles covered in this book allow each of us to achieve sustainable, scalable success. My prayer is that this book has allowed you to uncover your strengths and allowed you to begin to strengthen those areas of opportunity. You've been self-reflective. You've been honest with yourself. You understand how you see the world and how key experiences in your life have helped to frame your perspective. You have begun the necessary shifts in your mindset to give you the GOODS that are critical and foundational as you continue your success journey. My prayer is that you now have a strong core of resilience that provides you with the essential tools to overcome challenges and BOUNCE back from adversity. Finally, my prayer is that you put what you've learned into action through hard work, dedication, grind, and endurance to achieve the RESULTS that you desire. While your story may not be a journey of bullets, babies, and boardrooms like mine, you now know what I know. We share the same framework for success – one that is dependent on the right balance of mindset, resilience, and action to achieve success in any area.

So, here's my final charge to you. Give back! Pay the framework forward! Don't misunderstand me here; this isn't about book sales. This is about sharing the information. If you know someone who can also benefit from this framework becoming THEIR framework, make sure they get this information. Gift them the book. Loan them your book. Do whatever you need to do to be your brother and your sister's keeper. Now that it's written, share it! Be a blessing to someone else as I pray this book was a blessing to you!

CHAPTER 24

Epilogue

I admit it! I stole it! As a lifelong fan of Beverly Hills, 90210, the iconic 90s teen drama, I *had* to steal it! One of the most iconic phrases from the show stemmed from an episode when character Donna Martin, played by Tori Spelling, gets drunk at her high school prom and as punishment by the school board, was not going to be able graduate with her peers. The other students came from far and wide to gather in a protest where they chanted the now iconic phrase "Donna Martin Graduates"! So naturally, in December of 2017, when I was just days from graduating with my doctorate, I launched a campaign on social media called "Dr. A Graduates!"

The purpose of the "Dr. A Graduates" campaign was to create an easy-to-find and easy-to-remember website where family and friends who couldn't attend the graduation in person, could watch online. The official graduation date, December 9, 2017, was right around the corner. This moment was special for me, not because of the catchy "Dr. A Graduates" mantra, or the fact that family and friends could watch online, but because "Dr. A Graduates" was special for so many other reasons.

One major reason was that I was the FIRST in my family on either side to receive a doctorate, so yes, we said it proud – Dr. A Gradates! Another major reason was that on that Friday, December 8, 2017, the University of South Florida's School of Public Health held its private graduation ceremony where it recognized the graduates from its program, presented their doctoral projects, and presented each graduate with their awards. The was special because it marked 25 years to the *day* of when my mother was shot in front of my grandparents' house on my aunt's birthday in 1992. It took us *25 years* to find an occasion that would allow us to replace the memory of the traumatic events of that day, with something special – Dr. A Graduates!

Many of my champions were able to make it in person. My husband David, my mom, my dad, my stepmother Mel, my Aunt Saun who was celebrating her birthday in a new way that day, my older brother Aaron, one of my closest girlfriends Charita, my best friend André, of course, my son Nate! They were there in person on such a memorable day for us, a day that became iconic for our family – Dr. A Graduates! On that day, December 8, 2017, with several of my champions in person – 25 years after hearing my name being called on the phone when my other aunt said that my uncle was picking us up because my mother had an accident – my family heard by name being called as Dr. Angela D. Thomas at the University of South Florida's School of Public Health – Dr. A Graduates! The very next day on December 9, 2017 that same group of champions, plus a lot of other champions watching online, cheered me on as I walked across the big stage at the University of South Florida, to be hooded by my doctoral committee Professor as Dr. Angela D. Thomas – Dr. A Graduates! To top it all off, many of those same faces plus a few others were present when almost a year later to the day my son Nate walked across the stage at Coastal Carolina University to receive his bachelor's degree – Nate the Great Graduates!

So, WE'VE come a long way! WE held on to hope and used it along with some other key mindset lessons, some resilience, and a whole lot of action to realize our goals and our dreams! If WE can do it, so can you!

With Love and Blessings,
Dr. A.

Made in the USA
Middletown, DE
10 May 2022